# The Impossible Journey

# The Impossible Journey

## Thor Pedersen

ROBINSON

ROBINSON

First published in Great Britain in 2025 by Robinson

1 3 5 7 9 10 8 6 4 2

A CIP catalogue record for this book
is available from the British Library.

ISBN: 978-1-47214-976-3 (hardcover)
ISBN: 978-1-47214-977-0 (trade paperback)

Typeset in Adobe Garamond Pro by SX Composing DTP, Rayleigh, Essex
Printed and bound in Great Britain by Clays Ltd, Elcograf S.p.A.

Papers used by Robinson are from well-managed forests
and other responsible sources.

Robinson
An imprint of
Little, Brown Book Group
Carmelite House
50 Victoria Embankment
London EC4Y 0DZ

The authorised representative
in the EEA is
Hachette Ireland
8 Castlecourt Centre, Dublin 15,
D15 XTP3, Ireland
(email: info@hbgi.ie)

An Hachette UK Company
www.hachette.co.uk

www.littlebrown.co.uk

To the kind people in the world,
of whom there are many.

# Contents

# Prologue: You Don't Belong Here

*Cameroon, 31 December 2015*

We had set off that afternoon. I am in a taxi that I hope will take me in a big arc down through Cameroon, past its capital, Yaoundé, then deeper, further south, towards the border with Congo. If I can make it across, I'll then try to loop up through Congo, then into Gabon, and finally – if my luck holds – into Equatorial Guinea.

Getting into this tiny, paranoid petrol state has been an overwhelming obsession over the last couple of months. An obsession that has almost broken me. It wasn't supposed to be like this. I thought that my attempt to navigate a path through every country in the world without flying would be a great adventure. I thought it would be fun. But it hasn't turned out like that.

The bureaucracy, the corruption, the maddening chaos of Central Africa, that great devourer of people's souls, has humbled me. I am running out of money, and my relationship with the woman I want to spend the rest of my life with is almost extinct. I am feeling crushed and empty.

A few hours earlier I reached my lowest point and decided to abandon the project. In truth I am still feeling ravaged now, but I have also realised that there is only one way: forward. It does not matter if I want out of the journey, if I have come to hate it. I cannot go back. I must go forward.

We pass through towns and villages, forests and fields as light drains quickly from the sky above – the last sunset of 2015.

Almost every human being we see is partying: some dance in the streets to music – everything from Taylor Swift to Afrobeat – blasting out at high volume from enormous speakers on wheels; others simply scream '*Bonne Année!*' into the sky above.

Darkness falls and finally we stop in a village to look for food. The only place I can find is a stall with a woman serving soup. She hands me a deep plate. It is cold, in the glare of a nearby lamp I can see a fish head breaking the surface. I think to myself: *This is going to make me sick.* But I also know that it might be my last chance to eat for hours.

When I am finished we get back into the car. More miles disappear under our wheels. The surface beneath us begins to deteriorate, by the time we enter the jungle we are on little more than a dirt road. I can see that it has been prepared for tarmac or bitumen, but the builders haven't reached this far yet, so we are driving on a layer of dust. Almost immediately, clouds of it are thrown up, transfigured by the car's headlights. And as we pick up speed, even though the windows are closed, the dust begins to pour into the car.

Dust covers the dashboard, the seats, it spreads across our clothes and clings to any exposed skin. The driver and I cannot stop coughing. Our noses are running, our eyes are streaming. And all the time the driver's anger is mounting. He had borrowed this car from his brother to make what he thought would be easy money, but now he has realised how much cleaning he will need to do.

Several times we have to stop so we can open the doors, get out and breathe. For a moment we stand there, gasping, the hot moist air from the jungle pressing clammily against our skin, our ears filled with the relentless noise of an uncountable number of different insects.

We carry on, stopping each time we need to try to pull some clean air into lungs that feel thick, clogged with the red African soil. Occasionally the car's headlights catch something flitting across the road ahead of us. A couple of times I think I can see a big cat of some description disappearing into the thick wall of plants and trees that press claustrophobically on us from both sides of the road, but the dust, and the dark and the speed we're going, make it hard to be sure.

And then, as we approach 3 a.m., three slender shadows appear within the cones of the headlights. I can make out the sharp edges of a checkpoint. We slow down, before the driver halts the car. They shout roughly for us to leave our vehicle. We step out into the night.

Standing before us are three men in camouflage. They have assault rifles cradled in their arms and pistols strapped to their hips. What is also immediately clear, from the way that they are swaying and slurring, is that they are drunk out of their minds.

But not so drunk that they do not instantly clock that I am a white European. Something changes, as if a switch has been turned on. The man in the middle comes towards me. When I look into his face his glazed eyes suddenly snap into focus and I realise: *This man hates me.*

'You don't belong here,' he says. 'You've made a mistake.'

I have been in Africa a long time now. I'm used to checkpoints and soldiers. And generally I'm relaxed around weapons because I've seen so many. Most soldiers just have them hanging on a strap on their shoulder, or they leave them casually up against a wall.

There's no real threat, it's a power play – a chance for them to show that, for these few minutes of your life, *they* are in charge. If they're lucky, if they play the game well, they might even make a little money from the encounter.

You never know how long they will have been stationed in that part of the world, or how long they've got until their posting changes. You don't know how much or how little has been going on, or how bored they are. They, by contrast, know that as a traveller you will be on a tight schedule. You have transport to catch, contacts to locate, places to get to before your visa runs out. They have all the time in the world; you do not. It's in the gap between these two facts that their true power lies.

But this is different. Everything is already frighteningly out of control. I remember how when I did my national service in the Danish Army we learned to scan for certain things when confronted by armed men. How are they behaving with their weapons? Are the mouths of their rifles pointing safely down at the ground or at you? Are their fingers on the triggers of their guns, or resting on the sides?

The men swaying before us are thrusting their rifles forwards; I can see that their fingers are already exerting pressure on the triggers, as if they are preparing to fire. It's not clear what their intentions are, but even if they do not *want* to kill us, it is the middle of the night, they are full of drink, and all of them have been seized by emotions that they do not seem to be able to understand, or control. A tragic accident feels terrifyingly possible in this situation that seems to have taken on a bleary momentum of its own.

A recollection emerges of an encounter I'd had earlier in my journey, on a train in Croatia. Things were good that day. I was the only one in my compartment, having the time of my life sticking my head out of the window, when an old man came through the door. His desire to talk eventually defeated my desire for silence.

He was full of stories, about his job travelling from one university to the next selling books, about life under socialism. And then he told me about the night he had been held up at a checkpoint by some drunken Russian soldiers. They had opened fire on him. At this, he lifted his shirt to reveal a torso marked by the scars their bullets had left.

This memory only adds to my fear.

There is a quick scurrying movement as my driver takes a couple of steps back, stopping behind me so that he has almost disappeared from view. I am exposed and alone; he has made it clear that this is *my* problem, not his. The troops ask for my documents and we slip into a routine that has become familiar to me since I first entered Central Africa. Except that tonight there is a frayed, menacing quality to a back and forth that takes place in a jumbled mix of French and English.

'Do you have a passport?'

'Yes.'

'Is it valid?' The men are still a metre or so away from us. Close enough for me to catch the stench of booze and sweat flooding out of them. Their rifles are pointed squarely at my body, but they are not pushing me or touching me. From time to time, one of them stumbles away for a bit, and then comes back. I never lose sight of any of them. My stomach feels as if it has turned to liquid and I am so tired I can barely stand. I think with a quick flash of regret about the soup I'd eaten. Something inside me feels deeply wrong.

'Yes.'

'Do you have a visa?'

'Yes.'

'Is it valid?'

'Yes.'

'Do you have a vaccination card?'

'Yes.'

'Do you have this vaccine?' Everything they say has a kind of slurred aggression behind it. I know that they want to catch me out, because when they find an opening – an expired visa, a vaccination I've missed – they can exploit it. Although they're out of their heads, they are luxuriating in the power they have over me. Usually, the end point is clear, they will ask for money. But tonight I realise that drink has unleashed other desires. Suddenly, I am certain that they are going to kill me. I don't know whether I have minutes or seconds left, but I know, without any doubt or equivocation, that I'm going to die.

'Yes.'

'Do you have that vaccine?'

'Yes.' I'm frustrated by this tired charade, but I'm also painfully conscious that one careless word, or even the flicker of the 'wrong' expression, could lead to a bullet through my head, so I force myself to remain as submissive as they clearly want me to be.

'Do you have an invitation letter?'

'Yes.'

'Is it valid?' I imagine one of them allowing himself to be overwhelmed by the emotion and passion that have become concentrated in this little stretch of road and unloading a full magazine of bullets into my chest. I see myself fall to my feet before I am dragged into the jungle. This, after all, is a part of the world where people disappear. I'll be devoured by the creatures who live here and nobody will ever find my body. I have not told anybody where I am, or where I am going. This thought chills me. Once more, I feel terrifyingly alone.

It is possible that someone will trip, or press the trigger that fraction more strongly, or be startled by a noise in the dark forest around us. Or perhaps there will simply be a cold-blooded decision. The hatred in their eyes is not just because of the booze, or the circumstances. It is because I am a white European. Something about the situation makes me feel as if the entire history of colonialism is sitting on my shoulders. These men want to make me pay for the countless atrocities, the greed, the cynical, appalling legacy of more than a hundred years.

'Yes.'

'Where are you going?'

'Congo.'

'Do you have a visa for Congo?' They are shouting at me now, their voices made rough by rage and the night's festivities. Somewhere, not too far away, I can hear music and people laughing.

'Yes.'

'Is it valid?'

'Yes.'

They look more closely at my passport. One of them shoots me a look of wolfish triumph.

'No, it's not.'

'I still have seven days to go. Just let me deal with that when I reach the border. I'm sure it's OK.'

I struggle to keep as calm as I am able, even as inside I'm roiling with a mixture of terror and regret. I know that I've made a stupid, perhaps fatal mistake. I should never have got into that taxi, or asked it to drive through the night. And then I also think, what else could I have done? My visa was expiring, I had to get to the border.

My internal deliberations falter, replaced with one, insistent question: when is it going to happen? When is it going to happen? When is it going to happen?

And then abruptly, with the same aggression they have used through the whole encounter, they start shouting at us again. 'OK, go. GO. GO.'

The driver and I make our way slowly back to the vehicle. We are tense, convinced that at any second they will start firing.

I snatch a glimpse at my phone; it is forty-five minutes since we were first forced to stop. Still moving with painstaking care, we climb into the taxi, and then roll away, towards the border with Congo. A few seconds pass, I watch their silhouettes recede in the wing mirror. At a certain point, the driver smashes his foot down and with a roar and a flurry of dust we accelerate away. I realise I have been holding my breath. For the first time in I do not know how long I exhale.

A few minutes later I ask the driver to stop. I stumble to a big rock on the side of the road next to the jungle and slip behind it. My hands trembling, I pull my trousers down then empty myself. Diarrhoea pours out of me and all the time I'm shaking. Afterwards I crouch down for a good ten minutes. I'm still shaking. Finally, I compose myself. I get up and get back in the car and say, 'OK, let's go.'

CHAPTER I

# The Lake

*Denmark, Canada, USA, Denmark, Libya,*
*Thailand, 1979–2013*

When I was young I dreamed of becoming a great explorer. I wanted to be like Hernán Cortés, or Ibn Battuta, or Roald Amundsen, or any of the people I read about in the pages of a book my dad bought me which told the story of humanity's endless, restless desire to voyage to the furthest reaches of the planet. I read it over and again, obsessively, and I still have it now. My mind was filled with images of tangled forests, abandoned temples, lost empires in undiscovered tracts of land. I envied the way these men had been tested, how their expeditions had shaped them, or revealed their strengths and weaknesses. I wanted to have the same chance to live at the extremes of existence.

I'm from Denmark, the part of the world that the Vikings sprang from. Their blood is my blood, even if it's mixed with the blood of many of the countries they travelled to: Wales, Scotland, the Baltic nations.

I know that I carry within me their DNA, and sometimes I have fantasised that it is alive, that it is an active part of who I am.

9

I share with them the desire to explore, to see what's round the corner (though not their enthusiasm for killing or slavery). It is perhaps most accurate to say that I half believe it. It is fun to entertain the idea that part of what shaped my decision to embark on such an adventure was the fact that a thousand years ago, my forefathers had a similar urge to voyage across the ocean.

And yet I'm aware that in truth, what I've been most shaped by are my upbringing, my parents, the places I've lived, the things I've seen.

For most of my childhood we lived in a big house in Bryrup, a small town of little more than a thousand people hidden away in a valley that has a large lake at its centre. It was the sort of place where we all knew each other's business, where you couldn't do anything at one end without everyone at the other end finding out almost immediately.

Our home came with its own orange fibreglass canoe. That was my thing. As soon as I was old enough, I'd push it into the lake, with a rock on the opposite end to where I was sitting, as a balance, and set off on adventures. It became vital to me. I'd explore all the corners of the lake, and the little creeks that led off it. Once, I tried to find a mysterious fish, a 2-metre-long pike capable of biting your arm off, that was rumoured to lurk in its depths.

Mostly, I'd row to one of the lake's many tiny islands, so small that you couldn't even stand on them. It would just be me alone in my pristine natural sanctuary. I loved the distance it put between me and everyone else. All I could hear were the birds calling and the wind ruffling the trees. I could lie back in the canoe, look at the sky, breathe in the fresh, clean air and revel in the knowledge that I had come to a place where nobody could reach or disturb me. It was somewhere I could go to free myself of angry thoughts or frustrations.

On those days when there was too much wind or rain to take the canoe out, I'd disappear into the thick forest that surrounded where we lived. I wanted to discover it as fully as I could. I knew everything about the environment around us: the trees, the water, the marshland. The forest became another place where I could let my imagination run free. I'd pretend that I was on a quest, or that there were enemies hiding behind the trees. I climbed trees, built treehouses, and combed the forest floor looking for different sorts of ants and insects.

Sometimes, for reasons that even then weren't too clear to me, I'd run away from home. I'd walk out of our garden, then up a hill and into the forest that backed on to it and disappear. Usually, I'd be back in time for supper, but at least once I managed to travel so far that a stranger had to call my father to come to pick me up.

My relationship with an imaginary, adventurous world came from my mother, who took us into the forest, where we'd forage for mushrooms – she loved to cook – while telling us stories about people like Robin Hood and Ivanhoe, as well as her own childhood in Finland. They didn't have expensive toys then; instead they were able to take a pinecone and some sticks and transform them into a horse or a cow – enough animals to fill a whole farm. So even though, like all the other kids I knew, I had Lego and Transformers, there was another part of me that valued the sort of simplicity that my mother had told me about.

The other source of excitement in the house was in its basement. A gigantic model railway occupied the entire room, with what seemed endless numbers of tunnels and tracks and crossings: the sort of thing children dream about. It was nobody's idea of reliable. Some days it worked, others it didn't. Mostly I'd pull a couple of cords in an attempt to get it to work, pretending to myself I knew more about electronics than I actually did. But when it *did* work, it was like magic. The extra layer of intrigue came from the fact that the basement was supposed to be haunted. There would be times when I'd sit there, playing with the train, and then be hit by the strongest feeling that someone was right behind me, staring at me. What, or who, that was would remain one of the enduring mysteries of my childhood.

I was the first of three kids. My father Torben Pedersen, and my mother, Ylva Cederlöf, had met when they were thirty. Torben was a businessman, working for a Danish company that sold pillows and duvets. Ylva was Finnish, and had worked as a tour guide – that was how they met.

The bedding company was expanding rapidly, all across the globe, and so very early on in my life I found myself on the move, first to Vancouver, where they had opened an office, and then Toronto. After that, when I was four, we moved to New Jersey, in the United States, where we stayed for two and a half years before returning to Denmark's Middle Island just ahead of my seventh birthday. I came back with two sisters and a very shaky grasp of Danish, a language I essentially had to learn all over again. This early dislocation is perhaps why I have never felt completely at home in Denmark. Finally, we moved again, to Jutland, the peninsula that contains Denmark's mainland territory.

Back then, I was a little bundle of contradictions. On the one hand, I was very timid, afraid of spiders and the dark. I was a picky eater. I was a loner who rarely had more than one friend at a time. I also think that in some ways I was a bit slower at developing mentally than my peers, always a beat or so behind.

So perhaps it was no surprise that I got bullied. I remember when I started school in Denmark I had a hard time with the letter E. I'd use the English pronunciation of it rather than the Danish one. The other kids teased me mercilessly. I took this a bit too seriously, maybe because I was sensitive and anxious. Even the prospect of violence was enough to terrify me. Vague threats worked on me with terrifying force.

This meant that I was easy to control and bully. Bigger boys discovered that it was fun to chase me. For a while, they pursued me every day after school. I'd be on foot, they'd be on bikes and I'd never be able to escape them. Sometimes I'd try to evade their attentions by hiding in a creek – the wet shoes and trousers were worth it. This worked for a bit until they discovered they could just chuck rocks at me. Eventually my mother found out. Soon after, it stopped.

What was most upsetting wasn't the bullying itself, it was the sense that a village I had thought of as a sanctuary was no longer safe. I hated that loss of innocence.

This nervous, delicate personality sat alongside a belief that I was born for something else. I'm not sure I was able to articulate what was going to be different about my life, but that feeling was there. Some of it was rooted in the basic things that set me apart. For instance, I had a Finnish mother, and my early years in North America meant that I spoke fluent English long before anybody else. I saw it almost as a superpower.

The town we were in was small, but my mother made sure that the world outside was big. She told me that one day we'd go round the globe together. That sparked a fire in me that I guess is still burning now. We were proud of the beautiful community that we were part of. I still am. At the same time, there were lots of jokes about it being the sort of place that people got stuck in; that people couldn't make their way back up the valley's sides. I knew, from an early age, that I was not going to get stuck there.

I also deliberately did things that I thought would make me stand out. I wanted to show that I wasn't like everyone else. If others were wearing jeans, I'd wear different types of trousers. If they went to school on a bus, I'd cycle.

These were small things, I knew that. What I really wanted was to be known for something *good*. When I was still young my father told me about John Lennon being shot on his doorstep by a man, Mark Chapman, who did it because he wanted to be famous. He wanted to be known as the man who killed John Lennon. That resonated as something horrible within my head. I thought: *If I'm going to gain a reputation, it must be for an achievement I can be proud of.*

Perhaps this is why, when I was asked what I wanted to be when I grew up, I'd always say: I want to be the king of Earth. I wanted to be the person with the clear head who was in control, who made the decisions, who ensured a fair distribution of resources, who stepped in to remove any need for any nation or any person to go to war. I was absolutely serious about this, until I wasn't and it became a joke between my sisters and me. Later on, as I travelled through the world, I'd tell them that I was surveying my clients, checking where I'd set up my headquarters.

And there was also the life that began for me after night had fallen. My parents and their friends thought I was a polite sensible boy who was always ready to help them out, who never cursed, who would always do his homework, just like my quiet, placid friend Niels.

And that was true, except that I also had another friend, Kristoffer, who is my best friend to this day.

Kristoffer was different. He was not wild exactly, and nor was I, but whenever we met we would get into some sort of trouble. We'd egg each other on, each trying to be more daring than the other. As the rest of my family slept, I'd sneak out of my bedroom window, run across the rooftop and slide down onto the ground below, where Kristoffer would be waiting. We might go to someone's garden to steal some apples, then chuck them at cars we thought were going too fast; running away laughing as they braked violently, or lost control. We'd set off powerful homemade fireworks, detonate mailboxes. In the winter we'd toss snowballs at people's doors. I guess it was the sort of high jinks and mischief boys all over the world get up to – we weren't taking drugs or stealing anything – but having this other personality I could inhabit, one that came with a whole set of new possibilities, was important to me. Like the lake, it was a space that offered both sanctuary and adventure.

As I grew older, these places I could retreat to became ever more important.

My parents were a surprising couple in many ways, both a jumble of completely opposite qualities. It is easy for me to see what I took from each of them. My father is all the structure I have within my life. He has incredible confidence; he is the sort of person who you always feel is a step ahead of you. Perhaps because, in the most literal terms, he probably is. He wakes up early each morning so he can start his day before everyone else. He sets money aside for a rainy day. His mind is very structured, very organised. It's important to him to be prepared for every eventuality, and it's even more important to him that you always, always, follow through on your promises. If you say you are going to complete a task, there's no excuse for failing to do so.

This is allied to an unmistakable charisma. He's a salesperson but he's also an entertainer. He picked up a guitar the day I was born and before long he was bringing it everywhere. He'd take it to parties and write songs to suit whatever occasion was being celebrated.

My mother is all adventure and imagination. I can see clearly that there is no way I'd have been able to pull off the logistical feat of navigating a path through every country in the world without flying if I had not inherited traits like discipline and foresight and structure from my father. If I had just been my mother's creation, I'd probably have been stuck strumming a guitar on a beach somewhere.

But if I had been subject only to my father's influence, I don't know whether I'd have been inspired to set out at all. I needed the bit of me that is curious about different cultures and meeting people and tasting food I've never tasted before. The part that is desperate to find out what's around the corner. More than that, though, it was my mother who seeded that desire to become one of this planet's great adventurers. It's a very un-humble, very un-Danish ambition, but I cannot deny that it's there.

I sometimes wonder how significant it is that her name, Ylva, is a variation on 'wolf'. There's a Russian roulette quality to her: you're never entirely sure what version of this brilliant storyteller you're going to get. She was working as a tour guide when she met my father, and now, at the age of seventy-six, she's a tour guide again, taking groups to Italy to tell them tales about the Romans, or local wineries, or whatever these people are interested in.

I think too that of my two parents, she's the more volatile. My father always said that he didn't want us to fear him, but we had to respect him. I suspect that I did fear him, though. I certainly never wanted to upset or disappoint him. It was different with my mother. We'd have these terrible, heated arguments. I remember one time – I was just into my teens – when she slapped me in the face. Without thinking, I slapped her back. A friend of mine who happened to be watching couldn't believe what he had seen; he returned home that night traumatised. The awful thing is, I don't think we thought it was that strange an incident. It's not a defining moment in our relationship. Just another thing that happened.

The person she argued with most, though, was my father. By the time I was thirteen or fourteen they were fighting almost every night. They seemed to be trapped in a single, recurring incident in which my father stood there, calmly, as my mother screamed and cried. Sometimes I would creep over creaking floorboards, out of my bedroom, and partway down the stairs, where I would grip the banisters, pressing my face into the gap between them and listening to what was happening in the rooms below. As soon as they gave any sign that they might have registered my presence, I'd jet back to my bed. Then, one by one, they'd come in to check I was OK, while I lay there pretending to have been asleep all along.

Nobody was surprised when they told us they were getting divorced. I was fifteen by then. It was a relief; the marriage had long been beyond repair. But I think, even having seen them argue for so long, we were all a bit shocked by how vicious the aftermath was, by how much jagged, angry feeling swirled around us. One of my sisters described it as having been like a war. My mother took custody of my sisters and tried to get me as well. I think she wanted to hurt my father as much as she could. She was caught up in emotions, and we do terrible things when we let hurt or pain run our lives. But I decided to stay with my father, and so for a while we remained in that vast house, which now felt incredibly empty, until it could be sold.

We knew people were talking about us, though, oddly enough, for a few months it was hard for the local gossips to know what to pay attention to first, since four other families broke apart at almost the same time as ours did.

Very soon after the divorce my father met another woman, who already had two children of her own, and he moved in with them, instantly forming what looked to me like the ideal nuclear family. He had, very clearly, moved on. My mother, by contrast, couldn't stop talking about what a horrible deceiving human being he was.

And I was left by myself.

This underlined something that I had always felt, but perhaps not been able to articulate. My father's emphasis on organisation, on being there to support us financially, had come at a cost. I realised that he hadn't really been part of my childhood. He used to leave early in the morning and come back late at night. Some days I wouldn't see him. I barely ever talked to him. He was more like a bank than a father. I remember him asking, 'Do you need money? OK, I'll write it down. You can pay me back.' I don't remember him telling me that he loved me, or giving me a hug. He just wasn't that sort of man.

In the aftermath of the divorce I started to really struggle with this. I resented his absences, which meant I spent more and more time with other people's families. Some of my friends' parents became almost like surrogate parents for me; they filled the void that I thought my own mother and father had left. Because the question of which parent I'd spend Christmas with became a nightmare, I opted for neither and started spending that time with my friends and their families.

I'd sit there with my 'spare' parents and feel angry at my own for the fact that they hadn't stuck it out. I was pretty sure that the human beings I was sharing the table with had had their own ups and downs, and yet they were still there, still together. Why hadn't my family been able to do the same?

My father was the focus of my anger. Because, as I saw it, surely he knew better. I'd written my mother off by that point; I saw her as being absolutely hopeless. There were various things that contributed to this feeling, though the final straw came when I was sixteen and she and my sisters moved out of the house they were living in without telling me. The best part of a week passed without me knowing where my mother or siblings were. Then, after four days, they sent a postcard with their new address. It was too late. I decided it would be easier if I just cut her off. I told myself that I would not speak to that woman again, I didn't need her in my life.

Three years passed before I convinced myself that I still needed a mother, and we tentatively began to re-establish a relationship.

(What was odd is that it was only then that I noticed she spoke Danish with a Finnish accent.) I'd never been scared of telling her that she was a bad parent. I was cruel to her for so long, especially when I was a teenager. I regret that. Then my relationship with her began to change, became almost paternal. I'd let her know when I felt her behaviour had crossed a line; I called out her most blatant lies. It was easier to forgive her, I found, to accept that she wasn't going to change and to instead try to make the best of what we had. We had some hard years. And even today there are times when I find myself thinking, that's weird or that's strange, but we all only have one mother.

It wasn't until I was an adult, working in Libya on a project building a cement factory, that I was fully reconciled with my father. Out of the blue he sent me an email suggesting that he come to visit me in North Africa. I was so shocked that I had to read it three times to make sure I hadn't just imagined it. Our relationship was non-existent and now he wanted to come and *stay* with me?

I sent him a cold, business-like reply saying that if he wanted to come to Libya, he'd be more than welcome. One thing led to another, and we started to organise the trip. Once he arrived, I decided to take a few days off to show him something of the country. I hired a Toyota Land Cruiser, as well as a guide and another man who drove the car and cooked our meals, and we headed off deep into the desert. At some point on that trip, after days of driving on a paper-flat surface broken just once – by the extraordinary sight of Waw an Namus, a dormant volcano that contains three lakes, one red, one green and one blue – everything exploded. Until then there had been a sort of professional courtesy to the journey. We were less like father and son than we were colleagues. At times it felt as if he was measuring me up and I was trying to prove myself. He seemed impressed by the little bit of Arabic I spoke and the position I had obtained. Slowly, however, as we passed through an empty landscape with a dome of endless blue sky above us, the kind of land you could believe that God had forgotten about, our conversation turned to more uncomfortable territory. We started talking about our family and before we knew it we were in a heated argument. Once the fight had begun, neither of us could stop. He told me all the ways in which I had disappointed him, and I shared all my anger and hurt. I do not know what the two Libyan men must have made of this pair of crazy Danes.

Eventually, as we sped through that barren landscape of pebbles and dust, we reached a kind of understanding. We were here now, and there wasn't much we could do about it. We had both made mistakes, and though we could not undo them, we could at least try to move past them. It worked. Once I was able to strip all of the anger away, I could see him more clearly. It became easy to respect his cleverness and his competence and his bravery. I realised how much I could learn from him. We became best friends, or at least something close to that. My father has become far more emotional now – it's easy to make him cry, and it's easy to see how proud he is of me. I know my mother, who always loved us deeply, is proud of me too; she just shows it in different ways.

The time I spent in Libya had changed other things about me, too.

I went through most of my education without any real enthusiasm. To me it felt like I was just on the conveyor belt of life, being dragged towards the next thing. I think maybe I was waiting for a subject or passion to seize my interest, and in doing so transform me. This never came.

I carried on ploughing my solitary furrow. At business school I realised how vulnerable my loneliness was making me. How could I exist in a classroom if I wasn't willing to acknowledge the people in it? I willed myself into making a transition into somebody who had friendships across every clique, who was invited to every party. I guess I was a sort of class clown. I found that cracking jokes, being noisy and entertaining others came easily to me. (Around this time, I learned that the famous Danish writer Hans Christian Andersen had a reputation as somebody who could move effortlessly from one social class to another; as at ease with kings and queens as he was with factory workers. As soon as I heard that, I thought: *I want to be like that.*)

In my second year there was a kind of talent show. I devised a stand-up routine, and delivered it in front of hundreds of people. It was terrifying, but I found that I was hooked on the thrill that performance gave me. Still, it wasn't clear what I could do with that feeling.

After I had completed my military service, which I spent as part of the Royal Life Guards, one of the Danish Army's most distinguished units, I had a spell as a United Nations peacekeeper. The months I spent in a blue beret were eye-opening. It was my first trip to Africa; and I was going with a gun, to the Horn of Africa, not sunbathing in Egypt or Kenya. It was the first time I'd seen a dead person, an Eritrean lying there, his blood flowing out of his head into the sand. And there was that uncanny, uncomfortable sense of being a target: I remember driving through valleys in the middle of the night knowing that it was almost certain that someone I could not see had trained their sights on me. I had never been in such close proximity to violence. I was still a child then, really; unable to absorb the culture or history of the part of the world I had been sent to.

I returned home desperate to unpack all that I had learned of life and death. My friends would listen intently for a few minutes, then the focus of our conversation would shift. We'd start talking about someone's new toaster, and all the things I wanted to say were buried. I did not discuss those months with anyone again.

My friends were not interested in how I'd been changed by what I'd seen, they just wanted to know if I'd killed anybody. I learned that it's hard to keep people's attention.

After that, and a season in Austria as a ski instructor, I got into shipping and logistics. I thought that I'd lead a super-international life. No two days would be the same and I'd be swimming in money.

There was none of that. I spent four years working on a laptop in Denmark. The only thing that was international was the paperwork that crossed my desk. It was only when there was a change of management that I saw a chance to change things. I told my new boss that I was ready to leave if I couldn't go abroad. OK, he said, that can be arranged.

I expected that I would be sent to Singapore or London, New York or Rio de Janeiro. Instead, I was posted to Libya. Libya was one of those places, like Kazakhstan or Bangladesh or the Arctic, where you had more margin for error because nobody else wanted to go there. I knew that people got burned out there but, if I stuck it out, I'd be free to make mistakes without having to worry too much about consequences; I'd have a lot of autonomy. We were building a cement factory, so I picked up a lot about construction and logistics and all of those things. But what changed me fundamentally were the other lessons I learned.

During this time, I immersed myself in Arab culture – the world of handshakes and smiling and maybe telling the truth and maybe not – absorbing tiny details that would still be helping me a decade later. I discovered how much tea you had to drink, and how many cigarettes you had to smoke, to get inside a port, or a meeting with a man whose help you particularly needed.

I started reading the Quran and learning Arabic. I studied Libyan history to try to work out how the country had come to be what it was. I picked up Colonel Gaddafi's *Green Book* to get inside the mindset of this man who had come to power as the hero who liberated Libya from a king that nobody liked, then clung on to power for forty years.

That time is the reason I have a beard to this day. For the first couple of weeks in Libya I couldn't make anything work. Nobody listened to me or did what I asked them to do. Then I remembered that while I was in the UN we'd spent time preparing for a trip to Lebanon, where we'd been told that in some parts of the world there was more respect for men with beards. We ended up in Eritrea instead, but that fragment of information had stayed with me.

I stopped shaving and soon doors began to open for me. I don't know if it was a direct result of my facial hair, but one thing was definitely true: you can only get so far without trying to understand your environment. I had to understand how the culture worked, what was appropriate, and when. When was I offending people without knowing that I was offending people? In some countries, like Denmark or Britain, it is generally quite easy to know what another person thinks about you, even if some of what they feel is masked by politeness. But in much of the rest of the world the culture of hospitality is so dominant that you have no idea if they like you or not. If they need you or not. If they think you're funny or not. If you are polite or not. If you do not know the culture, then you will not know when you're stepping on someone's tail, because they're not going to tell you.

I also discovered a great deal about myself. Having pushed to be sent abroad I found myself in a swamp of difficulties. The fundamental explanation for my presence there was that people *weren't* doing what they were supposed to. When I realised that not only could I do the job, but I was actually good at it, something about me changed. I gained a new confidence. I discovered what it was like to be presented with a problem, and to then go away and try to find a solution, whether that was something technical or a question of finding the right person to help you.

I'd proved myself in this incredibly tough environment. I'd thrived in it. It made me feel as if I was capable of anything.

The project in Libya was interrupted by a dispute between my company and the Libyan government. I returned home briefly, and discovered that, for complex tax reasons, I literally couldn't stay in Denmark, so my company offered to buy me tickets to anywhere in the world I wanted to go. At this stage, despite my posting to Libya, I wasn't at all well-travelled. I'd skied in Finland and Austria, been hiking in Sweden and Norway, but everything else was just a dream.

What happened next showed how green I still was. I wanted to see Angkor Wat, the Cambodian temple complex. So, *naturally*, I asked for tickets to Bangkok. I arrived there still wearing a business suit and knowing nothing. At the airport I decided I would become a backpacker, and would buy everything there to avoid what I thought would be the chaos of trying to get hold of a bag and a water bottle and all the other stuff I guessed I would need in the city itself. I paid through the nose for these, as well as for a three-day tour of Bangkok and a limousine to take me to the hotel.

Everything changed when I summoned up the courage to step into the city's dizzying, crowded neon streets and got talking to Cam, an Australian backpacker who'd already been on some incredible journeys. After three days together in Bangkok we went our separate ways. He headed to India and I abandoned all the luxurious activities I'd booked and went to Angkor Wat on a bus. I got to walk around and talk to people and feel like Indiana Jones as I explored ancient, ruined temples, saw spiders and snakes and landmines, and caught cholera. It was liberating, it was transformative. And it put me on a new trajectory: I wanted more. I could feel the way in which this rush of new experiences was working on me, almost creating me anew.

For almost all my life I had worried that I lacked an identity. I was just an average person, maybe somewhat less than average. I wasn't interested in the things the people around me loved. This meant that I didn't have the sense of community enjoyed by people who, for instance, support the same football club. But these long journeys and complex foreign projects gave shape to something that had been inside me since I had first gone to Africa as a UN peacekeeper. I remember once, not long after my return from Eritrea, when I was working as a skiing instructor in Austria, a colleague had got a flat tyre while driving his expensive new Audi in the mountains. He came up to me and said, 'Hey, Thor, come over here, you've been to Africa, you can fix this.'

In some ways, it was an odd thing to say, and yet there was some truth to it. I did not realise it then, but I had become the sort of person that goes to unusual places, who learns how to do unusual things, who knows unusual things. I liked that. These were the sorts of things you might say about a real adventurer. I cursed my luck for having been born in a time when there were no adventures left.

CHAPTER 2

# The Last Great Adventure

*Copenhagen, Denmark, January 2013*

Over the years, the sense I had of having been born in the wrong century did not fade away. If anything, it became more acute.

It felt to me as if I was living in an era with little place for mystery. We know what causes thunder and lightning. There is nowhere, literally nowhere, you can go on this planet that another human being has not already been.

We live in a world haloed by many satellites – there cannot be any undiscovered continents. We have counted every island. New technology has allowed us to see into places that were once regarded as almost impossible to reach. Lidar, which emits a particular kind of light that can penetrate through even the thickest of tree cover, means that someone can fly a plane or a drone over the Amazon and, without having to set foot on the forest floor, locate the scraps of an old civilisation.

It's amazing. Of course it is. But I cannot help feeling sad about the way that things like this remove the need for somebody to wade through undergrowth, dodging snakes and spiders as they search for the crumbling wall, or abandoned trinkets, that signal that people had once lived even here.

I was longing for adventure. That instinct, that *attraction*, had been planted in me when I'd read about Mowgli in *The Jungle Book*, or Robin Hood, or Tarzan, or when I'd watched Indiana Jones.

As a boy I'd been able to escape into the forest. Then, Kristoffer and I had enjoyed our night adventures, paddling through canals and other lakes all the way out to Denmark's only river, which leads out to the ocean.

When I was young, all the things I'd read about in books felt thrillingly possible. I believed that one day I'd be able to stride out into Antarctica's snowy wastes, like Amundsen, or plunge deep into unknown tracts of jungle, like Henry Stanley. And then I grew up and realised that this was not true. I had become an adult in a world that no longer cared about these things. Once, news of Dr Livingstone had been the thing that prompted breathless news reports. Now what excited people was how fast a man was capable of cycling through France.

I'd tried to keep that thread of excitement unbroken, even as I understood that others had moved on. I remember one night, when Kristoffer had come to visit me in Libya; we'd gone out with a guide and a driver on an expedition into the Sahara.

The sun had long set, and everyone else had already turned in, but it was still only 9 p.m., and, we said, *who goes to sleep then?*, and headed out into the dunes. When you are this far into the desert, there is no light pollution, it feels as if you can see all of the stars in the universe. We walked and walked, entranced by what we saw above us, until we saw that we had crossed over a cliff, which meant that we could no longer see the footprints we had been relying on to help us find our way back.

Where was the camp? We knew it was within 300 metres but the dark, featureless terrain had disoriented us, we had no idea which direction it lay in. If we took the wrong choice, we might find ourselves 600 metres or more away. That could prove fatal.

Kristoffer had just become a father; he wanted to stay where we were, and wait until morning when our comrades would notice our absence. But I wanted to embrace the experience of being lost in the Sahara. It had activated something inside me; I felt as if the sort of adventure I'd read about in books had just fallen into my lap. We could head out alone into the wilderness! Navigate by the stars! In the end we did neither. Kristoffer remained in place, having turned his phone torch on, while I quartered the area around us, eventually locating our camp.

As avid as I remained for adventure, the problem was I did not know where I could find one. At the back of my mind, I feared that maybe this was because there were none left.

I had been idle for months when I got the email. It was January 2013.

Four years previously I'd set up as a sole trader; hiring myself out to people who needed a logistics coordinator. For a few years, everything went well. It got to the point where I was being offered jobs that I couldn't take because I could only be in one place at a time. I was beginning to consider expanding.

Then a project I was attached to was shut down and after that, everything was different. I had just bought an expensive apartment in Copenhagen but overnight my income had been liquidated. An accountant friend of mine told me: just find an income. So I took a job as a camp manager in the Arctic. The company I was working for was installing wind turbines in one of Sweden's most remote, coldest corners; I was in charge of running the mobile hotel they'd built fifteen minutes away from the site to house their workers.

We had to contend with wandering moose, blizzards and temperatures so cold that they froze the river we drew our drinking water from, and I was earning a fraction of what I had been used to, but it was enough, and I hoped that things would be different once I got home. They weren't. The phone stubbornly refused to ring. The economy was in a slump. Everywhere around me people were being fired. Who in their right mind was going to hire a consultant like me?

This worrying development was accompanied by another, slightly different train of thought. I started thinking to myself: *I've only ever worked on other people's projects.* Someone would call me, tell me that they had something they thought was a perfect match, and if I liked it I'd jump on it. But I hadn't given any consideration to what I wanted to do. This was followed by another thought, which was both liberating and terrifying in equal measure: what did I want to do? There was, somewhere still within me, the desire to do something spectacular, but I wasn't actively looking for an opportunity.

I was ready for a spark to set me off, I just didn't know it. And then it came. My dad forwarded me a link to an article about an incredible adventure by an Englishman called Graham Hughes. He had gone to every country in the world without flying. It felt to me like the most amazing achievement of modern times. It was exhilarating. But it also hit me like a punch to my stomach. I was angry and frustrated that I had only just learned that this feat had been lying there, waiting to be completed. But now somebody else – a man who I instantly saw as a legend, a hero – had done it.

Still, I was overflowing with enthusiasm. I couldn't stop talking to friends, family, anyone who would listen, about Hughes's journey. Until then, I had not realised that it was even possible for one person to visit every country in the world – I had known about a Danish man, a school teacher, who had died of old age when he'd been on the cusp of doing so; and I'd reckoned that if biology didn't stand in your way financial constraints might – let alone to do so without ever setting foot on an aeroplane. All I could think about, all I could talk about, was the buses, the trains, the borders, the epic scale of the four years Hughes spent on his journey.

My friends would listen politely, then move the conversation on to another topic. For me, it had become the world, I was already infected with the idea; they had other stuff to think about. The obsession grew. I found out everything I could about Hughes and his triumph. At first, this was just a question of trying to sate my curiosity, and then something started to happen. The more I learned, the more it became clear: the game is still open; I had stumbled across something that *still* had not been done.

Hughes had flown home several times during the journey. Sometimes there were good reasons for doing so (although once he had flown to Australia to see his girlfriend), but the fact remained. He had made things easy on himself by visiting seven countries in one day. He'd failed to get a visa for Chad so had persuaded a border guard to let him go across for just long enough to do a GPS plot. Even in the most generous interpretation his achievement had a big asterisk next to it.

I began to think about what a clean definition of the project might look like. To me, it was clear that you couldn't return home at any point. Because then it was no longer a single journey. Then there was the duration of time spent in each country. Most travellers' clubs – groups of well-travelled globetrotters that meet to share their experiences – demanded a minimum of twenty-four hours, which sounded good to me. Then, finally, most importantly, any form of flying, for whatever reason, automatically voided the project. If I fell sick with malaria and the authorities decided to put me on an aeroplane and evacuated me against my will, the whole thing would be over. You cannot say I went to every country in the world without flying, *except for that one time.*

What happened didn't spring out of me. I didn't really have the original thought. That was fine with me. Most things in the world build on someone else's ideas. Very few civilisations can lay claim to a great invention like writing or the wheel. They simply see what someone else has done, and then they adapt it, or improve on it, in the process making it their own. That's what I did with the project: I made it mine.

My mind started turning over, and I thought about my background in logistics. I realised that what Hughes had achieved was essentially a logistics project. Surely, I thought, I can do this better. There's a more optimal way of doing this. To begin with, I wasn't doing much more than daydreaming. I was thinking to myself: *I'm not going to do it, but if I* was *going to do it, how* would *I do it?* I remember buying a map, a blue pen and a red pen. Then I sat down with my younger sister, Tove, and we drew in Graham's route.

I like efficiency. I love the idea of the perfect system – something pure that works *exactly* as it is designed to. Much of my life has been spent hunting for the perfect system, and then being disappointed when I don't find it. I'd start somewhere like the Danish Army, an organisation that in theory has been refining its methods and structures for centuries, somewhere whose systems looked perfect on paper, and discover that nothing worked the way it was supposed to. It was all chaos, everything was done at the last minute. Then I went into the UN with the same high hopes, and they too were disappointed.

The project was my chance to build a perfect system. I thought I would have control. I could do the research and make the decisions. Should I take a bus or a train? Should I take the chicken bus or should I take the VIP bus? Am I staying at this place or the other place? How will I get there? How long will I spend there? I thought I could manage all of this by myself.

The idea that there might be flaws, or that something might go wrong, was anathema to me. That strain of thinking was so strong in me that when I read about the Danish Adventurers' Club – a highly exclusive band of travellers – who stipulated that one of their criteria for membership was that you had been on an adventure when something went wrong, I was outraged. What a bunch of amateurs! If you're good enough at what you do, nothing should go wrong. I'm going to go to every country in the world without flying and nothing will go wrong because I'm not an amateur.

After all of this thinking and dreaming I finally realised: *I can see a route through this. I can do this better than Graham. I can become the first to reach every country without flying.*

The list of the countries I would visit began with the 201 nations that Hughes had passed through (the 193 recognised by the UN, plus the constituent parts of the United Kingdom, Kosovo, Western Sahara and Taiwan, and the UN's two observatory states, Palestine and the Vatican). Once I was on the move, I'd also add the Faroe Islands and Greenland. I hoped to be able to pass through a country on average every seven days.

There is, I realise, something arbitrary about all of this and I have a hard time defending my own list. I know in some people's eyes it's silly to recognise Wales, Northern Ireland and Scotland as countries, as well as Faroe Islands and Greenland, but not, for instance, giving the same status to some of the territories that make up the Kingdom of the Netherlands, like Sint Maarten or Curaçao. Although I might also add that nobody who was trying to make their task easier would voluntarily add Greenland or, indeed, the Faroe Islands . . .

There was a great deal of strategy when it came to devising the overall route. I had this idea that if you're from Denmark, there's no news in being someone who's visited fifteen or twenty countries. Anyone can do that. So I wanted to get the country count up quickly in order to grab the world's attention, but also because I knew that later on in the journey my progress would be slower. Some countries are just impossibly big, or tricky to get into. Or both. So for those early stages in Western Europe, my plan was to stay for no more than three and a half days at a time. There was little novelty in places like Germany or Sweden that I had already visited, or could visit very easily in the future. I saw little point in lingering in them.

After that, I'd cross the Atlantic to North America. And again, that would be straightforward, because those countries are culturally similar. From there I'd go down through Central America and into South America for the first time in my life. I'd circle down the west coast, come back up the east coast then hop over to the Caribbean.

Then I'd return to the US, before travelling to Africa, which I would complete in one go, exiting to Europe (again). Next there would be Eastern Europe, the Middle East, and then from there I'd go to Central Asia, South-east Asia and East Asia. And then, finally, I would make my way into the Pacific, which would be the end.

I reckoned I could do it in four years, three and a half if I was quick.

For me, the saga in its purest form was a logistical masterpiece. I see logistics as an art form where the coordinator masters a vast amount of information and releases it to the right people, in the right quantity, at the right time. If that is done professionally then everything else runs smoothly. This can be applied to almost anything in life, from complex construction to organising your home and your relationships to those around you.

And looking back now, I'd say that probably 90 per cent of the plan I created in 2013 worked out. I'd still say that I had the right plan. What is also true is that the project ended up humbling me. That remaining 10 per cent contained more horrors, more frustration, more chaos than I could ever have anticipated.

What's strange is that although by the time the summer of 2013 came around my mind had been essentially colonised by the idea for months, I was still really just toying with it. I had a plan – a good one, I thought – but I remained uncommitted. Then my phone started to ring again. The first couple of jobs I was offered were either boring or unremunerative; then came something that seemed perfect. It was in South America, which I'd never visited, it paid well, it fitted with the time I had available. Every box was ticked and yet I found myself – almost as if someone else were speaking on my behalf – turning it down. That was the first moment that I knew this adventure was going to be something that I would actually do. Some part of my brain had reached that decision long before the rest of my consciousness had caught up. Everything was more serious after that.

All the stuff that had been hazy and hypothetical suddenly had to be forced into a more definite, purposeful shape. I started to have to think about a date. I'd already agreed to run a marathon in Berlin in September that year. Plainly it wouldn't be a good idea to leave the day after; it would be sensible to give my body a couple of weeks to recover. That put us in October. Why not the tenth? There was something about setting off at 10.10 a.m. on the tenth day of the tenth month. It was just a shame about the year. Still . . . there are some things you can't change.

With a date decided on, thing got busier still. I started to think hard about what I actually needed to have set up. What about sponsorships? What about a website (and how did one go about setting one up)? What was I going to put in my bag?

One thing was very clear to me. I couldn't afford to pay for this journey by myself, and I didn't want to go into debt in order to do so. This was where my friend Ann-Christina, who had a background in fundraising for veterans, came in. Over brunch I shared my plans. She, in turn, seemed to share my excitement. 'You have to do this,' she told me. 'We can definitely find you sponsorship; this is pocket change for these people.' By the end of the meal she had become part of the project group.

She was joined by another friend, Søren, who came on board because of the work he does with startups. He was the person I trusted to help me put in place everything I needed for me to promote my journey. This, we believed, would be a big part of the plan. Through contacts he'd made while his company was working with another client, he helped me build a website for free.

And then finally there was Parth, an Indian whom I'd met in Bangladesh who was uprooting his life and moving with his wife to Europe. He, too, appeared to be inspired by the idea. He is a graphic designer by trade, but that only tells part of his story, because I also think he is probably a genius. He's like a muse: capable of spitting out a thousand ideas every minute. Ideas so good that you actually want to follow up every single one. It was Parth who, as well as designing the look for the website and the uniform I was going to wear, suggested some of the most important elements of the project, like bringing a gift to every country, or taking a photograph of someone's eyes each time I crossed into a fresh nation.

Funding came from a company called Ross Engineering. They are leading figures in geothermal energy, and ever since I'd struck out on my own in 2009, had comprised the bulk of the business I had. It was a close relationship – they were almost like a family – so they were the natural people to approach.

My first step was to email them to say that I was available for any work they might have up to 10 October 2013, but after that I'd be away on my journey. They replied almost instantly: come to our office immediately, let's talk.

This riled me; I thought: *I have my own company. They can't tell me what to do.* But I also knew that I didn't want to lose them as a client, so I got on my bike and cycled over to see them.

I was ushered into one of their meeting rooms, where four of their most senior staff members were seated at a big table, waiting for me.

Before I'd even settled into my chair, they were on to me. It was like being savaged by a pack of wolves. The gist of their argument was: What *happened*? Did you hit your head? You're not really going to go through with this stupid idea, are you?

For better or worse, they were confronting somebody who was still head over heels in love with that 'stupid idea'. I mounted a vigorous defence of my plans, which saw them change their minds – 'This is brilliant, this is so crazy, we have to be a part of this' – but also gave them another reason to laugh at me.

I explained that I'd decided to work on a budget of approximately $20 a day; the consensus was that it would be tricky to get much done with any less.

'Twenty dollars a *day*? That's ridiculous. We'll obviously give you more.'

I made a brief attempt to argue, with little success, and walked out of the room with double what I'd asked for. All I needed to do in return was take a photo of a Ross banner they would give me each time I crossed a new border. And, of course, finish the project.

During the time before I committed to the project, I'd carried on thinking about what it was that I wanted to do with my life, and how I proposed to make money. I knew that I was still interested in logistics, and that there were certain immutable facts about the world – wars, natural disasters – that meant that there would always be a demand for people with a skillset like mine.

I searched the internet, juggling different possibilities, but the thing that really caught my eye was the Danish Red Cross's ERU, or Emergency Response Unit, who were trained professionals – doctors, camp managers, logistics experts, psychosocial support teams – who would be parachuted into disaster zones to begin the cleanup.

The problem was that you were only paid when you were deployed, so you also needed to have a job where your manager was comfortable with the idea of you leaving at a moment's notice. My view has always been that you should never feel as if you're too posh to pick up a broom and sweep the floor. I think you get further with that mindset; you're less likely to be left behind. So I was trying to see if I could work as a substitute teacher (they took me on, but I never actually got to go into a class) or collect tickets on the Metro (they never got back to me), and then the friend of a friend said that there was a homeless shelter that needed someone to do night shifts.

This gave me the opportunity to get close to the sorts of people – criminals, drug addicts, alcoholics – who I'd been afraid of my whole life. Now I was able to connect to them on a human level. I could give them syringes, spare clothes and a bed to sleep in. But I could also, maybe just for one night, be a steady, normal presence in their lives; perhaps the only one they had. In addition, I also worked nights at the Red Cross Asylum Centre.

Those two jobs gave me an income that helped me pay my bills as well as giving me space to do the Red Cross training and, it turned out, to start planning my big adventure. At a certain point I decided I'd approach the Danish Red Cross to see if they'd be interested in supporting the project in any way, which led ultimately to them confirming that I'd be able to travel as one of their goodwill ambassadors. I was passionate about being able to publicise the contribution the Red Cross and Red Crescent Movement makes across the globe.

Although they are best known for the important role they play in responses to natural and humanitarian disasters, as well as providing ambulance services, most people don't really know what the Red Cross does until they need help. In that moment, they learn a tremendous amount about them.

Their remit is, essentially, anything to do with humans. In some countries that will mean putting up streetlights to make it safer for women to walk after dark; in others they provide training for family counselling; in Orlando, Florida, I'd see volunteers knocking on doors in trailer parks to check that the residents had functioning smoke detectors.

I felt honoured and excited to be representing such an organisation. The arrangement was that I'd write an 'always present' story for the member societies in each of the 191 countries they operated in; in practice this would mean visiting every one of them, because how else could I write each article? In return, they gave me a letter of credit written by the secretary general of the Danish Red Cross, which explained my role and mission, and asked people for help and support.

After that, there wasn't a great deal to do.

I wanted to tell both my parents about my plans in person. I knew that my dad would take a lot of convincing – that it would be a hard sell – so I brought a map and the news that the Danish Red Cross had decided to make me a goodwill ambassador. As I spoke, I could see the disappointment in his face. Once we'd mended our relationship, he had come to be very proud of the career I'd built in logistics, and now in his eyes I was throwing it all away.

'Don't do this,' he said. 'I know you. You're a grown man, you're thirty-four, you make your own decisions, but if you want my advice, don't do this. No one will take you seriously after this. You might not be able to get a job.'

I carried on trying to sell the project to him. 'This isn't a hippy-ish kind of thing where I'll be on a beach smoking weed and playing a guitar. This is hardcore logistics. I'm travelling as a goodwill ambassador of the Danish Red Cross; even if everything else fails that gap in my résumé will be filled out as "Goodwill Ambassador of the Danish Red Cross".' I threw everything I had at it; enough, I think, to take him at least part of the way with me.

I didn't need his permission, but I did want his approval. I knew I'd be more at ease going into the world knowing that he was OK with what I was proposing to do. He told me that I would always have his full support, and I knew he meant it. He'd always be that person who I knew I could call if I had trouble of any kind. He'd make a call and set things straight. My mother, for all her many qualities, is a completely different story. And so, of course, we had a completely different exchange.

By this point she had moved to the south of Denmark's Middle Island, the part of the country where I'd been born. Her house was on a quiet street in a town called Svendborg. The two of us went for a walk. It was a beautiful autumn day, there was no traffic, birds swooped above our heads and she was talking, talking, talking, talking, because that's who she is. She was also pointing out interesting elements in the local flora and fauna, speculating out loud whether the apple trees we could see were evidence that there had once been an orchard on that site. I love this about her, she's really good at it; she sees the sorts of things others miss entirely. But eventually I interrupted her.

'I have something I want to tell you. I'm planning this extraordinary journey. I'll be gone perhaps for four years before coming back home. I'm aiming at going to every country in the world completely without flying.'

'Well, that's nice,' she replied in the same neutral tone she might have used if I'd told her I was planning a trip to the dentist, 'I also like to travel. Oh, look, I think there's another apple tree over there.'

Over and above all of this was one disturbing, exciting fact. I had fallen in love, with a woman called Le. The relationship had begun at pretty much the same time that my father had sent me the story about Hughes that had sparked my excitement.

We'd met at a wedding in Copenhagen. I'd flown in from the Swedish Arctic, where I was working at the time, put on a suit, and then found I was sitting at the same table as Le (we later learned that this was a piece of matchmaking that had been planned months in advance). We got drunk, realised that we had a connection, but within a couple of days I was back in Sweden.

I sighed, resigned myself to being alone forever, and then got on with my life. Three days later, she sent a Facebook friend request. What followed was not straightforward, but it also somehow felt inevitable. It was clear to me that Le was incredibly special; I already found it hard to imagine my existence with anybody else by my side. Alongside all of this, though, were my own experiences of long-distance relationships foundering because I was too far away, for too much of the time. I'd come back too many times to find that the other person had stopped waiting for me. Now I was proposing to spend at least three years, very likely more, on a quixotic adventure around the world.

I wasn't dumb, I knew others were poking her going, *Are you going to stay with this guy? You don't know when he's coming home. If he's not there with you, why are you investing time in him?* What they didn't know, and I think we did, was that we had something special, but we were so early on in our relationship, we had to work

41

THE IMPOSSIBLE JOURNEY

out what we were going to do. That's when Le, who was about to embark on a PhD, said: 'Let's stay together as long as it makes sense.' This felt to me like as good a plan as any.

It took me two days to leave Denmark. I had a party in a shisha café, inviting everyone I knew from the city to smoke, drink tea and talk. Then Le accompanied me to the station, where I took a train to Silkeborg, in Jutland, where I had a very grown-up dinner – red wine on the table and kids playing beneath it – with my friends from business school.

The next morning I woke up and, for the first time, put on the uniform I'd wear, pretty much every day, for the next nine years: a grey polo shirt with the Red Cross emblem on the left side of my chest, a long-sleeved T-shirt, a pair of combat trousers, Salomon walking shoes, and on my head a fedora-like felt hat that I'd bought from Copenhagen's oldest hat shop, having walked in with a crumpled photograph of one of my greatest heroes, Indiana Jones. There were practical reasons for having a hat. Eye contact is important to me, but my eyes are quite light sensitive, so I wanted shade without the loss of eye contact you get with sunglasses. I'm balding, so a hat offered protection from both heat and cold. More than that, though, it was a sign that this was an adventure – a baseball cap doesn't give that message.

I had with me two bags, one small one, containing the stuff I might need immediately, and then a larger duffel bag, which contained everything else I believed was essential. Among other things there was a sleeping bag, a hammock made out of the same fabric as a parachute, a mosquito net that would fit around the hammock, four sets of my uniform, socks, and twelve pairs of boxer shorts (I knew I wouldn't be able to do laundry every day, but I wanted, *really* wanted, to make sure I had clean underwear). There was also rope, some knives, a compass (because if you were going to every country in the world, why *wouldn't* you bring one? I didn't use it a single time), a Red Cross canister, and an iPad and phone and all their assorted chargers.

As the journey wore on, I'd acquire more electrical equipment, such as a GoPro and other cameras, which inevitably meant a heavy bag of cables too. I brought a lot of books, including Ernest Hemingway's *For Whom the Bell Tolls*, and a couple by Jan Guillou, featuring Carl Hamilton, the man known as the Swedish James Bond – thinking I would have lots of time to read, which I really didn't. Even then, I kept travelling with them as a kind of punishment, saying to myself: *If you want the bags to be lighter, read the books.* At various times Le would act as a kind of mule, bringing me new books from home, and taking back with her the few I managed to finish, as well as the various trinkets I'd acquired.

Still, I came home with a lot of books I hadn't read. Someone else would have brought a Kindle, but it was somehow important to me to have something that I could touch and smell, with pages whose corners I could fold. Although this still probably doesn't quite explain why I insisted on carrying the *National Geographic* encyclopaedia I bought in Canada, which had phenomenal detail about countries and their culture and religion, but was also extremely bulky. (Someone I met later stared in disbelief at its size: 'You are truly insane,' he said, wonderingly, 'why don't you just pull out the pages you need?' The same man made me line everything out on the floor really neatly in the military kind of style, so he could take a photo of me in the middle of all my crap. What he saw incensed him so much that he almost left the room. 'You're an idiot!' But that was my way to do it.)

My father drove me south to the border with Germany – where we would meet Kristoffer, who was living near there – stopping off en route to do an interview at a radio station. We arrived to find a journalist and his cameraman ready to film me.

I was red-eyed, exhausted, but full of energy and optimism. I had all the financial backing I needed! I was a goodwill ambassador for the Red Cross!

Everything felt bright and exciting. I'd found the last great adventure. I was going to go out into the world, complete that journey and write my name into the annals of history.

The journey, for me, was a chance to rank among names like Ernest Shackleton and George Mallory. I wanted to make a mark so that one day in the future someone would pick up a book that contained an account of what I had done and they would be inspired. I believed absolutely that I would become one of the most famous people on the planet, perhaps the most famous. The only question was, when? Would it take ten, twenty or thirty countries? I thought that my uniform would soon be covered in sponsors' logos, like the driver in a Formula One team. Money would pour in. I'd be picked up by friendly helpers in their private yachts. I'd have audiences with prime ministers and presidents.

I didn't consider the possibility I would fail. I knew that sometimes it would be fun, at other times it would be miserable. And I didn't really think it would change me as a person. Why would it? It was going to be a discrete chapter in my life. Once it was over I'd come home and return to my work in shipping and logistics. I knew I was good at that. I saw no reason why I'd do anything else.

Looking back now, it is slightly painful to think that I was delusional from the very first seconds of the project.

We'd chosen a starting point with historical significance: a windmill at Dybbøl Mølle, a little way from the border. The Red Cross had been founded in 1863, exactly 150 years before I was due to begin my journey. Its first mission was a war between Prussia and Denmark the following year. It had used that windmill as its headquarters.

The war had been a disaster for the Danes, who lost a great deal of territory. Nevertheless, the windmill had been woven into my country's national story, the subject of many songs and stories. For all those reasons, it felt like the perfect place to start.

The timing felt auspicious too. I wanted to set off at 10.10 a.m. on the tenth day of the tenth month. And my idea was that this precise moment could be filmed. It was a mild morning, above us the sky was blue, dotted with a few clouds, and it was pleasant to wait, each of us alone with our thoughts, for the clock to strike 10.10.

And then, about twenty minutes before the big moment, the journalist's phone rang. He walked away and had a brief conversation with whoever had called him, which I couldn't follow.

'Sorry,' he said, looking unapologetic, 'we've been called to cover another story.'

I looked at him in disbelief. 'You have to cover this. This is the big historic day. I'm leaving Denmark *today.*'

'So, can we just pretend it's ten past ten? Can you say goodbye to your father and your friend and then walk off and we'll film that, and we'll do a short interview with you and you can talk a little bit about why you're doing this. And then we'll jet off and then you guys can wait for ten past ten.'

There wasn't much we could do. My father, always the showman, insisted on a countdown.

I joined in, as did Kristoffer, then I walked off, waving at them. I'd taken a few steps when the cameraman called me back. 'Yeah, stop. That's far enough.'

After a hurried consultation, they decided to film my legs, then very soon afterwards we were watching their van disappear into the distance.

Fifteen minutes later, my father and Kristoffer started the countdown again. I took the first steps of my journey, then instantly slowed. I realised I didn't actually know what time the bus I was supposed to be catching was coming. I headed over to the bus stop and examined the timetable: another eight minutes to wait. Just as I was beginning to worry that there was something a little bathetic about the beginning of my epic adventure, the bus came round the corner. Its display read 'Number One'. For some reason, this restored my spirits. As my father took a flurry of photographs, I climbed on to the bus. I sat there and thought about how, in a strange sense, this moment on a windswept, anonymous border between Denmark and Germany would be the furthest I'd be from home at any point in the whole journey. Even then, I felt a sense of urgency bordering on impatience. Each day I set aside to rest, or visit some local site of interest, would push the date of my return back still further. For the moment, though, that didn't matter.

My journey had begun.

CHAPTER 3

# A Stranger Is a Friend
# You've Never Met Before

*Warsaw, Poland, November 2013*

I set off on my journey as somebody who believed themself to be well-educated and cosmopolitan, someone who knew a few things about the world. My objective was to tick off all of the countries one by one, then come home having hopefully had some amazing experiences along the way. I told myself that the world is so big, there are so many countries, that of course I'd return richer, even if just by default. I would taste things I'd never tasted before, see a shade of colour in a sunset that was completely new to me. I hoped that I might meet some nice people, but I wasn't invested in telling their stories. This was my narrative – I should be at the centre of it.

I didn't understand how big my blind spots were.

But I started to realise a few things early on. So many of the countries I passed through were not what I thought they would be. Even though in many cases I was only staying for a brief period of time, I could see that they had more value than I'd expected.

Sometimes it was the architecture, sometimes the people's clothing, sometimes the quality of the food or the smartness of their public transport. Occasionally it was all these aspects at once. At other times it was tiny, almost insignificant things, like the fact that everyone was carrying brand new smartphones in their hands. I'd feel a throb of embarrassment that I'd thought so little of that nation, and leave the country frustrated that I'd only just started to satisfy my curiosity about it, wishing I'd given myself more time to explore; that I wasn't impelled by this desire to visit as many nations as quickly as I could.

At that stage, I was so deeply conscious of the fact that my progress would be slowed dramatically once I had left Europe, that I was 'optimising' to a degree where I was losing weight because I wasn't eating enough. I wasn't sleeping very much, and I wasn't taking the time to actually see things or have meaningful encounters with the people I met.

The other realisation that hit me is that I had left Denmark without a particularly developed interest in human beings and the cultures they create. Quickly, though, I understood that countries are nothing without the people that live in them. It is people that make countries. The landscape can be beautiful, there can be the most sensational mountains, or lakes, or forests, but it's the people who live in and among those natural wonders who shape them and make them interesting. The whole locus of my attention changed.

This process was accelerated by the unbelievable kindness, openness and hospitality I received from the very beginning of my journey. The first leg had seen me cross the border into Germany, and then travel on to Hamburg where, somewhat to my surprise, I found that I was completely exhausted. I had not been sleeping a great deal and I had felt emptied by all my encounters with the press. I don't think I was used to the new, exciting sensation that the person training the camera in my direction was interested in *me*.

I found that my story opened something up in people. The guy at the hotel in Hamburg who gave me a free breakfast. The couch-surfing host in Bremen (at this stage I was using an app called CouchSurfing to arrange my stays) who excitedly showed me round his beautiful city. Ruud in Amsterdam, another couch-surfing host, who made me risotto with Danish blue cheese and took me on a tour of the Dutch capital on his old-fashioned bike, which included – on his insistence – a visit to its red-light district. 'You haven't been to Holland if you haven't seen a peep show,' he told me. I worried he'd be offended if I didn't take his invitation up, so I went, though in deference to the ideals of the Red Cross, I taped over its insignia on my uniform. Or there was the young persons' choir in Liechtenstein who I met through my Finnish cousin who happened to be in the area at the time, and who sang for me on their bus.

And it wasn't as if people needed the project as an incentive to do something kind. In Andorra, where I had carelessly left my GPS tracker (which was essential for proving I'd actually been where I said I had) on a bus, a bus driver not only took me to the depot to help me recover it, he diverted his vehicle on to a completely different route to do so – and not a single one of his passengers complained. He didn't know that I was doing something different to any of the hundreds of people he'd driven around that day – he just saw somebody who had a problem and went out of his way to fix it.

None of these moments were very big in themselves – little fragments of generosity and warmth – but they had a cumulative effect. It made me start to question whether I would be capable of offering the same if I'd encountered these people in Denmark.

Then came Poland. It was already late November by the time I arrived in Warsaw, and temperatures had plummeted. I was also experiencing my first meaningful delay of the project, because it proved harder than I'd expected to get a visa for Russia. This was a significant obstacle. In order for my plan to work, all the logistics needed to fit together. I was travelling from Poland to Lithuania, and then on to Belarus with a transit visa, which I could only get if I had a Russian visa that proved I was travelling on to somewhere after Minsk. In hindsight, my frustration at being held up for four days seems faintly comical. Compared to what would follow, four days was *nothing*, but I was going mad at what I saw as time slipping away from me.

And after all the kindness I'd experienced thus far, the cool reception I got at the Russian embassy gave me a jolt. It seemed to me as if the women working there had decided to shun me.

'Is it not possible I can get something by tomorrow morning?' I asked the woman behind the desk when she told me how long I'd have to wait.

'No, no. There's no way,' she informed me, her languorous desire to take things slowly smothering the urgency I felt. 'This is the process.'

The next day I decided to draw on my experience of the sorts of gifts that had helped keep things moving when I was working in Libya. I returned to the embassy, this time with some chocolate. I thought that if I could befriend the women there, then maybe things would go more smoothly.

I pushed the chocolate across the counter and stepped back, looking expectantly to see how they would react. They paused for a second, then started laughing. They didn't actually say, 'You have no idea what you're doing,' but then they didn't need to. It was written all over their faces. And yet it did do something. Now we had a little connection. It wasn't enough to speed up my visa application, but it did change the tenor of our interactions. Everything became warmer, more friendly; they no longer looked pained at the mere sight of me.

The delay gave me the time and space to look around me a little: I went on a walking tour of the city, visited the cinema several times, drank shots of vodka over which somebody had draped a slice of ham spread with mustard, ate kebabs and sushi, and lay in my room watching TED Talks. It was winter, so I was alone in the hostel. I liked the solitude. And it was sometimes easier to not be the sober thirty-four-year-old surrounded by partying twenty-year-olds.

By the time I eventually had the visa in my hands, I was desperate to leave. It was late in the afternoon but the idea of waiting until the morning had become intolerable. I spoke to the helpful people at the hostel I was staying in. They said that if I set off that night, I'd be able to make it to Suwałki, in the north-east of Poland. They even managed to telephone a guy who lived there to arrange somewhere to stay for me. 'He's insisting on being paid the exact money, the *exact* money, and didn't sound very friendly, but it's just one night, so you'll probably be fine.' This was far from perfect, but I didn't have any better options.

Three hours later I stepped out of the train into dark, snow-covered streets and was instantly reminded of a joke I'd been told earlier that week about Suwałki being the coldest city in the whole of Poland. Suddenly, as I tried to sink deeper inside my winter jacket, I felt on the wrong end of a punchline.

I also encountered another problem. I'd been given my host's address on a scribbled piece of paper, but had no way of actually locating his home. At that stage of the project, I was trying to get by without acquiring a new sim card each time I crossed a border. You could usually rely on finding wi-fi somewhere, but not, it turned out, in Suwałki at eleven in the evening. I had alighted from the train alongside a number of other passengers, all of them swathed in heavy winter clothing, but they had soon slipped into the darkness, taking with them any chance I might have had of asking for directions. I looked around, hoping to find a shop or a kiosk that was still open. Nothing. I cursed myself for forgetting to look the address up on Google Maps and saving it on my smartphone before I'd left the hostel.

What I *had* managed to find out was that Suwałki was a city of some 20,000 people. And yet none of them appeared to be awake. I had travelled enough by this stage that I was generally able to get a feel quite quickly for the geography of a city. It's always possible to sense where its centre is by looking out for church towers and tall buildings, or watching the flow of traffic. Not here. It was dead. There were no moving cars, not a single person walking the streets.

In the hushed silence of this snowbound, sleeping city, I was beginning to worry that I was edging towards something difficult, or uncomfortable. Spending a night out in that frigid cold was deeply unappealing, but what was I going to do with no map, nobody to ask and no landmarks to help me navigate towards signs of life?

I decided the best, perhaps the only, thing for me to do would be to pick a direction, and then simply commit to it. I tried to orient myself using the railway as a guide, figuring that if I could walk away from the direction I'd arrived in, I'd give myself a fighting chance of finding *something*. Still, I knew that it was essentially a coin flip.

I pushed on for fifteen minutes before I reached a T-junction. Standing under a streetlight as snow gently fell on my hat and beard, I looked down the street at the houses and parked cars, trying to decide which way I'd go next. There was nothing to distinguish the street from anywhere in the world. I could have been back in Copenhagen. Its only notable feature was its lifelessness.

It was then that I saw a door open two or three houses down from where I stood. A woman stepped out on to the stairs that led down to the street below, her slim figure silhouetted by a blaze of light coming from behind her. This was my opportunity. What did I have to lose? I lumbered across to her, my heavy bag crashing against my shoulders.

I cannot imagine how shocked she must have been to see this strange, snow-crusted foreigner emerge without warning from the darkness, and yet she appeared unruffled. Instead, she smiled down at me, as if waiting for me to speak. In that moment, I suddenly realised how profoundly exhausted I was. The idea of taking even a step further began to feel impossible. 'Hello,' I said, more in hope than expectation, 'do you speak English?'

'Yes,' she replied. I looked at her more closely: she was middle-aged, wearing jeans and a thick woollen jumper. Her face was kind, framed by brown hair that hung down to her shoulders, 'I'm an English teacher.' There are parts of the world where you do not expect people to speak English, and this provincial Polish town was probably one of them, and yet here I was standing in front of somebody who actually taught it.

'Can I ask,' she said gently, 'what you're doing here?'

Questions like this always required me to decide how much I was willing to share. I had to weigh it up: is it an advantage for me to let people know what I'm doing? If they're excited then that could really help. That might give them an incentive to go a little bit further – maybe by giving me a bed to sleep in, or helping me across a border – so that they could feel as if they'd played a role in the project. But sometimes, if they could smell my desperation, it could devolve into yet another power play.

I would usually just have a few seconds to work out what camp the person I was speaking to fell in. Over the course of the journey, meeting more and more people, I got better at reading people; my intuition improved. It was never as straightforward as a list of signs or tells, more a feeling that: *If I tell this man the truth it will make their day*, or *If I tell this woman too much she will make my life hell*.

In this case, I decided it would be better not to complicate matters, so I simply told the woman that I was travelling, that I needed to go to Lithuania the following day, and that I was looking for the home of the man I was supposed to be staying with.

I handed her the scrap of paper that had the address scrawled on it. She looked at it briefly then back at me. 'Yes, I know where it is, it's not far. But wouldn't you much rather stay at my house?'

I remembered what the people at the hostel had said about how unfriendly the host they had spoken to had been. But that was what had been organised. He was expecting me. On some level I felt an obligation towards him. And who was this woman? Everything about her seemed pleasant, and yet could I really walk into her home and spend the night in whatever bed she was willing to offer me? She was a stranger. I'd never done anything like this before. The couch-surfing was different, that was all arranged; there were safeguards, email chains, online ratings. What if there's some enormous beast of a husband hiding around the corner, ready to grab me by the throat? But it was late, really late. And she was standing there before me enveloped by the warm glow of her home's interior. Just a handful of steps would take me out of the biting cold and into that calm, quiet space.

All of my confusion emerged in the fractured words that spilled out of my mouth. 'Well, no, I can't do that, you see there's this man that's expecting me . . .'

'But look,' she said, pointing at the scrap of paper with his address I still held in my hand, 'there's his telephone number, I can call him to tell him that you're not coming. I have a guest bed. It's not a problem.' She looked at me expectantly. As she waited, I tried to take a second to think as quickly and clearly as I could. *I'm going to go to every country in the world. I should be more open to people and experiences. This seems safe. I mean, she's obviously a kind woman. I should just go with it.*

'OK,' I said, 'let's do that.'

'Fine,' she said, then smiled before explaining that the reason she had opened her door that night was because a storm was sweeping across Europe from west to east; it had already caused untold damage. They were expecting it to hit this part of Poland later that evening and she was worried that some of the nearby trees might break and fall on her car. Leaving me on her doorstep she hopped down the stairs to her car, moved it, then returned, beckoning me to follow her inside the house.

As I kicked off my boots I realised that we still did not know each other's names. She had no idea who I was or where I had come from, and yet she had seen that I needed a bed. That, it seemed, was enough for her. While she bustled around in the kitchen, I brushed the snow off my jacket and bag, then joined her.

I decided to introduce myself. 'My name is Torbjørn Pedersen,' I'd shorten my name later on in the journey, 'and I'm Danish.'

'I'm Maria,' she said. 'You must be hungry, it's so late.' She was right, I was hungry. The meal I'd had on the train now seemed like a very long time ago. But I felt reticent about saying yes – I'd already imposed so much on her evening. 'No, thank you.'

She did not believe me. 'Oh, rubbish, I'll warm something up for you.' Almost before I knew it I was sitting at a well-loved wooden table with a plate of potatoes and eggs in front of me, and she'd handed me a cup of tea. As I ate, we began to talk more. I told her about my journey, and she revealed that she was a member of a travellers' club. The night drew on, I became more and more comfortable, and then suddenly a woman in her early thirties came down the stairs. She looked confused, then instantly launched into a long, antagonistic conversation with Maria that rattled on at immense speed. Occasionally she would gesture in my direction. I spoke no Polish, but I could follow the drift of things closely enough to establish two things. First, that she was Maria's daughter; and second, that she thought her mother had gone crazy.

I tried to look as unobtrusive and harmless as I could. Eventually, the daughter calmed down. It turned out that she spoke English too. She was a lawyer and was sick. Our conversation had disturbed her, and she was worried about who had been invited into the family home. Now at ease with the situation, she returned to bed.

A little later, after I had finished eating and had helped her with the washing up, Maria showed me down to the basement where a guest bed was already made up. Once we had said good night I slid under the heavy duvet, laid my head on the pillow, and drifted off before I could even begin to process the twists and turns of my evening. I slept deeply, undisturbed by the storm that raged all around the house.

When I woke the next morning, Maria and her daughter were already up. They made me breakfast then offered to drive me to the stop where I'd catch the bus to Lithuania.

We drove through slushy streets to the bus terminal. I stepped out and was struck instantly by the cold – the temperature had dropped a few degrees overnight. As I stood there, my feet slowly freezing, Maria helped me buy a ticket, told me how nice it was to have me to stay, and then resolutely refused to accept anything in return.

Later on, safely inside the warm bus, I began to reflect on what had just happened. I was struck by how unlikely it was that we ended up meeting in that way. I had essentially rolled the dice when I walked away from the train station. But I was at that intersection at precisely the moment she opened her door. If I had taken a left rather than a right, if she had delayed checking on her car by five minutes, our paths would never have crossed. I don't believe in fate, or destiny. I don't think we have our futures mapped out in the stars, but sometimes it's hard to look at how things turn out and *not* be assailed by vertigo.

More than that, though, was the hospitality she showed me. My thoughts returned to something I'd already been considering. What would I have done if the situations had been reversed, if I had been at home in Denmark and somebody had stepped out of a snowstorm with an address in their hands. I know that I was the sort of person who would have cheerfully given them directions. I might even have offered to drive them to their destination, as long as it wasn't too far out of my way. But would I have invited them in and given them a bed to sleep in? No. And even if I had been willing to do that, there's no way I would have cooked a meal for them in the middle of the night. At best, they might be offered a glass of water.

Maria, with her unthinking generosity, changed something in me. Now, ten years on, I like to think I'd react more like she would if faced by similar circumstances. She encapsulated, for me, the meaning of the saying, 'A stranger is a friend you've never met before,' which is something that would go on to be very important to me as the project wore on and I was presented, time and time again, with similar instances. It doesn't mean that every single human being you walk up to has the potential to be your friend. Some people aren't pleasant, or kind. Some people will hate you because of the odd accidents of your birth, or some part of your personality that you can do nothing to change. Some people will try to cheat or hurt you. That's humanity, for better or worse. You can't befriend everyone. But that sentence does give an indication of how you can, or should, behave when you meet somebody new. Do you look them in the eyes? Do you remember their name? Do you allow them to speak? Are you polite or do you push them aside? The idea is to behave as if every person you meet is *already* your friend.

There was a kind of calm confidence about Maria. For some reason, she felt able to trust me immediately. I am sure I was not the first person she extended that kind of generosity to, and I am equally confident that I will not be the last.

In fact, Maria was a living embodiment of another concept that I came up with over the time I was finding my route through every country in the world.

In Northern Europe we exist in this weird space that makes us unlike maybe 90 per cent of the rest of the planet. When we get on a bus, we take a seat that places us as far away as possible from any other passengers. You only sit next to somebody else if you absolutely must. You will not ask: how was your day? What's your favourite colour? How many children do you have? At a push, it's acceptable to ask when the next stop is. I can see the argument in favour of this approach: it's a way of respecting others' privacy and preserving our own.

Still, it feels to me as if we've got this wrong. Almost everywhere else on the planet does it differently. If you're the first person on the bus, you get to pick whichever seat you want. But when the second person climbs on, there's only one 'right' seat – the one that's next to you – because it's the only seat that allows them to begin a conversation. For them, the *worst* outcome from that encounter is that they'll have a pleasant conversation. But they're far more sensible of all the places that it could lead to. Maybe they'll come away with a new job! (My experiences with couch-surfing showed me something similar: if I wrote to ten people in Paris, my expectation would be that they'd either ignore my request or reject it. In West Africa, by contrast, everybody you contacted offered you somewhere to sleep: the issue was how to turn down kind invitations.)

There's an African proverb: if you want to go fast, you go alone. If you want to go far, we go together. When I set out from Denmark, I needed to go fast, so I went alone. It did not take me long to realise how wrong I was. Over the course of the nine years that I was on my journey, I met hundreds of men and women who, like

Maria, went out of their way to help me. Whatever it was that I achieved was built on the shoulders of others – the people who lifted me up and brought me through the project. There's no way I could have pulled it off on my own. The idea that *anyone* could travel to every country in the world, let alone without flying, and not rely on the contributions of other human beings, is delusional.

People like Maria understand implicitly the idea that it took me years of travelling to absorb: when you're dealing with people, it's like you're playing a lottery in reverse. In a conventional lottery you buy a ticket and you expect to lose, even if you hope to win. And, of course, it's overwhelmingly likely that you will lose. With human beings, it's different. The odds are reversed, it's as if the whole game has been rigged in your favour. When it comes to people, you're constantly winning.

## CHAPTER 4

# Master of Nothing

*Reykjavik, Iceland, May 2014*

My journey began to get a bit complicated in the spring of 2014, a little over six months after I'd left home.

I'd spent about a third of that time in Greenland, which had been tricky to get to in the first place, and even harder to leave. I needed to reach Canada, which meant crossing a few thousand kilometres of the Atlantic Ocean. My first plan had been to hitch a ride on one of the fishing trawlers that operate in the waters between the two blocks of land. The fish they catch is offloaded in Greenland, and then the boats return to Canada before winter comes and closes everything up.

But I was too late for the ship that had agreed to take me. With little prospect of being able to find another berth, I reluctantly returned to Iceland, which felt like a better springboard for the next stage of the journey.

I didn't necessarily mind having to retrace my steps like this – I liked Iceland, it was Viking country after all – but I was disquieted by the fact that my progress had slowed from a sprint to a sludgy crawl. This was my second visit to Iceland. In the same time period, I'd managed to pass through thirty different European countries. I didn't like that, nor did I like the fact that it felt to me as if I was losing control. I was at the mercy of events, and there was no amount of persistence or ingenuity that could make things go faster.

For the first time since leaving home I found I had no desire to explore or meet people, I just wanted to hide by myself. I was beginning to realise that I had set out on a journey that was nothing like I thought it was going to be. The task I had set myself felt easy when others reflected some of my enthusiasm for what I was trying to do back at me. But not everybody in Iceland seemed to share my excitement.

I remember a woman in a bank who I decided to tell about the project. I suggested that she might want to follow me on Facebook, or Instagram. She looked at me disbelievingly. 'Why?' Her indifference was so intense that it felt almost like antagonism. I was taken aback. Still, I tried to explain: 'Well, because I'm showing you all these different countries that I'm going through.' 'But I can find that on the internet.' I walked out, disheartened.

The blunt fact was that if I wanted to make progress, I needed to be able to 'sell' the project to strangers. I could not leave any of these countries when I wanted to. I could not choose between different options for transport. I could not plan my long-term future activities because I was at the mercy of strangers and their willingness to 'buy' what I was selling. Without that, I was a master of nothing.

Over the next few days, I continued to run into the same attitude. The worst moment came when I approached a shipping company that had routes to Canada. I thought that perhaps if I turned up at their offices and offered them a free speaking engagement they might ask more about my story. They would get to know me, and hopefully like me, and then want to support what I was doing.

I walked up to the reception desk, told them a bit about why I was there, then waited while they called somebody from the offices on the floor above. That was when she appeared on the stairs. You could feel the world around her turning grey as she descended. Everything about her was miserable. Strange things seemed to be growing out of her face; hair sprouted out where it shouldn't, and she appeared incapable of smiling.

She fixed me with her shark-like eyes and looked at me as if to say: what? She wanted to show me that I was an inconvenience in an already unpleasant existence. She succeeded. Still, I was here now. I summoned up all the enthusiasm and energy I could. 'Hey,' I said brightly, 'I got this far. This is country number thirty-nine. I need to get on board a ship and continue.' I told her what I was able to offer in return, then waited.

'Why would we want to listen to that? What do you have to tell us?'

'Well,' I said, feeling something lurch inside me, 'I have had different adventures, I've met different people—'

'Yeah.' There was no sympathy or interest in her voice. I could tell that all she wanted was for me to walk out through the door and never return. Every second I was here I was polluting her existence. 'Do you know that the kinds of people we usually have as speakers here are people that have been to the top of Mount Everest?' Her words stabbed into me; they were like a physical assault; I felt as if I'd been struck by an ice pick.

Almost in a daze, I handed her my card. She took it and told me that she'd get back to me in a way that left me absolutely convinced that she would not waste a single second on my proposition. Then without saying anything more, she walked away.

I trudged back to my hostel. I still wasn't putting sim cards in my phone at this stage, and there was no wi-fi. I couldn't contact anybody to try to process what had just happened. Instead, I was alone with my thoughts. The walk was longer than I'd remembered. I could feel my feet dragging. It was as if they, too, were beginning to wonder whether there was any point to everything I had been doing.

I cannot now recall how long the journey took; it could have been forty minutes; it could have been four hours. But I do know this: for the first time since I had left Denmark I was beginning to consider giving up. I'd already been to almost forty countries, which seemed like a lot of progress until you began to consider how far there was still to go. All the biggest challenges lay ahead of me. And yet what was the point if nobody cared? Not even me.

I had set off convinced that I was engaged on a world-historical challenge and yet the support and attention I'd hoped for was barely there. I started to wonder whether I had spent the last months in a bubble, telling myself I was doing something amazing when, in fact, I'd just been wasting my time. Was this an illusion that I'd created for myself? Does it have any of the value that I think it does? Does it have the significance? What is the point in reaching every country without flying? Is it simply enough that it has not been done before? Nobody has tried to live off coffee alone for a month before: is that reason enough for someone to give it a go?

I plodded on. Something inside me had shifted. It was like getting a completely different perspective. Maybe, I thought, I'm not one of the great explorers. Maybe I'm not in that calibre. Maybe I'm just someone who is taking backpacking to extreme lengths.

As soon as I got back to the hostel, I turned on my iPad, logged on to the wi-fi and searched: how many have reached the summit of Everest? It was over five thousand. I was taken aback, I had not realised so many people had made it. I looked to see how many had made it to every country in the world: around two hundred. This made me feel better; it was fewer even than the five hundred who had been to space. I imagined someone in the not-too-distant future looking up my achievement and seeing just one name beside it: mine.

Still, that left another problem. That woman in the shipping company's office did not know or care how rare was what I was attempting to do. Nor did she appreciate how hard, or complicated, the endeavour would be.

Most people only recognise two types of travel. You're either on holiday, or you're travelling for work. The distinction is that if it's a holiday, then you're the boss. You do whatever you want, you wake up when you want to, you see and do whatever you want, and you pay for it. And if it's work related, then it's highly confined. You will be charged with some form of task, you'll probably spend most of your time in airports and conference rooms. It's mostly routine and dull, and at best you might have a couple of hours off where you can go and see a temple or a bar.

I could understand why someone would look at what I was doing and say, it's definitely not work. Going to every country in the world without flying is not a job. So it has to be a holiday, or something close to it.

But I would argue that there is a third category. Here you cannot escape the travel part, but the travelling itself is not the target; it's a mix between the two, but really it's a third and different creature. Running a marathon is travel, but no one in their right mind would call it that. You cannot reach the top of Mount Everest or the International Space Station without travelling, but we don't see mountaineers or astronauts as travellers. The project wasn't about travel. The overall aim was to reach every country in the world without flying, something which cannot be done without travel.

I was not a tourist or a traveller, that was clear to me. Finding a label I was happy with was harder. What eventually seemed best was either a Modern Viking, or a Modern-Day Adventurer. I liked these, but, in truth, they did little to help clarify my situation. I'd still get people saying, 'I wish I had your life. I would love to see every country in the world and do it without flying. You must have met so many people . . .'

There were other adventurers whose journeys were far more legible. People saw them sweat and struggle along as they tried to run across Africa and it was immediately obvious what they were doing, and also that it was pretty tough.

It was never as easy for me to convey the scale of the challenges I faced. Not in the few seconds you get in a TikTok clip. How do you communicate the frustration you feel at being turned away yet again from a border crossing, or the difficulty of getting a spot on a container ship? Those things don't lend themselves to easy explanation.

I was not spending my days lazing around on a sunbed. I wasn't drinking local booze into the early hours. I was working. Working so hard I'd often curse that there weren't enough hours in the day.

But what all of this reminded me was that I *was* doing something unique, that had never been completed before. It still felt to me like the last great adventure, and surely that was something worth finishing.

I did not hear from that woman again, but I was fired with a new enthusiasm for what I was doing, so I decided to walk down to the port and see what I could make happen. In most countries it is almost impossible to do this. Ports are surrounded by layers of security; the very last thing anybody involved in shipping wants is for random men or women to saunter into their property. And the romantic notion that you can work your passage on a container ship is long gone. These days you can't just hop on to a ship, offer your services as a welder, or as a chef or whatever, then allow it to spirit you to the other side of the world. You need permits, insurance policies and a contract; all stuff that takes a while to acquire.

In Reykjavik, though, things were different. I spotted an open gate manned by a bored-looking guy in a uniform. Here was my chance. I wasn't supposed to be here. I wasn't wearing a hard hat or protective shoes. Everything about me was off. Or, at least, it should have been. I took one step. Then another. Then another. Then, I realised: nobody is going to shout at me. All I need to do is carry on walking as if I know what I'm doing and where I'm going; as if I'm *supposed* to be here. As long as I don't turn around, I'll be OK. What I learned that day is that you can get away with a tremendous amount on this planet just by being a little bit cheeky. If you can look authoritative while you do it, all the better. Or, as someone once told me: walk like a king. If you look timid, you'll make yourself a target. You need to give the impression that you own the place.

Over the course of the journey, I refined this method. In particular, I trained myself to not react when I heard loud noises. I wouldn't turn my head immediately, even if I heard a loud bang or a scream. Instead, I'd let two, three seconds pass, then calmly turn my head.

This time, though, my success left me almost giddy with disbelief. Feeling as if I'd pulled off one of history's great heists, I approached the gangway of the first ship I saw. My feet clanged up the metal until I met a guard, who this time did seem interested in stopping me. 'Who are you?' he asked me. 'What's your business?' With all the authority I could muster I informed him that I was here to see the captain. 'OK,' he said. They called the captain then pointed me to the bridge, where they said I'd find him. With each step I told myself thinking: *I can't believe I've got this far. This might just work.*

Andriy the captain was a slim young Ukrainian, whose kindness was immediately apparent. He was also eager to help, but aware that he did not have the authority to let me on board. Instead, he gave me the contact details for the shipping company who ultimately owned the ship: although the *Westerkade* was being operated by the dreadful lady's company, it did not actually own it.

'We're sailing tomorrow,' he said, 'I hope you'll be with us.'

I walked away full of hope and immediately called Jesper at Ross Engineering, who then contacted the shipping company. It was better this way. If you've got somebody who can vouch for you, it's so much better than just being a random guy approaching a massive corporation.

A deal was quickly struck. I'd get a berth in exchange for $60 to cover my insurance and $15 a day for meals and accommodation. We calculated the journey would last eight days, so I paid accordingly, and got ready to leave Europe.

'This cannot be true,' Andriy said as we stood there together on the bridge overlooking the horizon. 'I don't believe it.' The sun was setting, the water around us glittered, and above us a handful of birds flitted in the darkening sky, each searching for a final meal before night fell. It was a moment of serene beauty.

'It's never this calm,' he told me, adjusting different panels, pressing buttons and getting us ready for our departure. Somewhere far below us, the ship's huge engine rumbled into action, everything around us rattled gently. 'You must be a lucky omen for us. People think travel on ships like this is a fairy tale, but it's not: the work is hard and we often encounter rough conditions. Tonight, though, the conditions could not be more perfect.' He beamed at me, and I smiled back.

Some people, like Andriy, are built for a life at sea. Others, like me, are not. Andriy was typical of the hardworking men who lived and worked on these ships. He was passionate about both what he was paid to do, and the environment he performed those tasks in. I am nobody's idea of a natural sailor. I get seasick, I have no sea legs, I'm painfully aware of how big oceans can be, and how insignificant we are in comparison. And although I'm able to build a tolerance for being at sea, that tolerance starts to perish as soon as I return to solid land. So that cheerful reaction was exactly what I needed; I began to look forward to a stage of the journey that I'd been actually dreading.

And for the first few days, everything was fine. We rarely saw the sun – just a monolithic grey sky which reached all the way down to the horizon in every direction – but nor did we encounter huge waves, high winds, hard rain or any other harsh conditions. We existed in a binary world: everywhere you looked was either grey skies or dark ocean. There were no other vessels, we had seen no aeroplanes, and the only wildlife we'd spotted were the seagulls who hovered above us or occasionally rested on the vessel's cranes. Otherwise it was just us, the engine and the sound of water breaking against the ship.

One day followed another. The cook continued to produce thousands of breakfasts, lunches and dinners, catering for two different types of stomach. The Filipino sailors liked rustic, spicy food that reminded them of home, the kind where you end up gnawing sauce from bones. They also adored rice; consuming mounds of it. The more senior crew members, like Andriy, generally wanted something plainer, like chicken breast and fries. But nobody lingered. The sailors came, ate, and left. They were worked hard while they were at sea, so there was no time for deep conversation at mealtimes, and most finished their food within ten minutes. Still, there were moments that made you remember that alongside all the freight were complex, impressive human beings. There was the twenty-year-old Filipino cadet. I asked him what made him want to be a seaman? He didn't have a say in that matter, he replied. His parents made that decision for him in order to provide for the family – I'd learn that this was a fairly common occurrence.

Suddenly my ambition to travel to every country in the world, *because I wanted to*, began to feel like an extreme luxury.

Or there were the ship's three Ukrainians. Each of them was trying to cope with being cut off from any information about their family and friends at a time when Russian-backed rebels were seizing great swathes of their country. I thought about how I would manage, probably not as well as the chief engineer, who told me with a light smile, as if he was telling a joke, that he was a former Ukrainian: recent events had made him Russian.

This kind of deep, often intimate conversation happened a lot when I was on container ships. The men (and it was almost always men) who sailed on them worked punishing hours, sometimes as much as seventy hours a week for three months at a time. That was what they were on board *for*. I represented a break from that routine.

But that openness wouldn't come immediately. The crew generally weren't informed who I was, or even that a passenger was on board at all. They'd be left to guess. Often they'd start off thinking that I was another officer, or superintendent, which could make them cautious, as if I was there to check up on them.

Once they discovered that I was just this oddity passing through their existence for a few days, they became curious. They'd ask me questions and start talking about their own lives. It wouldn't take long for some to start confiding in me. Especially those who were having a hard time, perhaps because there was something on their minds that they didn't want to share with their mates, or because they were being ostracised for one reason or another. For the brief period I was on board, I became their outlet.

On some journeys, I'd sit in the common room, so that they knew that I was available, if they wanted to talk to me. I liked this role, but as I got deeper into the project, I noticed that I saw fewer and fewer people in the communal areas. When I talked to old hands they told me that it was a change that had been coming for some time.

It used to be different, everybody knew each other, would be able to tell you the names of their comrades' wives, and knew how many children they had at school. In the evenings they'd play cards, gossip and drink.

Alcohol has almost disappeared from ships now, though it depends on the company's policies – some still allow the odd beer if the captain gives permission. The biggest change, though, has been the proliferation of cheap laptops and then, slightly later, the arrival of the internet at sea.

Instead of discussing which movie to watch in the common room, they're holing up in their cabins to watch alone. It's great that they can talk to families and friends at home, but that means they have far less time to bond with their shipmates.

If there is an exception, it would be the Filipinos, who I thought were amazing. They'd have barbecues, there would *always* be karaoke, and they'd just generally be together in a way that many other crew members didn't. There are some nations whose default setting seemed to be happy; that was definitely my experience of Filipinos, who rarely complained, and seemed to greet any challenge with unruffled cheerfulness.

When, while on board the *Westerkade*, I tried to make a video of the whole crew dancing (a doomed attempt to go viral) it was the Filipinos who helped me out. Initially nobody was interested. So I went out on deck and did it myself. I showed the footage to some of the Filipino guys. There were a couple of seconds of what I feared was embarrassed silence – my time in Africa has made me a better dancer, but I'm never going to be mistaken for Fred Astaire – then one man spoke up, 'I'll do it.' Soon, almost everybody else followed him, and performed the routine immaculately. Or, at least, better than me, which was enough. After that, I'd have people knocking on my door, asking if we could do another.

The only holdout was the captain, Andriy, who refused point blank. He was much more typical of the Ukrainian men I met. They didn't like taking selfies, or anything else that they feared wasn't masculine. Andriy had the odd combination of gentleness and hardness I'd noticed in his fellow countrymen, as well as Russians and a lot of people in Central Asia. I always had this sense that these people spent their childhood wrestling bears, and had been brought up in a strict society, where there wasn't always enough food on the table, and their homes were too cold. In comparison to them, the rest of the world seems soft. And yet there was also this gift for true, almost immediate friendship. You are immediately confident that they want the best for you, that they will be there for you if you need them. Except, that is, if you want them to do a choreographed dance in their workplace.

There was never a moment during the project when I found myself longing to sleep in my own bed, surrounded by my possessions. For me, one bed is generally as good as another. And the *Westerkade* was not the newest or best-loved ship I would travel on. Everything that could be damaged in my cabin, was. At some point the sink had broken in half and been glued together, a chair was missing a leg. But it was a real pleasure, after months of living out of a bag, to be able to arrange my possessions on the shelves of my cabin's closet. I liked having my own couch, window and shower.

Most of all, having been in constant movement for so long, I relished the chance to take a break. On this ship, indeed on every ship like this I travelled on, I was left to my own devices. Everybody but me had a function to fulfil. For the first three days I busily cleaned equipment, repaired clothing, edited photos and drafted emails that could be sent once I was online again. After that I pretty much ran out of tasks.

Without internet, television, a telephone, or the pressures of trying to arrange the next stage in my journey, I read, slept (a great deal more than usual) and played endless games of solitaire on my phone.

More than anything, I was excited. This transition between two continents was a big thing for me. I was doing it all without flying. It felt momentous. After all the anxiety and stress I had felt in Iceland, I believed that I was succeeding. I was on the ship. We had left the port and there was no turning around.

Then came the fifth day of our journey. The morning had been pleasant, but early that afternoon the sky once again turned grey and it started to rain. The swell started to pick up and the *Westerkade* started to roll more and more. Once in a while, I would lose my footing and grab the walls to stop myself from falling. Waves smashed against the hull, as if testing its strength, then the bow would crash down in a spectacular spray of water. Torrents surged across the bow and containers. Suddenly this behemoth of a vessel had begun to feel tiny and frail.

I talked to the first officer, our voices struggling to be heard over the thunderous noise of the sea outside. He told me the swell had already reached 3 metres. By early evening it had doubled in size. Rowdy waves had given way to utter chaos. The thunder and lightning outside was so intense it was if the sky were being split apart.

I had been uncomfortable before, now I was *afraid*. It was impossible to stand upright unaided. Anything that was not tied down would be sent hurtling across the deck. At times it felt as if we were being repeatedly hammered by a gigantic iron fist. But at others it was more like the ship was sliding along the surface of the Atlantic. There was no telling when you would be knocked off balance.

By this point in the project I had been on six other ships coming across the Atlantic. Trawlers, container ships, fishing boats. I'd been stuck in ice, and on ships that had rolled and pitched. But this was something completely different. Night fell and it became impossible for me to estimate the height of the waves. I just knew that the wind was screeching and the ocean appeared to be trying to drag us all down into its watery depths. The worst moments were when the *Westerkade* was lifted up by the waves then dropped down at the same time as another wave or swell came from the side.

I have only a limited knowledge of physics, but it seemed to me that this ship could not withstand what was being inflicted on it. I thought: *There is no way we are going to make it across, we are going down, we have been caught up in something that is totally out of control.* We were pitching so violently that each time the front of the ship plunged down, the propeller emerged from the ocean, and, meeting no resistance, started spinning so fast that it threatened to overheat the engine. In response, the captain ordered that we should proceed at a speed of no more than 4 knots, around 7 or 8 kilometres per hour. We were effectively crawling through the storm.

Realising that I was too scared to even feel sick, I staggered up to the bridge. The higher I climbed, the more I could feel the wild movements of the ship. When I could, I would cling on to the rail that ran alongside the steps, desperately holding on to it with all the strength I had left, my arms strained and stretched beyond what I had thought possible as the rest of my body was pitched backwards. At other times another sickening lurch in the ship's gravity would throw me against a wall.

I reached the bridge. Usually these are fairly sparsely populated, especially after dark. You might expect to see just two people keeping watch on the ship's progress. Tonight, there were seven officers. The sight of them lined up together triggered a new, violent surge of fear in me. Were they about to ready the crew for an escape into our lifeboats? What was going on? Why were they talking in such a calm and composed fashion when we were minutes away from plunging to the bottom of the sea?

It was not as if they could not see what was happening. The bridge offered an unparalleled view of the mayhem outside. The lightning streaking across the sky, the rain being hurled at our windows, the great white stripes running across huge swells.

I thought: *This is no good. This thing, this adventure, was a stupid idea. I should not be here. Why did I ever leave home?*

The crew continued talking unhurriedly to each other. Although I desperately wanted to ask one of them what was going to happen, I also knew that this was not a time when it would be sensible to interrupt them. I stood there, one hand on the ceiling, the other gripping a metal rail, just about remaining upright until there was a lull in the conversation. This was my chance.

Gently, anxious not to reveal too much of the alarm that had consumed me, I asked, 'Is this normal?'

The two men closest to me turned round, sniggering. I had not been prepared for this. 'This is nothing, son. Just make sure you don't go outside, we don't want you falling overboard. Everything's going to be fine. We've seen much, much worse than this.'

I'm not sure I've ever been so relieved to be laughed at.

The storm lasted for another four days. Four days when it was hard to keep the food that had been served to you on your plate because it was moving around so much. Four days when, once you finally have the food you want on your plate, you have to sit holding on to it, otherwise it slides across the table and smashes messily against a wall. Four days in which, in addition to holding on to your plate, you must also hold on to the table to stop your chair from falling over. Four days in which you realise you do not have enough pairs of hands to eat your meals.

There was never a time when I was not holding on to a wall or railing with at least one hand, which made even mundane activities more challenging than usual. It is not until you're in a storm that you realise that there are things that absolutely demand the use of both of your hands, like closing your belt buckle, or putting toothpaste on your toothbrush. Still, the sailors' confidence meant that even when somebody mentioned in passing that we – who were not in an ice-class ship – were passing the spot where the *Titanic* had sunk, and that ice had been spotted in the area, I felt no anxiety, just mild historical curiosity.

Steadily, a world in which nothing was behaving as it should began to feel almost normal. I no longer raised an eyebrow when I opened my cabin door and saw three pairs of shoes and a doormat sliding past me in the hallway. I learned how to walk in a ship that was continually rolling from side to side at a 20–30-degree angle. My falls became increasingly rare.

I slept, when I was able, in the recovery position. A night of painful trial and error had taught me that this was the best way of staying in your bunk during a storm. I also learned why my cabin was arranged with the bunk following the length of the ship, while the sofa ran from side to side: it gives you options depending on whether the ship is rolling (in which case you move to the sofa) or pitching (you can stay in bed).

Nevertheless, several times during those four days I woke up sliding on the floor. One night I watched as my cupboards were thrown open and the shelves inside them were tossed across the room, crashing against the wall.

Showers were equally challenging. You would turn on the shower and then try to make sure you were standing wherever its crazily pitching spray landed. And I never got used to having to cling on to the toilet when I needed to move my bowels. Even putting trousers on became a complex affair.

On the night of our seventh day at sea, the waves and wind finally settled down. For the first time since the storm had struck, I slept well.

I woke, rested and relieved, in time to witness the ocean do something that I'd never seen before. It was many, years until I saw anything like it again. There were various moments in my time on container ships when I felt lucky. There is no light pollution that far away from land. On a clear night you will see more stars than you've ever seen in your lifetime. And then there is the humbling scale of the endless ocean. But this was something else.

The unimaginably big expanse of water had turned into a mirror: a thick, smooth, dark blue. It was as if it was made of oil. It was so still that you knew that every time the surface broke, you were seeing signs of life. Suddenly there were whales and dolphins and large fish that I could not identify frolicking before me. I stood on the bridge staring wonderingly. It was an image of utter, heartstopping beauty. And there was more. That night I stood out in air cold enough to cloud my breath – we had left the Gulf Stream behind, so the temperatures had plummeted – and watched as the unearthly glow of the northern lights above us was reflected in the perfectly calm water below.

Was this, I wondered, what it was like to float through time and space?

I began to think about everything I had already experienced, and everything that lay before me. It had been jarring to encounter the scepticism and doubt in Iceland, and some of the delays that had slowed me down made me think that perhaps this journey was going to be harder than I'd thought. But it was so exciting to think of all the people and cultures I would encounter, all the wonders I would see. For a few minutes I stood there, a feeling that I initially could not identify flowing through me, and then I realised what it was: joy.

On the day we were due to arrive in Canada I went back up to the bridge. The reduction in our speed had slowed our progress across the Atlantic and I realised I had never gone so long before without seeing land. We were just four hours away from our destination but there was still no sign of it, just a horizon of pure, unbroken ocean. North America was hidden from us by the curvature of the Earth.

And then suddenly an intense, resinous smell drifted up to us, it was unmistakable: forest. The wind had blown pollen across the water to us. Canada was the only country I smelled before I saw it.

CHAPTER 5

# Do You Need a Boat?

*Puerto La Cruz, Caracas, Venezuela, October 2014*

Mostly, my journey down through North then Central America had passed without incident. I experienced great kindness from people on American trains, at Brazilian bus stops, at the border between Ecuador and Peru.

It was hard work, harder than I'd thought it would be. At the same time, I was making progress. The number of countries I had visited was ticking up all the time – already over sixty by the end of my first year. I'd gone through Central America at lightspeed, and though my pace had dipped in South America, I was still rattling along at a decent lick, spending no more than a handful of days in each nation.

Some people following my progress began to suggest that I'd been pessimistic when I'd said it would be a four-year project, that I'd be home in just two. I wasn't so sure of this. It had taken for ever to cross the North Atlantic – my urgent pace now was an attempt to recover some of the ground I'd lost – and I knew that I still had many logistical and bureaucratic challenges ahead of me. But I was having good experiences, it felt as if I was on track.

Everywhere I went, people seemed willing to go out of their way to help me complete my journey. Not everything was easy, or pleasant. I remember sleeping with one eye open when I had to spend the night on a bench in a bus terminal in Honduras. And in Panama City I accidentally walked through one of the most dangerous urban areas in the whole world: a single Danish traveller in a fedora surrounded by burned-out cars, gangsters, men brawling in the road and people staring as if to say: what are *you* doing here? I was eventually found by two policemen wearing full riot gear. They called me over and spoke to me in Spanish. I could not follow what they were saying, but caught the word *loco* several times.

The fact that I generally felt safe was a constant source of surprise to almost everyone I met in Latin America. When I entered a new country, its inhabitants would tell me that I was lucky to have survived in the place I had just come from. And then they would warn me about how dangerous my next destination would be. Everyone seemed to think that their neighbours were entirely compromised of criminals or terrorists or snakes, or some combination of all three. Nothing I could say could ever persuade them otherwise.

Although, if they could agree on one thing, it was that Venezuela was the most dangerous country of them all.

Whenever I told someone about my project, they'd say something along the lines of, 'But you're not going to Venezuela, are you?'

I'd reply that I kind of had to, and they'd look at me with the mix of sympathy and fear usually reserved for the insane. This attitude was reinforced by the media I'd consumed about the country, which showed it in a permanent state of violent chaos, and what I was told by many of the travellers I met. There was one Israeli guy in particular, who I met on a bus going through Bolivia. Now, I like Israelis as much as the next man, but a lot of Israeli men that I've met have been very sure about the knowledge they possess. This man was no different. He took what I thought was an unseemly amount of pleasure in informing me of the exact numbers of people who had been kidnapped, tortured or had simply disappeared in Venezuela over the last year. By crossing the border I'd be signing my own death sentence.

For the first time since I'd left home, I was beginning to feel frightened about visiting a country. This anxiety was partly soothed by an encounter with two young Venezuelans studying dentistry in Brazil, who I met on a bus in the north of the country, heading towards Venezuela. They were intensely curious about why I was going, and far more blasé about the risks involved. 'Just be careful, keep your head down and you'll be fine.'

Still, a queasy sense of apprehension sat awkwardly in my belly as the bus trundled on. We crossed the border into Venezuela without any difficulty, and before long we stopped at a roadside café to get something to eat. The two dentists remained by my side, keen for me to try everything and providing a running commentary on each delicious morsel I put in my mouth, explaining what part of the country it came from, and how it was made. Most of this went over my head, but I felt welcomed. My fears began to diminish.

I bade them farewell at the next stop, and the bus continued up into the middle of Venezuela. We passed through astonishing landscapes. I remember in particular one moment when everything opened up. We were high up the side of a hill, gazing down into a gigantic, grass-covered valley. Every so often there would be a cluster of palm trees that looked like an island within an ocean of green. In the distance I could see the outline of mountains soaring upwards into heavy, slate-grey clouds. It was enough to make me feel as if my soul was being filled up by the beauty.

My bus eventually stopped at a city called Puerto La Cruz, which sits on the country's northern coast, looking over the Caribbean towards the islands of the West Indies. I had time to kill before the next leg of my journey, so I decided to explore a little.

At first, I felt tentative, I still had a thousand warnings echoing around my brain. And yet the streets were full of life. People ate arepas in improvised-looking cafés in which plastic tables were crammed on to the pavements, shops were open. At one point I was approached by a tiny, maternal old lady who barely seemed to reach my knees. She looked up at me with a face creased with joy and asked: 'Where are you from?' When I told her she immediately started speaking in a cheerful jumble of Danish, German and English. I made out enough to understand that she had a friend in Denmark who she had never met but to whom she wrote and spoke on the phone. She invited me to her home, offering to cook for me and appeared genuinely sad when I told her I did not have time.

The friendliness and bustle could not entirely hide the signs, which were everywhere, of a country that was struggling. After travelling through sixty nations, I was learning that it was possible to 'read' a country when you first stepped into it, and that the more experience you have, the less distracted you are by things that truly do not matter.

A greenhorn who arrives in a new country that seems exotic to them will be distracted by everything: every sound, every smell, every sight. Their senses are overloaded. But as you go through more and more countries, you learn to cut some of that noise away and start to see, if you want to, what a country is worth.

I'd always try to visit a country's national museum, and I was interested in worship. If someone ever asked me, 'Do you want to come and see how I pray?', I'd always say yes. (My feeling was: if it means so much to these people, then I should try to learn where they're at. More broadly, I was surprised by how religious the world still is. I left Northern Europe where churches were closing all the time, and I assumed I'd encounter the same story wherever I went.

And yet the opposite was true. Even if one attributes attendance to tradition, we remain a very religious planet. Some people, in some places, are becoming more secular. Faith rules everywhere else.) But, generally, I was not experiencing places in the same way as a tourist. This gave me different eyes. You see different things when you get tangled up in another nation's bureaucracy, or travel on their public transport rather than by Uber – you would be surprised by how much you can learn from staring out of a bus's window.

Eventually, you get to the point where you can 'read' a country.

You look at the pavements to see if they're actually paved, or are just dirt paths on either side of the traffic. You look for potholes in the road. You look to see if children are wearing school uniforms or not. Are there garbage trucks? Are there waste bins for litter? How often do the buses come? Do the buses have windows? You can ask locals about their schools and hospitals. These are all small things in themselves, but they help you paint a picture of what kind of country you are in. How modern and developed it is, how well it functions. And the more countries you go through, the quicker you get to paint that picture. You have more practice, and more data to use as a comparison.

The more you understand your environment, the more respect you get from locals, the safer you feel in that environment, and the less likely you are to make a mistake. This extends to cultural stuff, like the way that in the Arab world it's considered rude to point the bottom of your feet towards someone, because it is tantamount to indicating that the other person is beneath the feet you use to step in the filth and dirt of the streets. Nobody expects you to know everything, but the more you're able to fall into the atmosphere of a country, and the less you draw attention to your foreignness, the more you'll get out of your encounters.

It was always important to me to blend in as much as I could, to become, as far as I was able, part of the environment. I felt I'd be less of a target that way. It's why in Central Africa, for instance, I never wore a wristwatch, tried to ensure that the only phone people saw me using was an old Nokia, and avoided giving away unnecessary information about myself, which extended to where I was staying: I'd really have to trust somebody before I told them the name of my hotel. The less you can give people, the less likely it is that you'll get hustled.

It was obvious that Venezuela had once been rich, or at least parts of it had been. The buildings were beautiful, the municipal architecture was impressive. And yet it was also obvious that this was a nation whose economy had almost crashed. The situation was not irrecoverable, society had not collapsed, but life had clearly changed here, become less easy or straightforward. Even before they opened for business there were queues for ATMs that snaked for several hundred yards. Later I would see similarly long lines for basic goods such as flour and milk.

I saw, too, that corruption had become more or less formalised. A sailor I met directed me towards the place where I could change my money on what was essentially a black market. This was not in some shady backstreet, but rather a smart, glass-fronted office on a busy road. They clearly felt no need to hide their operations from the police.

I felt conflicted about using this service to change my Argentine pesos. I was adamant that I never wanted to participate in active corruption, like bribing officials. But this was more of a grey area. I didn't want to further destabilise a currency that was already teetering, and yet surely there was a benefit to putting money into the pockets of locals.

Having found I couldn't use any of my credit cards, I decided to use this office. They even gave me a receipt.

And there were hints of something more. Later that day I'd be surprised by how strict the security was around travelling on an intercity bus. Usually in South America, these sorts of services would stop constantly. At each halt some passengers would get off, but we'd also be joined, briefly, by hawkers trying to sell us fruit or plastic trinkets. Here there was no question of anything like this. We went from one city to another, and nobody was able to step out of the vehicle at any stage, with one exception: me. The air-conditioning pumped so much cold air around that I was actively worried about freezing (in almost all warm countries they set the air-conditioning to penguin mode). I begged to be able to recover my jacket from my bag in the hold. Eventually, grudgingly, I was allowed.

It was hard to put my finger on it exactly, but there was an unstable quality to the atmosphere in Venezuela; a sense that anything could happen at any time. I knew about the demonstrations, the mass arrests, the stories about violations of international law. None of these happened while I was there, and yet they were undoubtedly present each time someone smiled and warned me to be careful.

There were other things that defied my understanding. Puerto La Cruz had an incredible beach. White sands, palm trees, the image of tropical perfection, and yet it was abandoned. Strange, I thought. At the same time, there were no signs warning me off, so I thought I'd go to sit on it. I found a comfortable spot and started enjoying the view. The sea glistened and whispered soothingly, there were boats on the horizon. But every jogger that passed stared meaningfully. It was as if I was sunbathing in a radioactive zone. Then one stopped: 'You can't be here, go somewhere else. You're not safe here.'

It was hard to know what to do. I felt as if I was the punchline of a joke that I could not understand. The stubborn part of me wanted to stay, duelling with all the warnings I'd been given about Venezuela. Then, suddenly, the sun was blocked out. I looked up and saw four policemen sitting massively on horses that loomed above me, casting me into a dark shadow.

'What are you doing here?'

'I'm a traveller,' I told them, deciding to keep my cards close to my chest.

'You'd better move, you shouldn't be here.'

I clearly had no choice. Thirty minutes later, still none the wiser, I was shivering on a bus that would take me to Venezuela's capital, Caracas.

I never found out why I had been forbidden from lying on that beach, or why everyone else in the city was avoiding it. But these warnings remained a constant refrain while I was in the country. People would issue blood-chilling threats about what would happen if I walked alone, or went to a particular part of a particular city . . . and nothing ever happened. At the Caracas Metro I stopped to ask staff for directions to my hostel. And then one of them insisted on escorting me for the whole twenty-minute journey, all the while issuing instructions about what I was to do if I saw riots or protests (run in the other direction). We walked through busy streets filled with children chasing birds, men and women calmly going to the shops or work, and the elderly reading newspapers. In the parks there were people eating picnics, reading books, practising elaborate gymnastic moves and ballroom dancing, playing football, or simply sleeping in the shade.

I had expected to find the population cowering in their homes while thugs roamed. It was like he was discussing a city that was thousands of miles away rather than the one right under my feet. I kept asking myself: *What am I missing?*

I returned to Puerto La Cruz, again by bus, then managed to get a lift in a private car to a fisherman's village called Güiria, further up the coast. Petrol in Venezuela was, for obvious reasons, virtually free, and people seemed to have a lot of time on their hands, again for obvious reasons. So if someone was in the mood they'd be willing to take you pretty much wherever you wanted. In my case, a cheerful guy with grizzled white hair called Luis had agreed to take me and a couple of others on a leisurely journey east, stopping off along the way to have a cold coconut-based drink.

I had originally hoped that I'd be able to get a ferry to Trinidad and Tobago, but in Güiria I learned that it had long since stopped operating. Trinidad hovered somewhere out of sight off the coast of Venezuela, tantalisingly close. I reckoned a speedboat could make the journey in three hours, maybe less. There had to be a solution, I just needed to find it.

Luis found me a cheap local hotel. The long slow journey in a hot car had left me drowsy. I headed upstairs to my room to try to take a nap. It was a large room, simply furnished, and painted entirely white. I lay back on my bed, staring up at the ceiling, trying to work out what I was going to do next. I'd got this far, but how was I going to cross over to Trinidad? I tortured myself by looking again at my map. It was so close! And yet there was no obvious route to it from Venezuela. My Spanish was almost non-existent and it was hard to find anybody who spoke much English. This mutual incomprehension had rendered my meeting with the local Red Cross almost farcical, and now that I was several hundred miles away from the capital my chances of being able to communicate what I needed, or even find somebody who could help me, seemed minimal. It was also Friday, and I struggled to believe that anything would be open over the weekend.

Time passed. I drifted in and out of sleep. Whenever I woke, I'd turn the problem over in my head. Then, at around 3 p.m. there was a knock on the door. I came to, sharply. For a moment I wasn't sure where I was; the room's bare walls offered few clues. Slightly unsteadily, I walked over to see who had roused me.

I found a diminutive, smiling man with a square face. Without any preamble he asked in English so broken that the sentences barely held together: 'Do you need a boat?'

Sleep and surprise had left me slow and uncomprehending: 'What?'

'Do you need a boat? I have a boat.'

'Are you going to Trinidad?' I asked keenly, beginning to understand what he was offering.

'Yes, OK, I have boat. I'm going to Trinidad. Follow me.'

*What*, I thought to myself, *is going on?* This man had arrived, almost miraculously. It felt too good to be true. Still muzzy, I tried to decide what I should do. On the one hand, this man said he could take me to where I needed to go. On the other, I had spent weeks being warned about this country. Caracas hadn't been the hellhole I'd been told it would be, but perhaps I'd just been lucky. Did I really want to push it? How on Earth did he know I was here? And how did he know where I wanted to go next? I'd stayed safe so far on my journey by being careful. Was this a risk too far? He looked at me, expectantly. Was I going to regret this? Maybe. And yet, did I think another opportunity like this was going to fall into my lap? I nodded and he smiled back. After I'd secured my bag in my room and locked the door carefully behind me, we walked out of the hotel together.

Waiting in the street below was a beaten-up car with another man behind the wheel. The little man said, 'Get in.' Instantly the doubts that had assailed me only minutes earlier returned. For the moment, I was in control of the situation. As soon as I got into the car, that would change. There were two of them; I had no idea where they were proposing to take me. Once again, I realised I had few options.

We drove in the late afternoon heat. The short man introduced himself as Simón, but we had too few words in common for him to be able to communicate what we were doing. Still, neither he nor the driver showed any signs of turning nasty. I began to relax. After about ten minutes we pulled up outside a little two-storey house with a staircase leading up to the first floor. Simón hopped out then ran over to knock on its door. A woman emerged. She looked out, obviously recognised the car, then disappeared back inside for a couple of minutes before returning clutching her purse, and then accompanying Simón back to the vehicle.

After another ten-minute drive we arrived at another building. Simón and the woman got out. Simón leaned through my window and asked for my passport. For the third time that day, I wavered. I had not let my passport out of my sight at any point in the journey so far. And for the third time that day I decided to surrender to fate. I passed Simón the document and watched him and the woman disappear inside. *What am I doing?* I thought. *How have I found myself here, sitting in a vehicle with a man I don't know, while these two strangers do God knows what to my passport?* Ten minutes passed, then fifteen. There seemed to be no sense to the situation.

I tried to ask the driver what was going on, but faltered as soon as it became clear that neither of us could make ourselves understood. Eventually, the door opened and Simón and the woman stepped back out into the sunshine, then climbed into the car. I was relieved to see them, along with my passport, and yet still none the wiser. We dropped the mysterious woman back at her home and said farewell, then headed to my hotel. As we slowed to a halt, Simón leaned around to hand me my passport and tell me to be ready at 6 a.m. the following morning.

They sped off, and I trudged up to my room, to try to piece together what had just happened. Slowly, as I leafed through my passport and saw that I'd been stamped out of Venezuela, it dawned on me. Luis, or one of the other passengers I'd travelled with that morning, must have made enquiries on my behalf, which had led them to Simón. He, in turn, had taken us to the woman, who worked in immigration. We had driven to her office, where she completed all the necessary paperwork before the weekend. For a moment I was stunned. This would never have happened in Denmark. It *couldn't* have happened there. And yet here, it had. They had all expended a great deal to help me and I had responded with suspicion.

I was ready at 6 a.m. on the dot the following morning. So too, unusually for South America, was Simón. We made the brief journey to a small marina behind the hotel. A few ocean fishermen's boats were tied up on the wharf, but there was barely anybody else about to enjoy the gentle early sun. I stopped for a moment to take in the smell of ocean and seaweed, and the squawking of the gulls; it was hard to believe that I had made it this far. Things had seemed so hopeless the day before.

Simón led me to a little red motorboat. It was wooden, no more than 5 metres long, with four engines at the back and a scattering of equipment, like canisters, in the hull. It bumped happily against the wharf – I looked out and could see that the water was calm. Another man I'd never met before stood inside the boat, offering me his hand. I allowed myself a final moment of panic. I was aware that across the Caribbean there had been several incidents where people who had appeared friendly and helpful had invited people out in boats to go between islands or to go fishing. Once the boat was far enough from the coast, they would rob their passengers then push them into the water. Not many made it back.

Simón gestured impatiently. I wondered if he knew what was running through my mind. I clambered in, handing my backpack to the stranger. We puttered out of the harbour and then, as soon as we were in open water all four of the engines roared into life and we started to blast across the ocean. Although it was so noisy that any conversation was impossible, Simón tried to act as a tour guide, pointing out what I guessed were sites of local interest. I nodded politely to show I was grateful for his effort.

An hour or so into the journey, with Trinidad still too far away to spot, Simón's fingers extended in the direction of a small dot on the horizon. Smiling, he shouted, 'Coast guard!' and our captain cut the boat's engine. Within what felt like seconds the coast guard had come alongside us. Everything about our new interlocutors was professional and purposeful. They were dressed in matching uniforms, accessorised with matching shades, life vests and rifles. One guy manned a menacing-looking machine gun that I felt glad he'd pointed up into the sky.

They quickly turned their attention to me. 'Do you speak English?' I confirmed that I did. Then, 'Do you work with the Red Cross?' They followed this with a set of specific questions about my itinerary. I did my best to answer them.

Once satisfied, they hauled themselves over to our boat and proceeded to take apart almost everything on board – every little can and jar – but left me and my possessions alone. It was clear that we had nothing in the boat that would trouble them, and we were allowed to fire up our engines and continue our journey. We sped off, leaving them bobbing in the water, watching our progress through binoculars, just in case we decided on a last-minute change of route.

Simón's last act after we had docked in San Fernando was to hand me some money: 'Go and get yourself some breakfast and have a nice journey.'

The tools I use to help me work out what a country is *really* like were useful throughout the project. But I never let myself believe that they told me even half of what I needed to know.

It was my experience of being in places like Venezuela, places that are routinely portrayed as chaos-ridden nations crushed by authoritarian leaders, that gave force to my desire to show every country in a positive light. This is not the same as pretending that bad things do not happen in these places. They manifestly do. Venezuela is run by a corrupt, repressive autocracy that has presided over a collapse in the living standards of millions. It continues to deprive its population of civil liberties we take for granted, and is guilty of unspeakable cruelty towards anybody who stands up to the leadership.

All of this is true. But it is not the only story that can be told about the country, because a country and its rulers are not one and the same.

I was in Venezuela for a week; I travelled hundreds of kilometres within it. I was safe, I ate well. None of this is a reflection on, or an endorsement of, its government. It was the amazing people I met who made it possible.

The world is by no means a perfect place, but it is a far better place than the reputation that it has. And I don't think this framing helps.

Human beings, even smart ones, are easily manipulated. If you are in a relationship and your partner tells you day in and day out that you're beautiful, amazing and talented, that they don't know what they would do without you, this will build up your confidence. If the opposite is true, and you're constantly told that you're an incompetent, ugly moron with bad breath, then you're likely to fall apart. If you're told the same thing every day, you start to buy into it. And what we are told every day is that this planet is on fire.

From morning to evening the media is full of earthquakes, corruption, child molestation, school shootings, climate change and the danger of imminent war. And then, at the end of the bulletin, they'll say a woman outside of London is growing carrots and has found a sustainable way to live. This is what they call balanced news. To me it's insane.

We are constantly being shown terrible images of terrible things. But the thing is, the cameraman is usually safe. If he were to turn round, he'd probably capture a series of entirely different images: taxis driving about; children in school uniforms; the markets overflowing with vegetables and fruits. Life continues. The news reports we get hugely underplay the resilience of pretty much anyone who lives in those places. Their ability to keep on going. The fact that they are not simply trudging from one day to the next, but actually trying to grab moments of joy and pleasure where they can.

During the Arab Spring, our televisions were full of things going bonkers in Cairo. Tanks were rolling out, people with pots and pans on their heads were throwing rocks. And yet it's a city of ten million people. It's big enough that, were you to walk just a few streets away, you'd see that life doesn't stop. People are still going shopping and cooking and cleaning.

We should be made aware of the worst elements of the world, because we need to know that we still have work to do. But we can't let that undermine our sense of how normal the planet is. If the world was as cruel and inhumane as it is portrayed, how did I come home in one piece with every tooth in my mouth and without a scratch? If the world was such a terrible place, then I would have to be the luckiest guy on the planet. And, I promise you, I'm not. The world is far safer than people realise.

I felt this when I went to North Korea. When I talked about my visit to others, who had never been there themselves nor met anybody who had, their first reaction was always to focus on how weird and closed and horrible it must have been, or point out that everyone there is a machine, that civic life is a charade. It was interesting to me that they could only conceive of the things that were negative or strange. I think that speaks to the human default setting.

Nobody would deny that the country is run by a highly authoritarian government, but that is not the biggest part of the picture. If North Korea were to open its borders for a week and offer anyone who wanted it the chance to leave, then our assumption is that the country would be left empty within days. But I would guess that perhaps 15 or 20 per cent of the population would try their luck in South Korea, or China, and the remaining 80 per cent would stay. People are generally attached to the soil they grew up in. They know the landscape, they know the insects and animals and plants, they know the seasons, they know the food, they know the language. This is where their parents grew up. This is where their family and friends are.

They are not idiots. They know it's not a perfect system. They know it's not normal that when there's an election, there's only one name on the voting slip, and that if you do not vote for that name, then your family and your friends and your neighbours will be punished. They also know that they cannot go against that system. When I was there, I saw a mother walking hand in hand with her daughter, who was desperately trying to come over to the group of Westerners I was with. She was curious! Her mother was pulling her back because she understood the likely consequences. But I also saw men standing on the street corner sharing a cigarette, talking, laughing and joking. I saw two boys in school uniforms with their school bags on their backs scrambling around in the road, one kicking the other's legs out from beneath them. The sort of horseplay that you see in any street in any country. Life is being lived in North Korea.

Unless we acknowledge this shared humanity, we risk reducing other human beings to ciphers, or victims, and we stop seeing what we have in common. My desire to promote the positive aspects of every country I passed through became increasingly important to me, even more so once my enjoyment of what I was doing faded.

The further I got, the value of being the first person to travel to every country in the world without flying diminished. I needed motivation, something that would provide a reason for me to carry on; this seemed to provide it.

## CHAPTER 6

# Famous People Come Here All the Time

*Havana, Cuba, February 2015*

A strange thing happened to me as I was walking, surrounded by other people, along a pavement in Havana. I had been admiring the crumbling colonial buildings that rose steeply on either side of the street, their bright colours supercharged by the sunny blue skies above us. Then, suddenly, there was a hard *thump*. I looked down and saw a black puppy splayed on the hard flagstones. Its tiny flanks quivered pathetically; otherwise it was still, probably paralysed.

I gazed up at the three-storey block it must have fallen from; there was no sign of what had happened. Had it slipped? Had somebody tossed it over the side? It was impossible to tell. A handful of pedestrians collected around the stricken dog. There were calls of '*Qué pasó? Qué pasó?*' but no one did anything. The puppy just lay there on its back looking back at us. My first instinct was to lean down to put it out of its misery. This was followed by another thought: *This isn't my country, I shouldn't interfere.*

A young man picked it up, cradled it in his arms for a few seconds, whispering soothingly into its ear. He was acting as if it was the most normal thing a person could do. Then he put it down next to a litter bin, out of the way of the feet striding up and down the pavement. Life continued. Everyone started walking again. For days, the experience stayed with me. It could have happened anywhere. It happened to me in Cuba.

This was the time in my journey when I was slowly beginning to understand that the world holds too much history for any of us to comprehend it all. Maybe this was an effect of being in this country that sits so close to the relentlessly modern behemoth of the United States, and yet also seems to exist as a political and temporal dead end, one of the curious wrong turns history sometimes takes.

I fell in love with the country quickly, although it was hard to avoid the sense that this was somewhere that was better to visit than to live. (In Denmark you are limited by the abundance of choice, in Cuba by the absence of choice – though I could see myself growing old happily in its countryside, where the farmers seem to be left mostly to their own devices amid the most stunning scenery you can imagine.) It was a privilege to be somewhere that you knew was changing by the second, even if that privilege was shaded by a deep sadness.

The decaying buildings in Havana symbolised all of this. Many of them had been built in the 1920s, avatars of the country's wealth and modernity. Now, almost a century on, those outside the main tourist areas were derelict, or at least faded, with tattered paint and decaying plasterwork. In many cases their balconies had tumbled down from the building's façade, or looked as if they might do so imminently. The blocks of stone outside their front doors that acted as steps up to the entrances were worn into smooth valleys by the passage of thousands of pairs of feet. But they remained beautiful; you could see how their structure and architecture were a homage to a time before a house was simply a 'machine for living in'. And if their inhabitants could not stop them falling into disrepair, then their constant cleaning and sweeping – with tatty, almost improvised-looking brushes – showed how deep their pride still ran.

If Cuba really opens up in the ways it probably needs to in order to improve living standards, it's likely that these quiet, empty streets of houses and the heritage they represented will be bulldozed.

When people talk about how everything used to be better, what they often have in mind is something like Cuba. It felt to me as if there is more time for people and culture. Cubans still value things like speaking to their neighbours, playing baseball in the streets, listening to music, meeting strangers. The only McDonald's in the country is in Guantanamo Bay; you don't see people mainlining soft drinks, and there is hardly any traffic: so much so that you quickly lose the habit of looking left and right before crossing the road. The contrast with the rest of the Caribbean, where it felt to me as if these things have spun out of control, is stark.

Although technology has brought changes with it – young people have tattoos, they listen to pop music, they stare at smartphones – they have not been as profound or as widespread. That smartphone is unlikely to be connected to the internet. Instead, there is an intranet which, along with the telephone, telefax, telegram and postal service, connects Cubans.

Illegal connections are subject to severe punishment. It's possible to buy a limited amount of wi-fi in a limited number of places, but this is offered at prices that are prohibitive in a country whose average monthly salary is around $30 to $40 (in Mexico, for instance, it's $500 to $600). In major hotels the price can be $10 an hour. A woman told me of a place where I could get internet for as little as $4.50 an hour, an official government 'internet café'. After waiting in line for about an hour I learned that there was no wi-fi: the only way to access the internet was through their authorised desktop computers. So, I left again.

I was surprised by how affected I was by this absence. I felt starved; it was an almost physical loss. Since leaving Copenhagen I had been so used to being able to access the internet at every hostel, tourist office, most cafés and other places. Of course, I was also aware of the impact that being able to outsource most of my memory had had on my atrophied brain. It was striking that in Cuba people were able to give you answers to questions without resorting to Google. In Denmark, or anywhere in the West, that dog would have quickly been surrounded by human beings wielding smartphones, desperate to record this oddity without having a clear sense of why.

I'd gone through a lot of the early stages of the journey conscious that I could not spend my time thinking too far ahead. If I was in Poland there was no point worrying about how I'd get to Japan. That's something I could deal with when I had arrived in China or Korea. Otherwise, I knew the scale of it all would become too grand and daunting. I had to divide it all up into small pieces, and deal with one at a time.

There was another factor in this: the world was changing, usually in ways that made travelling without flying harder. There wasn't a war in Yemen when I set off. There was by the time I arrived in July 2018. I left home having researched ferries that serviced a few of the island nations I needed to get to. But I'd turn up in the country in question and find that the ferry company had gone out of business. Across the planet, ferries are disappearing and being replaced by aeroplanes. A lot of countries will give you a visa on arrival if you fly, but if you want to cross a land border they'll make you jump through innumerable hoops. I can see why: it's far more expensive for any given nation to operate twenty separate border posts than it is for them to have just one in an airport. If they can make it hard for you to cross borders by land, they only need to buy that expensive scanning machinery once.

A lot of the time, immigration officials are downright perplexed by any traveller who doesn't want to fly into their countries. It took me two extra weeks to get an Iranian visa because I wouldn't fly there. And they are suspicious if you arrive without a ticket back to your home country, or don't know how you're planning to leave. Sometimes I'd have to buy a dummy plane ticket.

All of this felt particularly acute in the Caribbean. Getting to Cuba had been easy. While I was in Jamaica, I'd discovered that there was a cruise ship that travelled to Havana, and managed to talk my way on to it. Even obtaining the visa had been a breeze.

This was a huge surprise, because I'd found that travelling from one island to the next in the Caribbean was infinitely harder than it should have been. Thirty years ago, there was an efficient network of ferries that shuttled from one island to the next. But since then, the airlines had paid to shut the ferries down, or found other ways to make the routes they had followed impossible.

The population's only option was to pay a fortune to travel by plane. Sometimes I'd be talking to a local about getting to the nearest island, and it would be so close you could *see* it, and all they would say was: go to the airport. I'd say, 'If you gave me a boat I could make it,' but I knew what their response would be.

In order to make things happen you had to dig deep, keep talking, make as many contacts as you could. Drink a lot of rum with a lot of people. Eventually someone would say, 'Oh, actually I have a cousin. He's a fisherman. Do you want me to call him?' The cousin might not be able to help himself, but he might know a guy, who knows a guy . . . who has a boat.

Eventually, I'd find some form of floating transport – during this time I sailed on everything from cargo ships to sailboats, through to banana boats – but the relief was always tempered by the knowledge that very soon I'd have to undergo the whole rigmarole all over again.

The ease with which I'd arrived in Cuba was matched by the difficulty I encountered in leaving it. After all, this was something that a lot of people had been struggling with since the Cuban Revolution in the 1950s. The government does not exactly encourage people simply to sail away from the island. My frustration was compounded by the fact that I'd had a breakthrough, which meant that time had suddenly become even more precious. Maersk, the world's largest operator of container ships, and also a Danish company, had agreed to help me get back to Europe, which I was going to use as the jumping off point for my journey through Africa. I had a berth on the *Sea Land Eagle*, which was setting off from Miami on 18 February 2015. I just had to get there before it sailed. The problem was, this was easier said than done.

I began asking around in Havana. Most people pointed me towards Marina Hemingway, an enormous network, almost an ecosystem in itself, of jetties, which housed many hundreds of boats. It was like contemplating a giant amphibious parking lot.

The harbour master was one of a long line of human beings I talked to during the project who greeted my explanations of what I was doing with an air of benign indifference, neither engaged by my romantic mission nor interested in actively obstructing it. 'Go for it,' he told me. 'There are boats from Florida, from all over the Caribbean, moored here, you're more than welcome to try. Just don't, whatever you do, bother anybody. If they tell you to go away, then you go away.'

Fine by me, I thought, before heading down the first walkway I saw. I realised a couple of things quite quickly. You needed to be close up to any given boat if you wanted to speak to its guardians. And this meant a *lot* of walking. Many of the boats were vast – they were ocean-going vessels – which meant you'd have to travel a tremendous distance to get proximate enough to somewhere you might be able to hail its occupants.

I spent the day on my feet. In many cases, I'd find that there was nobody aboard, so I simply moved on. I'd stand there for a bit, shout, 'Hello? Anyone? Anyone?' Then I'd look at the dirt on the hull and realise that the boat had been there by itself for a while.

At other times, I'd be invited aboard to sit with the crew. There were a lot of laidback hippy-ish types – none of them were exactly clear-eyed. We'd talk, it would become clear that they couldn't, or wouldn't, help me, and so I'd try to find out as much information as I could. Maybe they knew someone who could open things up for me. But by the end of the day, when it was time to return to the city, I was still empty handed.

I returned the next day and settled into the same groove. The morning came and went; no luck. As darkness fell that evening, I still hadn't found anybody who could help me. But I came back the following morning. One thing I told myself when met by these frustrations was: there is always a door. There's always a solution to every problem, it is just a question of being sufficiently persistent, of knocking on enough doors. And, halfway through the third day, I found myself standing beneath a yacht so big that there was space on deck for both a Volkswagen Beetle and a crane.

I'd learned as I'd made my way through the Caribbean that, if somebody had money, *proper* money, they'd be far less likely to help you. The people who could do most for you, who had spare cabins, who could absorb extra costs without even noticing, were the people you'd never be able to speak to. A lot of the time they wouldn't even be on their boat. Somebody else would have been paid to look after it, and they certainly weren't going to put you in touch with their boss. My rule became: forget about the rich.

It was other kinds of people that I came to rely on. People with less cash to hand, like the family that had sold everything else up and now lived on their boat. Or adventurers, like two young Norwegians who had repaired a boat and were now sailing it around the Caribbean. Then there was the booze-soaked British guy who divided his time between sailing his boat topless, smoking a lot of weed, and trying to impress girls.

In fact, this was true wherever I went in the world. Generally, the less people have, the more they are willing to open up and help. Maybe because it gives them a good standing with God, maybe because they have less to lose, maybe they were just better placed to understand how precarious and difficult a voyage like mine could be.

All of this meant that when I stood there looking at this great white yacht, with a *Volkswagen Beetle* perched on top of it, I did not hold out much hope. Still, I thought, I was here, I might as well try.

I called out a couple of times then waited. A few minutes later a man emerged from the cabin. He was in his sixties, barefoot and somewhat incongruously wearing a white suit whose trousers were rolled up to his knees. He exuded wealth and eccentricity; you could tell he lived in the kind of privileged bubble upon which normal people's problems never impinged.

'What do you want?' he asked, more warmly than I'd expected. His voice was difficult to place, but sounded French. Almost before

I'd finished my spiel, he'd beckoned me up. 'Lovely, lovely,' he beamed. 'My name is Dunavan.' Then, more peremptorily, 'Take your shoes off.' I looked down at my grubby shoes, then up again at the gleaming interior of his yacht. He had a point.

We sat down and he offered me a drink. There was Coca-Cola and Fanta, not what I usually drank, but it seemed churlish to say this. A deckhand appeared soundlessly and poured half a glass for me, leaving the can and a napkin in front of me. Everything about the experience was uncanny, and yet there was never any sense of threat. Dunavan seemed like a man used to curious specimens. I was just another one to examine and hold up to the light.

I sipped my drink and told him what I needed. 'Oh, we could surely find a boat for you, surely. Follow me!' He seemed baffled that I'd had so much trouble, as if it had not occurred to him that anybody ever could.

We walked back out of the cabin, leaving our barely touched drinks behind us. Once we had clambered down on to the walkway, and he had slipped a pair of the least practical-looking shoes I'd ever seen on to his feet, he explained that he was a ship's architect, which meant that he knew all of the ships in the marina. He began gesturing to different ships. It seemed he had designed almost all of them, and owned six himself. 'Here, take this,' he said, pressing a white business card into my hand. I turned it over, it read: 'Gérald Dunavan, Ingénieur Naval, Havana.' No telephone number, or address, or any other way of contacting him.

'You should talk to these people,' he pointed out one of the bigger yachts I'd seen, 'And I can definitely help you out here.' His finger extended in the direction of a still bigger yacht. Then he stopped, with an air of triumph, in front of a high-performance yacht called *KORE*. 'That one there, that one comes and goes all the time. You should go and talk to that captain and say hello from Dunavan.' He made to follow me around the edge of the boat, then evidently thought better of the effort involved and instead waved me off. 'Good luck!'

It was a fine-looking boat 60 metres long. Something about its sleek lines made it seem as if it was travelling fast even as it stood still. It was clearly a vehicle that was built for speed.

I could hear noise on the boat. Someone was up there. I shouted up then stepped back to see who came out. A Caribbean guy in a cap sidled up to the boat's edge, then looked at me fiercely.

'What?'

Sometimes the best way to get what you need is to act like a king. Sometimes, and this was one of those times, it's best to act as if the *other* person is a king. I told the man as politely as I could who I was, what I was doing, and how I was hoping he might help me. I finished by asking him if he was the captain.

'No, I'm not the fucking captain.' He smiled as if he had just remembered the punchline of a good joke. 'But he is.' Another figure had manifested on deck without me noticing. I looked at him and knew instantly that he was Italian. He was the personification of that nation; its spirit present in every movement he made, every sound that came out of his mouth, the way that his hair looked simultaneously stylish but also as if he might have just had a nap. I do not believe that anybody has ever been more Italian.

'Who are you and what do you want?' he asked, his accent as thick as I'd expected. I explained then paused, waiting for his reaction. I looked at his eyes, I could see that he was thinking. But whatever decision he was making did not take long to reach.

'My name is Ciro.' His rrrs rolled sensuously. 'I find that we live in a world where people do not help each other when they should, and I do not like that. I am going to help you. But I cannot help you right away.' For a second it seemed as if he had suddenly thought of something that he didn't want me to know. 'It'll be several days. Here's my number, let's stay in touch. When we leave, I'll take you with us. We're going to an island in the Bahamas.'

This was perfect – the last country I needed to visit in the Caribbean. That boat builder had really come up trumps.

'Oh, and by the way, Dunavan said hello.'

Ciro stared back at me uncomprehendingly. 'Who's Dunavan?'

A few days passed and I heard nothing from Ciro. I began to think: *What if he leaves without me? Has he changed his mind? Has he forgotten about me?* I returned to the marina to put my anxieties to rest. He greeted me warmly and assured me that he was not planning to let me down. There had just been some complications that I didn't need to trouble myself with.

A conversation began – something about me had piqued his interest – and I gushed about the beauty of Cuba, and the kindness of its people. He looked at me askance, like a professor regarding a keen but naive pupil. 'There's a dark side to this country. You need to see the real Cuba. Let's go.'

We got into his car and drove back towards Havana. For a while, he talked and I listened. This was fine by me. Ciro was a practised raconteur, feeding me wild stories about his time as a captain of a yacht used by the rich and famous, then instantly swearing me to secrecy. The bright flow of gossip and scandal continued until we overtook a beautiful young woman walking alongside the road, very clearly minding her own business.

Ciro moved his hand to the gearstick, as if preparing to stop the vehicle. 'Do you want to fuck her?'

Taken by surprise, I blurted out, 'No.'

'You can. Everyone is ready to fuck you. They don't even need a lot of money to do it. Everyone here is willing. They're desperate for money. Anyone will fuck you. You want to fuck her? We can stop and ask. She'll fuck you right now in the car.'

'No, no, I'm OK. I'm fine.' We drove on. I thought about what I had seen since I had arrived here, and the ways in which the disparity between the wealth of those visiting Cuba and the relative poverty of those living there – tourists spend five times in a day what their hosts earn in a week – had distorted everyone's behaviour.

Most of all, there was the incident I'd witnessed in a bar one day. A band was playing traditional Cuban music to a mix of tourists and locals. People were eating and drinking happily in the sunshine. Weaving through the tables was a Cuban man, who approached customers with a small basket asking for a few coins. Some people paid him. Others pretended he didn't exist. Then a male tourist leaned forward. The Cuban eagerly stretched out the hand holding the basket. I had not been paying close attention until this moment, but I felt instantly that something in the bar's atmosphere had shifted. The tourist flicked ash from his cigarette into the basket and reclined back arrogantly into his seat. The Cuban man smiled helplessly and moved to the next table.

It is hard to categorise the night that followed. We ate extraordinary Italian food at a trattoria that felt as if it had been transplanted lock, stock and barrel from Bologna. The chef, holder of a Michelin star, was, of course, a friend of Ciro's. They spoke quick, impenetrable Italian and occasionally glanced in my direction. At one point they broke off and the chef asked me what I wanted. I said, slightly vaguely, 'Oh, whatever's on the menu.'

He stiffened, an arrogant smirk creeping on to his face. 'No,' he said, 'I asked you what do you *want*? Whatever you'll want I'll make it.'

I asked him what he'd recommend. In response he rolled his eyes, then made me some of the best pasta I've ever had in my life.

After dinner, we went to an old factory that had been turned into an art installation.

'Famous people come here all the time,' Ciro said, expansively. 'I bet you there are famous people here right now. Different bands will come here, movie stars.' We milled around for bit, surrounded by chic people smoking and drinking wine from small, fancy glasses. I felt divorced from the Havana I'd spent the last few days moving around in. Occasionally he would point to a piece of art and we'd admire it. Weaved in among all of this, he told me more about himself and the boat he was in charge of.

They couldn't leave because his yacht was filled with valuable art; they were waiting for a Cuban to pick it up and take it to the national museum. Their employer was a Cuban woman who had married a Brazilian man. They'd made a fortune together setting up communications companies, and then divorced. As part of the settlement, she'd demanded the boat. She'd also moved back to Cuba. Determined to maintain the lifestyle she'd enjoyed in America, she was using the boat to bring in stuff under the radar. They had already made forty-two runs between Cuba and the US. The yacht could outsprint a helicopter, but this speed came at a price. It was so fragile that it could only really operate in the calmest of waters; even a few waves could prove fatal.

It was this that caused a further delay. A cold front moved between the Bahamas and Cuba. For the first time since I had left Denmark, my journey was being held up by the weather. I suppose I should have felt lucky, but my plans were falling to pieces. I'd wanted to reach Nassau in the Bahamas for my US embassy visa interview. That was now impossible. And the Maersk Line container carrier that I was supposed to be catching in Miami in mid-February was looking increasingly unlikely. I spent my days exploring the city – I went to the Hemingway museum in the writer's former home and a bar in Havana where a statue of the great man sat on a stool – but really waiting for a call from Ciro.

Then, a few days later, he rang: we were ready to set off. The first leg of the journey was relatively sedate. We hugged the coastline of Cuba, then spent the night in an exclusive marina – unlike Marina Hemingway, there were very few other boats there – where we could take on fuel.

We woke the next day to a bright, clear sky and a sea as flat as a duckpond. The yacht eased out into open waters. Ciro stood at the steering wheel, the engines rumbled then bellowed and we leaped forward. It was almost as if we were about to take off.

It is hard to compare the noise made by a high-performance yacht to anything you would hear in your day-to-day life. All of that super-abundant power. It's like sitting on top of a space rocket's engines. You move through the environment at bewildering speed: in what feels like the blink of an eye, the massive boat that had been looming over you when you were docked alongside it becomes a small blur, then merely a speck on the horizon. A normal sailboat would take about two days to complete our journey. We did it in three hours.

Our destination was North Cat Cay, a private island, where Ciro would leave the boat – he wanted to return home to Italy to see his son Hugo, who he doted on. The island had once been the home of disgraced US president Richard Nixon, now it was the sort of place inhabited by billionaires and the people employed to make their lives as frictionless as possible. I spent my time there feasting on lobster and dipping my feet into the crystalline waters of empty beaches. Then, after six days, my time was up. I managed to talk my way on to the *Captain Duckie*, a stone-crab fishing boat crewed by a group of fun, skilful men who also all gave the impression they belonged in a swamp. They were headed for Freeport, a city in the Bahamas. Their job involved pulling the crabs out of the ocean, tearing their claws off, then throwing the rest of the body back into the ocean. One of the fishermen noticed my curiosity about what I'd just seen.

'Now what?' I asked.

'Don't worry,' he said breezily, they'll grow new claws.'

'But don't they need their claws to defend themselves?'

'Yeah, it will have a hard life for a bit, but then the claws will grow out again. We'll probably catch it again someday.'

I realised something on that island. Perhaps for the first time. The amount of money you have in your pocket does not always decide where you end up in life.

I had very little cash, and yet here I was in this crazy place. I'd arrived here on a high-performance yacht. If you can read the person who is sitting across from you at the table; if you can work out what story they want to hear, then you can go a long way. That's the question I always asked myself when I met somebody new: what do they want from me? Is it the version of my journey where I'm a Red Cross ambassador? Should I focus more heavily on ambition, on my desire to become the first person to travel through every country without flying? Or perhaps they are interested in human connections, in which case I can talk about my belief that strangers are just friends you haven't yet met. What do I say to that person to make a connection, to engage them, to make them want to play a role in this saga?

And yet I knew this was not the whole story. The time I'd spent in Cuba had been one in which I'd seen extremes of wealth and poverty forced together in close proximity. The country was a place where billionaires could retire after a failed relationship, and a theme park for wealthy Westerners. It was also home to eleven million beating hearts, 90 per cent of whom lived in extreme poverty. No matter how clever or talented they were, the overwhelming majority would never get the chance that I had to charm my way into a luxurious island existence. The people in Cuba I met were graceful and engaging, and yet you were always aware of an underlying resilience that only comes from having survived hard times. This is a nation, after all, who, starved of parts for their cars, repair them with material they take from old dishwashers and washing machines.

A constant refrain from men and women I encountered there was, *What's garbage in the USA is gold in Cuba*, which reminded me of something I'd heard in Bangladesh, *Garbage is not garbage until six people have gone through it*. In Dhaka there would be people who sifted through scrap heaps. Objects that we in the West see as disposable, or obsolete, have incredible value for those who aren't, like us, swimming in abundance. The first wave of finders searches for copper wire, the next for plastic. And this process continues until anything of even remote utility has been stripped out and taken away to begin a new life.

It wouldn't be impossible for the richer members of the international community to bring living standards up in places like Bangladesh or Cuba. But of course we don't, because if they received remuneration on a par with ours, the products that they make, and we rely on, would become prohibitively expensive. We do not want to pay $30,000 for an iPhone. We cannot pay for the lives we have if everybody has the life we have.

The billionaires who owned North Cat Cay were barely present; they only spent a few weeks there a year. I wondered how many other homes they owned, in London or New York, Tokyo or Paris. What I did know was that the people who ran their private paradise were paid very little. Some relied on handouts of things such as clothes and shoes from wealthier colleagues, like the generous Ciro.

Perhaps this was why even these people, so far from the top of the economic pyramid, understood the power of cash so acutely. One night, I was walking in the grounds with the gardener, who was nice, a young kid really. He was giving me a tour of the house, telling me a bit more about the island's history. Offhand, almost as an afterthought, he told me that it used to belong to 'some American president'. 'Which one?' I asked. 'I don't know,' he said. 'Presidents don't have so much money, they're not important.'

CHAPTER 7

# C'est Compliqué

*Brazzaville, Republic of Congo, October 2015*

I love Central Africa, and I hate Central Africa. I have a passion for the region that I'm somewhat afraid of. It is one of the most astonishingly beautiful places I have ever been to; I cannot begin to express how overwhelming the range of flora and fauna is; the way every animal or plant seems supercharged by an excess of energy and colour. It produces incredible musicians and artists. The people are kind and funny, and all seem blessed with an instinct for hospitality and open-handed generosity.

The food is extraordinary. I still think about the way they would grill a saltwater fish on a barbecue and serve it with manioc pounded into a paste and a mess of onion and chilli; then you'd eat it with hands. To begin with, doing this felt almost too foreign to me. And then, while I was in Cameroon, I realised that doing this enriches your experience of eating. In addition to the smell, taste, temperature and texture of a meal, you can feel it through your fingers as you pull flesh from bones or peel off skin. It brought new senses into play. I loved this dish and had it over and again. I'd go back there, I'd *fly* back there, just to eat it again.

And you could experience this version of Central Africa quite easily for yourself. You would fly in and be met by a handler or guide. You would stay at a hotel and follow a rich, entertaining itinerary. You'd sit on beaches, go on tree walks in forests, where you might also see mountain gorillas. You might perhaps climb a volcano, or run a marathon, or visit a casino. You would eat brilliantly, visit museums that reflected the extraordinary cultural history of the region. But you would not recognise the Central Africa that I saw.

Because Central Africa is my also nemesis.

It is full of good people trapped in a hard part of the world, with minimal safety and security, where the system is choking them every day. It is a place where if you have a good idea, you're unlikely to succeed unless you know powerful people or are willing to corrupt yourself and others. Most people must sit with the knowledge that because of the nature of the polities in which they have been raised, they will go nowhere, just as their parents went nowhere themselves, and just as their children will also go nowhere. There is almost no sign that anything is likely to change for the better. They can look at the countries that surround their own, but there is no point crossing the border because they are also going nowhere. The best hope for most is to go to South Africa or, if they're extremely resourceful or lucky, Europe or the United States.

The weight of all of this can, at times, bend the human beings who live there out of shape. It can push them to display the worst of themselves; force them into venal, petty, malicious shapes. It is the hardest place in the world to accomplish something, to get anywhere. As I was told hundreds of times by people unwilling, or unable, to help me, *'C'est compliqué.'*

The problem for me was that this all came as a surprise. I had gone through the early stages of my journey bracing myself against the prospect of taking on the Pacific. I thought that it would be its huge expanses of water that would be my biggest challenge. I approached Central Africa thinking that I'd be able to run up the tally of the countries I had visited so that I would have made it through a hundred by the time I had been away for two years. I reckoned I could buzz through it in five, maybe six weeks.

I did not realise how wrong I was.

Perhaps I should have been more aware of the toll that the malaria had taken on my body. I had caught it while spending the night in a petrol station in Liberia. I had been desperate to see Le in Ghana, where we were due to spend three weeks together, but my progress had been strangled by concerns about the Ebola outbreak. When I finally made it to Accra, a week later than planned, I almost immediately collapsed. I sweated so much that even my mattress got soaked. I was torn up by nightmares and hallucinations. Le forced me to go to a clinic, where I was diagnosed with malaria. When I failed to respond to the first course of medication I'd been given, they upped my dose dramatically. They also put a piece of paper and a pen in front of me and told me to write my name. This upset me, I thought: *Can't they see how sick I am? Everyone here knows my name. If they need it in writing, Le can do it.* But I did as they asked, or at least tried to. I took the pen and drew the vertical line of a T, then my hand stopped. I had an image in my mind of what a T looked like, and yet I was incapable of the coordination needed to finish the letter.

This was what they needed to confirm that the parasites had spread into my brain: I had cerebral malaria. Untreated, it can kill you within a couple of days. Le nursed me, washed the sheets and duvets that I had soaked with my sweat, and made sure that I took the right pills at the right time. I lost blood (malaria destroys the

117

blood platelets, you end up urinating them out) and muscle mass, was too weak to even carry my luggage, but after twelve days I recovered. Two days later, Le flew home to Denmark. Her holiday had been ruined, but she had saved my life.

Even now, several weeks later, I was still weaker than I had been before I'd contracted it; occasionally those telltale tremors would still shake my arms. And perhaps I should have paid more attention to the warnings I'd received about the rampant corruption, the bureaucracy, the fact that most governments figured in their subjects' lives as a kind of inefficient mess.

The thing was, there was so much else going on. It was a time when I was beginning to worry whether what I had planned to do was even going to be possible.

Ross had been an incredible partner for almost two years. But now the world had changed. Oil prices had tanked and they were beginning to lay off employees. I knew the pressures they were facing, so I wasn't surprised when I received a polite, almost apologetic email saying (effectively): we're sorry, we love what you're doing, and we know we said we would be with you until the end, but we can't let people go and keep paying a guy with a beard and a hat to travel around the world.

*Yeah, sure*, I thought, *that's another thing to deal with*. It wasn't an immediate crisis; I still had money in my account from my days working in shipping and logistics, which I used until there was nothing left. Then, there really was a problem. I began to struggle to see how I could afford to go on. That meant calling my father to ask for cash. *I know I'm in my thirties, an adult*, I told him, *but can you help?* I hadn't wanted to do this. It was embarrassing, and yet as a friend who I spoke to pointed out, taking out a loan from a bank and paying them interest was insane. One thing led to another and quite soon I owed my father 100,000 Danish kroner.

There were other pressures too.

For the sake of brevity, you can assume the following is true for almost every moment of my time in Central Africa: it is hot, loud and dusty, and the air is intensely, almost unbearably humid. Although I am drinking litres and litres of water, I am permanently thirsty and on the verge of overheating. I am sweating profusely but this no longer bothers me; I have long since resigned myself to this fact, as has everybody else around me.

It is highly possible that I will be the only white person in any room I find myself in, or street I walk down. Months can go by without me seeing another European face. This fact will rarely go unremarked. Often, people will shout at me from the other side of the street: 'Hey, Le Blanc,' or 'Hey, Whitey.' There are many different words for pointing out I have a different skin colour.

I'm treated differently in other ways. In rural areas especially, watching me eat local food has become almost a spectator sport, akin to watching aliens land. I will be routinely misquoted prices on anything and everything. I will also always be offered the front seat in any mode of transport I travel in, a mark of my status as a guest in their country. In order to obtain the right price, I have developed a system. Before it is time to bargain, I will find another vendor, selling something unrelated. While I am buying fruit, I will also ask how much the shopkeeper thinks it will cost to travel to Bamanda. Since someone who sells bananas doesn't profit from a taxi driver's tariff, I know I will get the 'right price', which is what I will aim for when it comes to the actual negotiation. It's simple and it works.

After a while, this all becomes a part of everyday life, although I never become comfortable with it because it robs me of a comforting fiction: that I have managed to blend in.

Some people will be pleased or intrigued to see me, others will seem antagonised by my presence. It is my job to listen to the inflexion of their voices, or watch the gestures they make with their

119

hands, to work out as quickly as I can which category my interlocutors fall into, and then respond accordingly. Sometimes this is straightforward. Other times, this can be rather more complex. It is a process that is fraught with its own complications and, *in extremis*, dangers.

I will be experiencing a kind of bone-deep exhaustion; the result of a combination of several things. The lingering effects of malaria; the draining slog of getting anything done in this part of the world; the fact that the stress I am experiencing about all of this is eating into my ability to sleep. I am covering huge distances. Thousands of kilometres in one journey (Africa is so much bigger than most people imagine: Sierra Leone is closer to France than it is to Kenya), which takes far longer than it should. What you might complete in fourteen hours in Europe takes two days here.

I am thinking too much; I have already done much, and yet I always feel as if I have not done enough. My existence has narrowed to a relentless grind of activity. Get visas. Cross borders. Find a boat. Find alternative to the first boat you discovered because the ferry service was discontinued three years ago. Navigate checkpoints. Post regularly on social media. Research for social media posts. Reply to messages from social media. Communicate with Le. Arrange visit to the next Red Cross office. Obtain sim cards. Locate somewhere to stay. Try to make contacts who will be useful in this country. Try to make contacts who will be useful in the country you're planning to visit in three weeks' time.

Despite all of this, I was about to embark on what would be the biggest challenge of the entire journey.

Travelling in Africa during an Ebola outbreak had had its moments. There were many times when I felt deep, almost painful frustration. But I had anticipated this and was broadly content with the progress I made. Since landing in Morocco in April 2015, I'd snaked down the west coast of the continent: Western Sahara, Mauritania, Senegal, Cape Verde, Guinea-Bissau, the Gambia, Mali, Guinea Conakry (Republic of Guinea), Sierre Leone, Liberia, Ivory Coast, Ghana, Togo, Burkina Faso, Niger, Benin and, finally, Nigeria.

So far, so good. I was ticking countries off the list, and it was around that time that I realised that it might, just might, be possible to reach that target of one hundred countries within two years. I hoped that might be the thing that punched through and grabbed the world's attention. I needed this, because no matter how hard I tried, I had not managed to turn my project into something that enough people cared about. My dreams of being greeted by crowds of cheering supporters each time I crossed a border seemed incredibly far away. But maybe the BBC would pick up on it; then I could really build momentum and a profile.

I wasn't completely ignorant, I was aware that there would be difficulties, and yet it felt so close, it felt doable. The biggest challenge, I knew, would be getting into Equatorial Guinea.

Generally, it's fairly easy to get a visa for a country you're planning to visit. You show up with one, maybe two passport photos, and copies of your vaccination card and passport. (For some reason, if you can supply this stuff in colour, you can really improve your chances.) Then you fill in a form and wait. You might hear back that same day or a week later. Most of South-East Asia is like that. These are gentle countries; the officials are professional, they smile at you and thank you and wish you a nice day. Dubai is an excellent place to get visas. It's efficient and easy going.

Equatorial Guinea is different. It is a hard country surrounded by other hard countries. The quality of life enjoyed by its population is reflected in its officials, who I found obstructive, rude and occasionally cruel. That's if they were even in their offices for me to see them.

I was familiar with the country's reputation as somewhere that was difficult to get into. They are a paranoid petrol state run by a military dictatorship who, despite their close ties to the United States, are generally convinced that any Westerner visiting is likely to be trying to topple their government. My plan was to attempt to obtain the visa as early as I could. I'd start in West Africa, then keep on trying as I travelled through the other nations that made up Central Africa: Angola, Central African Republic, Chad, Democratic Republic of Congo, Gabon, and São Tomé and Príncipe. I thought this would give me the best chance of getting the document in good time to help me maintain progress.

I made my first attempt in Nigeria. The Equatorial Guinean embassy told me, in the bluntest terms, 'We will not give you a visa here. Try when you get closer to the equator in a country that's closer.' I had a similar experience in Mali. The next country I tried was Cameroon. Specifically in the capital, Yaoundé, a teeming, bustling city that smelled richly of cooking food, flowers, spices, sweat, oil and dust, where the contradictory forces of both Cameroon's energy and its corruption were made manifest in the form of the grand, unfinished construction projects that loomed over its skyline. I was staying here in a damp, bare concrete room, in a bed that bore the signs of the thousand other people who had laid their heads down there before me, in a neighbourhood called Madagascar, a cacophonous, rubbish-strewn warren of irregular-sized buildings that was supposed to be one of the city's roughest areas. A man I'd met on a bus had arranged it for me. There were probably nicer places to stay, in more upscale parts of the city, but it was cheap and infinitely superior to slinging my hammock in a noisy bus station, which I'd been doing far too often recently.

Because Yaoundé is in the French-speaking section of the country, I'd enlisted the help of a local woman who could translate for me. We arrived at a two-storey building, Equatorial Guinea's embassy. We knocked on the door and stepped back to wait. To our surprise, the reply came from a window that opened abruptly above our heads. 'We're out of visas,' a woman shouted down to us. 'Go away!' Registering the disappointment on my face she paused; not quite sympathetically, but with at the least the look of someone willing to give us a chance. 'Are you a diplomat?' she asked, looking squarely at me. 'No,' I said, figuring we'd be unable to bluff this one out. She shut the window: another route closed. I tried a couple more times in Yaoundé but could never get through to anyone.

My frustration at failing to get this visa was compounded by the difficulty involved with securing others. The problems came when, for whatever complex reasons, the person behind the desk decided that they didn't like you, or wanted to squeeze something out of you, or both. At one border, I had filled out the form using capital letters. It was clear as day. And yet the official went through a pantomime of asking me to spell out every single entry on that sheet of paper – 'What does this say?' – then painstakingly writing over my words. I had been travelling by bus, everyone was waiting for me, and yet he did it for the entire form.

In another embassy, in the Republic of Congo, a francophone country, I walked in and said, in my best French, doing everything I could to ingratiate myself, 'Hello, how are you?' The woman at the desk stared at me and said, also in French, 'Come back when you know how to speak French, or at least bring someone who speaks French.' I spun on my heels and left, perhaps thirty seconds after I had come through the door. Luckily, I was able to call on the help of a Lebanese woman, Marie, one of the most charming people I have ever met (the Lebanese are maybe the most charming people on the planet, but they can also be vicious: you want them on your side). She translated for me on my return to the embassy. We paid $10 to get the necessary form, which was actually the copy of a copy of a copy of that form. It was barely legible; a kind of bureaucratic ghost.

We filled it in and handed it over. It was instantly given back to us: 'You used a blue pen, you're supposed to use black.' Another $10. (Some countries were insane about these tiny details. They would not accept $100 bills that had been folded down the middle, no matter how crisp and fresh they were.) Once they were satisfied with this, it was time to give them my passport photo. Another problem. In the shot in question, I was wearing a long-sleeved T-shirt. This wasn't good enough, I needed something with a collar. So I had to go back out on to the street, put on my polo shirt and find a guy who did passport photos.

All of this stuff goes on until you reach the moment you know that everything is finally going your way. None of these immigration places can receive money, the risk of corruption is too high, so they instead send you to the bank to make your payment. Once you have a receipt, you can be sure that within a matter of days your visa will follow. That bit is easy; it's the dance you have to do to get to that point that sends you crazy.

The secret, I found, was to see if you could make the officials laugh within the first few seconds of walking into their office. Everything would be easier if you managed that. The other thing that really greased the wheels was being respectful to the point of being submissive. You don't enter an office until you're told; you take your hat off before you step into a room; you don't sit down until they say you can sit. Anything that helped reinforce a hierarchy in which they felt they sat above you. It was all nonsense, really, but it worked.

While I was in Cameroon, I secured visas for Gabon, São Tomé and Príncipe, and the Republic of Congo (Congo-Brazzaville), as well as invitation letters for the Democratic Republic of Congo (DRC) and

Angola. I decided to bypass Equatorial Guinea for the moment and instead mapped a route that would take me to Gabon, São Tomé and Príncipe (an island nation, so I'd need to find a boat), Gabon again, Congo-Brazzaville and the DRC. That would bring me up to 100 countries, hopefully before the anniversary of my departure, on 10 October. If all else failed, I thought, I could try to sneak illicitly across the border into Equatorial Guinea; I might end up in prison but as long as they didn't send me back to Denmark on a plane, I figured it was a risk worth taking.

Things initially had felt more hopeful in Gabon. I was accompanied by a Gabonese woman to the Equatorial Guinean embassy in Libreville. It turned out that she was from the same tribe as the guy sitting behind the desk. Good news! I watched them talking for a while, unable to follow the drift of the conversation but allowing myself to believe that I might be about to get a break. And then, without warning, the man from the embassy stood up and starting shouting. My guide turned to me and said, 'We better go.'

Once we had stepped back out into the street, I asked her what had happened. 'Nah, he doesn't want to give you a visa.'

Nothing was going my way. All the ferry services to São Tomé and Príncipe had been cancelled and it was now obvious that I'd fall short of my target of reaching a hundred countries before October 2015. So instead I passed through the Republic of Congo's wild green hills on the way to its capital, Brazzaville. I thought I'd be able to cross the Congo Delta and get to Kinshasa in the DRC. That would make it ninety-nine in two years. Perhaps that would be enough to get some headlines?

Brazzaville itself was pleasant, even if its proximity to the equator meant that it could be almost unbearably warm. I'd entered the city on a long road that began somewhere to its north before sweeping elegantly south. I was later told that it had been constructed to make life easier for the president's son, who lived near where the highway began. Brazzaville felt suspended, happily, between its past and its present. More than most places in the region it was safe, calm and well-organised; free of the shouting and horn honking that plagued other cities of a similar size. There was a great deal to explore, most of all its monument to the man after whom the city was named, the French-Italian explorer Pierre Savorgnan de Brazza. Visiting that felt like an opportunity to pay homage to an older generation of adventurers.

When I was roaming the streets, I found it hard to resist buying local delicacies: chunks of grilled meat, served in a newspaper with a small, fiery mound of spices; there was also a paste with a jam-like consistency, made I think with a local plant, which appeared in a variety of different colours. I never knew quite what it was, but it was a perfect accompaniment to bread, meat or fish.

The problem was that I had all this time to explore – a month in total – because I was finding it so hard to make any progress. I tried everything that would get me from one side of this river to the other. I repeatedly called the embassy to see if anybody could help; they never answered. There were days when we were given assurances and the signs looked good. But nothing would come of these promises. Instead of progress, there was just silence, or another reason why unfortunately my application could not be approved. I would be granted a meeting with a high-ranking official who I was told could help me, then rush to their office only to learn that they had long since left for the day. Even the Red Cross, which generally kept their distance from me, tried to exert whatever pressure they could on my behalf. It made no difference.

Then on 10 October, two years since I had left Denmark, a woman at the DRC embassy in Brazzaville told me that the only way I could get a visa was if I was a resident of Congo-Brazzaville, or by applying from my home country: 'Go back to Denmark and get your visa and then come back.' I was surprised by how vindictive her tone was.

'But Denmark is five thousand kilometres away. Where I'm trying to go is less than a kilometre from here. You're telling me to go five thousand kilometres, then come the same distance back so I can go one kilometre?'

'Yes.'

She said that I would also need a second document, which cost $50. I needed to have it signed and to provide the original copy. It was more than double my daily budget, but I thought, *Fine, what choice do I have?*

'Where do I get it from?'

She wrote the address down and slid it across the counter to me.

'But this is in Kinshasa? And I can't get there without a visa. This is madness.'

'That's just the way it is.'

It was two years since I had set off. I stood on the shore of the Congo Delta looking at the cars and people and lights on the other side of the noisy, choppy river. It looked far too rough to even consider swimming across. Around me walked men in loose shirts and jeans, sandals on their feet. The women were wrapped in vibrant dresses. Most were in sandals too, but a brave few were in high heels; something that felt almost insane to me in a region where one was almost always walking on cracked, dried-up, uneven surfaces. This was a country where the sky usually seemed bigger and bluer than anywhere else in the world. Now, though, it had begun to rain, heavily, and water streamed down my face. Every part of me felt tired, heartbroken. *What the hell am I going to do?*

The anniversary passing intensified my emotions. I didn't miss Denmark itself that much. I missed the people I loved, like Le, and close family and friends, but I never spent that much time thinking about Denmark. Life is an accumulation of choices, and that means you're always going to have a shadow existence – the world you *could* have built. The question for me was: am I spending my time on something that outweighs what I'm not getting?

The jobs I'd had before, where I'd spent long stretches abroad, meant that I was already used to missing birthdays and weddings and graduations. I wasn't bothered by the fact that, mostly, I spent the major celebrations in any given year by myself. You could say I was lucky, I guess. All the time I'd spent away working or travelling, and also my parents' divorce, meant that for the most part I'd been desensitised to the loneliness that comes with spending events like Christmas or your birthday alone, or in unconventional circumstances. And, in fact, I've never been big on birthdays. I do not care about my own birthday. I do not want people to celebrate it.

It was undeniably hard knowing that I could not be there to support people when they were hit by depression, or were the victims of crime, or lost their job. It was equally hard not being able to show up for the good stuff: the promotion, the night someone meets the love of their life, that moment when someone learns they've been given the all-clear from cancer. Those things add up over a decade.

But as important as they were, they were all ordinary. You can get bucketloads of that stuff. What I was trying to accomplish was unique and special. And the experiences that I was getting as I was going on my way were unique and special to me. I was in cultures and seeing things and learning things and growing as a person in a way that I wouldn't be if I was back home. At least, that was the theory. The nightmare of Central Africa was beginning to make it fray.

What I really missed was the ease of home, the sense of knowing where everything is and how everything works. Because each time I moved to a new country, I would have to try to learn those things all over again. Everything was a challenge. How do you pay for this? What is this meat? How do you activate a sim card? What is the system for queuing for buses?

In fact, the only specific thing that I really longed for was the taste of Danish milk. I think that the milk you grow up with automatically becomes the correct taste of milk. They have great milk in France and Canada, but it's not right for me. Milk tastes right in Denmark.

It was more that I was lonely; stranded in a foreign country, in a culture far from my own, leading a life in which every day contained its own disappointment or frustration. I'm fortunate in that I'm capable of distracting myself by getting deep inside a conversation, or throwing myself into work (and there was always plenty of that), or going for a run. And yet this phase of the project was tremendously solitary. There was no team or travel companion. The closest I ever got to that were those occasions when I met another traveller on their way to the same border as me and we would join forces because we both understood it would make things easier that way. But then you'd get to the first town once you'd crossed, there would be a quick 'Have a nice journey,' and then you'd go your separate ways.

I felt lonely when I was sick, because it is not fun to be ill when you are away from home. I was lonely when I was struck down by the migraines that were becoming an increasingly regular part of my existence as a result of the stress I felt; lying there in a strange room, my head feeling as if it was coming apart. I was lonely when I was trying to come up with the solutions I needed to make progress. I was lonely when people asked me questions like, why are you doing this? Why don't you just go home? Why don't you just fly? What's the point?

And I felt lonely when I was forced to defend the project to myself. Why was I fighting so hard for something that I believed in less and less? Had this actually been done before? Can I communicate to the world what makes my journey different? Can I make them care?

I don't think anyone ever really appreciated the scale of the resources that I had put into the journey. Sometimes I wonder what would have happened if I'd put the same energy into building a company. I treated what I was doing as work. So, although I'd met a lot of extraordinary people and seen a lot of extraordinary things, it wasn't a pleasant existence. That gap between people's perceptions of what I was doing, and what I was actually experiencing on a day-to-day basis, was the thing that made me feel most alone.

I stayed in Brazzaville, and put my application for residency in motion. I was told it would take a couple of weeks, and that I didn't need to be in situ while they processed it, so I decided it would be best to return to Gabon to try to find a vessel that could take me to São Tomé and Príncipe, as well as making another attempt to get a visa for Equatorial Guinea.

My failures were eating me up from the inside. I cursed myself for overlooking small details, for not having anticipated how difficult it would be to persuade countries to let me cross their borders, but these thoughts were chased by another, more frightening one: maybe there was nothing I could have done differently; maybe there is no way through.

CHAPTER 8

# It's No Good

*Brazzaville, Republic of Congo; Libreville, Gabon; Douala,*
*Cameroon; Kyé-Ossi, Cameroon, October to December 2015*

I trudged to the bus terminal and was greeted by a scene of complete chaos. Men were trying to climb on to overloaded vehicles. There was shouting, pushing, an incredible noise. Usually, wherever I was in the world, I paid attention to local media. As I was going from country to country, it was of value to me to know if there was going to be an election next week that might get nasty. Or, equally, that a local sports teams had triumphed and everybody was super proud – knowing that was the sort of thing that helped formed connections. But I had been so focused on trying to obtain my visa that I had not noticed that Congo-Brazzaville was in the middle of a political crisis. A controversial referendum about a proposition to change the country's constitution had been announced, which prompted a wave of furious protests. People were fleeing the capital, afraid of further violence. Every single ticket for every single seat on every single bus and train out of the city had been sold.

There were no taxis, just a swarming mass of human beings all trying to escape.

Amidst the melee, I managed to team up with Miriam, a beautiful young local who I had started talking to. Sometimes this would happen on my journey: I'd find someone, or they'd find me, and there would be an unspoken understanding that we each had something to offer the other. Miriam suggested that we would get further if we worked together. Although in truth I think she was just trying to help me. In the hours that followed, she was far more of an asset to me than I was to her. She spoke French and the local dialects; she was familiar with the idiosyncrasies of Brazzaville and the country around it. I thought perhaps I'd be able to protect her if events took a nasty twist. Although I hoped this would not be put to the test.

Miriam was exploring the possibility of finding a flight out of the city. This was something I obviously could not do, and it soon became clear that it was a dead end for her too. The options were narrowing; there would be no transport at all from tomorrow onwards – if we were to travel, it would have to be today. The sun continued to climb, we all began to wilt in the heat, and both Miriam and I were becoming more desperate.

That was when they rolled out the trucks. These were what savvy businessmen brought out for desperate situations: open cargo trucks on which you could buy yourself a place. The whole system was chaotic, but Miriam got our names on the list for a truck going to Dolisie in the Republic of Congo, from where I could try to travel on to Gabon. After a lengthy wait, we were allowed to climb on board our vehicle: a yellow lorry with a deep, wooden cargo bed and metalwork turned red by the unforgiving climate in which it operated. Half of it was empty, the other half stacked high with luggage. We had been told that the empty space would soon be filled with as many as forty people, who would have to stand, crammed in among each other, holding on to metal pipes for balance, for two days. This sounded unappealing, so we opted to scale the 5-metre mountain of luggage and sit precariously on top of the lorry.

To begin with it looked as if we'd made the right choice. But then more and more passengers joined us, the men in old T-shirts and baseball caps, while many of the women were swathed in more traditional, brightly patterned dresses and headscarves. There were so many that I was worried we'd end up being pushed off the other side.

At around 10 a.m. we set off; we had 300 kilometres to cover before nightfall. To begin with, spirits were high. People were gesturing and screaming and smiling. My presence up there was the source of widespread hilarity, as was my appearance. When I'd first entered Africa, I'd decided on a whim that I wouldn't cut my hair for the whole time I was there. I thought it would be a bit of fun, and it wouldn't last that long. By this point, my hair was straggling down to my shoulders. This, combined with a bushy beard, proved an irresistible target. I'd get constant shouts of 'Jesus.' Today was no different. They waved, and I waved back.

As we trundled into the country, the road deteriorated. Tarmac gave way to red dirt. The truck shuddered and crashed over bumps, kicking up dust that covered us all in a thick film of muck. We were breathing the dust, and it was soon also filling our ears, noses, hair, skin, eyes. I looked around, my fellow passengers all looked like ghosts.

I was utterly drained, and close to sleep. Fearing that I might topple on to the road if I nodded off, I tied myself to the truck with some rope from my bag. The people around me laughed uproariously at me. An hour later, as they began to feel drowsy, they asked if I would consider tying them up too. I allowed myself a small moment of satisfaction before agreeing.

In truth, there was little fun to be had. Everyone's high spirits had long since worn off. It was uncomfortable sitting on awkwardly shaped boxes and bags; the sun was beating down upon us. People were dirty, hot, hungry, scared, and all of them looked like they were in pain. The landscape around us was stunning, and yet nobody gave it a glance; we were all just hoping that this journey would end as soon as possible.

We carried on inching forward, painfully slowly. At some point, the truck broke down. After a few hours it was fixed but we had to stop at the next village for more repairs. I had an app that helped me track our progress. Each time I looked, I thought: *This is going to take the rest of my life.* I was sick of the attention I was drawing, every part of my body hurt.

And then something beautiful happened.

The woman behind me started banging her empty plastic bottle with her hand to make a simple rhythm. She began to sing, beautifully, in a language I did not recognise. Slowly, more voices joined her. First another woman, then a man. Before I knew it, everybody else on that truck, perhaps sixty others in total, was singing with her. The sun was setting, and rays of light streamed eerily through the landscape around us. It was truly magical: bliss washed over me.

The singing stopped as the sun finally disappeared beyond the horizon. We all returned to our misery.

After nightfall, we stopped in the town square of a small village – a grand name for what was in truth just an open area of dirt. I checked my app: we had travelled a mere 100 kilometres, just a third of what we were supposed to have covered. But the truck was still ailing and needed more work. More pertinently, it was not considered safe to travel by night because of the bandits that were believed to be operating in the area (something similar had happened to me when trying to cross the Ivory Coast; my taxi driver refused to travel after dark in case we were ambushed). We would start again the next day at 6 a.m.

Somebody spread out a large sheet of tarpaulin for us to sleep on. I ate some manioc and lukewarm fish that swam in a muddy-looking broth whose surface glistened with droplets of fat, and then joined the others in trying to find a space to curl up in. Sitting there, with my legs folded in the darkness, in this remote, unknown village, surrounded by people speaking languages I couldn't speak, I suddenly felt stabbed again by loneliness. Miriam was still with me, but she had her own stuff to deal with and I knew that we'd part ways as soon as this stretch of my journey was over. It was more than that though: the feeling of being misunderstood and ignored, and knowing just how much land and sea separated me from the people I loved most.

Just then, a little girl, no more than six years old, came up to me. Her bright eyes shone as she indicated that she wanted me to lift her up. She touched my beard and my hair and the skin on my face. Later, she just wanted to sit in my lap. I felt the warmth of contact with another human being, and in that instant I realised how much I'd been craving it. It made me think that children have a gift for perceiving, or understanding, things that adults have lost.

The bodies collected on that tarpaulin that night were rowdy and fractious, as if they had struggled to shake off the discomfort and angst of the day before. And though bone-achingly tired I struggled to sleep. Several times I was woken by loud, angry discussions. At 3.14 a.m. almost everyone stirred and began packing, before climbing back up on to the truck. A few of us held back, puzzling over this decision to move themselves so much earlier than they needed to. We waited for 6 a.m. Nobody's mood improved. A little while later we were disturbed by a commotion. Two men on the top of the truck were hurling punches at each other in an oddly exaggerated way, like they were in a bar fight in a

Western movie. This eventually subsided. We continued to wait. And then another inexplicable noise, the sound of water hitting the ground. Had a pipe burst on the truck? Miriam and I turned to see what had happened: a man was standing on top of the luggage with his pants down, a bright arc of piss cascading on to the ground beneath. I sighed and said: 'These people are not normal.' Miriam nodded silently.

On reaching Gabon, I discovered that there was a consulate right on the border with Equatorial Guinea. It was somewhere between a half and a full day's travel away, which would inevitably involve at least twenty checkpoints. It would be a hot, uncomfortable journey but I was assured that it was as close to a sure thing as was possible. Some of this would prove to be true. The journey was hot and uncomfortable. The checkpoints were tiresome and – as always – totally unnecessary.

But the woman who handled my application once I arrived was perhaps the ugliest human being I have ever met. I do not mention this to be cruel. Rather she was an example of how sometimes the way a person looks on the outside can be a sure guide to the sort of person they are on the inside. She seemed to take active pleasure in telling me that the visas she issued were only for residents of Gabon.

I hauled myself back onto the bus that would take me back to Libreville, cursing the fact that nothing here ever worked out the way it was supposed to.

Two months later, I found myself in Cameroon again, this time in Douala, where I decided to attempt a different approach at the Equatorial Guinean consulate. I'd tried four different places and had been rebuffed by each one. This was potentially my last shot and I needed to do something different. Perhaps if I swapped my hat and uniform for clothes that marked me out as an expat I would stand a better chance. I was aware that my uniform, with its Red

Cross emblem, sent one kind of signal, and my hat another. Neither were necessarily positive. And I'd been an expat before, in Libya and Bangladesh; I was familiar with that mode of being which mixed arrogance with good manners. More often than not, behaving as if you *expected* people to do what you wanted them to led to them *doing* exactly what you wanted them to do. I felt as if I could deliver a passable impression of this.

I went to the nearest market and bought myself a blue shirt, which I put on, taking care to undo the two top buttons. The look was completed with sunglasses (an essential component of the expat uniform), which I clamped on my face and kept there for the duration of our encounter, and an official-looking folder that I cradled under my arm.

Then I marched in, a picture of busy efficiency, firing questions at the man behind the desk: how many passport photos do you need? What currency do you want me to pay in? When they asked me why I wanted a visa, I said that I worked in the region. A friend had had an amazing experience in Equatorial Guinea, I told them, so I was here for a holiday. Just for a few days. What's more, I had already booked a hotel and bought a flight ticket. A few minutes later I had a visa to Equatorial Guinea in my hands. And a few minutes after that I'd thrown the shirt away and cancelled both the hotel and my plane.

For the next twenty-four hours I was in a state of near exaltation: I now had the visa I'd been ripping my guts out for months to obtain. It had been so *easy*. And I'd only paid the local rate, which was many times cheaper than what foreigners were usually expected to shell out.

This joy lasted precisely up to the point when I tried to cross into Equatorial Guinea and was informed that the border was closed because there had been (another) coup attempt. A high-ranking military officer had tried to seize power. After his revolt failed, he went on the run, trying to evade a manhunt in this tiny country of less than two million people. Nobody was allowed in, and nobody was allowed out. There was no indication when it might open again, but the chances were that it wouldn't be until after my visa had expired in thirty days' time.

Worse still, I was being refused re-entry to Gabon, even though I'd been there before without any problem at all. Gabon was far better organised than its neighbours and I had a large list of contacts I could rely on, so I'd persuaded myself that it would be easier crossing into Equatorial Guinea from there than from Cameroon. Now that opportunity had been snatched away. It also meant that my big bag, which I'd left there thinking I'd only be gone for a few days, was stranded in the apartment I'd been couch-surfing in. I did everything I could to resolve this border madness. I returned staggering under the weight of piles and piles of paperwork: a valid passport, a valid visa, a valid invitation letter, confirmation that I'd been given all the vaccines I needed and some more besides, confirmation that I was a goodwill ambassador for the Danish Red Cross. I'd also printed out articles that had run in local newspapers about my journey the last time I had been there, which I could point at to show that I'd been saying positive things about their country.

None of this was enough. They ignored what I'd brought and asked for a range of documents that I didn't have, even though I knew, and they knew, I didn't need them. This meant a two-day bus ride back to Yaoundé in Cameroon. I then embarked on a marathon between different offices to try to secure these irrelevant documents. I jumped through hoops, filled in forms, waited patiently for people to return from bloated lunch breaks; smiled and agreed to return the following morning even though I knew they were perfectly capable of helping me *right then*; and finally emerged, several days later, with a sheaf of stamped and signed papers.

I stood there, blasted by sun and exhaustion, and suddenly felt faint. I realised that the long hours I had been spending sitting on public transport, or in meetings, or waiting for meetings meant that I was barely eating. Skipping meals was becoming a habit, but I kept on reminding myself that the project was my priority. There wasn't time for anything that wasn't directly helping me to make progress. So I put these worries to the back of my mind and I hauled myself on to a bus for the two-day ride to the border.

I took a lot of buses when I was in Africa (and would travel on 351 long-distance buses in total during the whole project). They were often delayed, or cancelled, because rain had churned the dirt roads into an impassable mess. When they did run, you'd bump along pitted, cracked roads – sometimes so uneven that it would actually be hard to focus – with thick jungle pressing claustrophobically on either side of the route. And because as a rule the vehicles themselves were imported from Asia, where people tend to be smaller, my 193-centimetre frame would feel uncomfortably cramped. But the buses were social places. You'd chat and share food with the other passengers. People were interested in me and what I was trying to do, and often they wanted to help. There were many nights when I found a place to sleep because I was sitting next to somebody who could offer me a space on their floor (or if I was lucky, I'd get their bed while they slept on the floor). In Cameroon, I remember taking a minibus called 'the Vatican service'. The driver conducted prayers before we set off, before blasting out Christian music from the radio at extreme volume.

So, generally, I liked buses. What I didn't like were the frequent checkpoints, where men in uniform would stop us, theoretically in order to check our documents, but actually so they could shake someone down.

The worst were always at dark. A soldier would clamber on then stride down the aisle, clearly on the hunt for *something*. Then, finally, inevitably, they would get to me.

It was always me that was ushered outside. It was always me who had to present my paperwork and answer a fusillade of petty, devious questions. Do you have a valid passport? Do you have a valid visa? Do you have valid vaccine certificates? Yes, I would answer, yes, yes, yes. But the charade would continue until the moment you eventually said no, I don't have that. This meant they had you. The mood would change. In a mix of exaltation and menace they'd threaten to call the police, and begin talking ominously about how much time you'd spend in a prison cell. At this point, I was supposed to offer them a bribe, but I had resolved never to do this. (They would never explicitly ask for a bribe, but they always knew, as I always knew, where the conversation was going. Only once did I actually tell somebody I wasn't going to give them any money. He responded with outrage, doing an extremely good impression of an honest man trying to do his job who would never lower himself to corruption.) I hate corruption, I think it's a cancer that eats away at a country's wellbeing. And I knew that if I handed over money while wearing the emblem of a goodwill ambassador for the Red Cross then I would create a destructive expectation that other people working for the Red Cross would do the same, which could cause terrible trouble for relief goods passing through that checkpoint in the future. I also, more plainly, didn't have enough cash to pay what these people wanted.

To begin with these experiences rattled me. I always felt a prickling, hot sense of injustice when they singled me out. The sort I remember experiencing at school when a teacher scolded me in public for something I hadn't done.

As time wore on, I still resented them, that never stopped, but I realised that they were a game and the best thing you could do was try to work out how to win it. Sometimes, when I played it particularly well, I could escape after just five minutes and we would part as friends, each with a selfie of the other saved on our phones.

What I learned is that the soldiers had to feel as if they were in control, even if I was actually in control because I knew exactly how to handle the situation. I'd experienced so many checkpoints, I'd heard and seen almost anything one could hear or see in that context. It was always Groundhog Day for me. I knew what to say, and when. I knew I had all my documents in order. I had responses ready for any question they could ask, and whenever it looked as if we were heading towards an unpleasant place, I was good at shepherding us on to safer ground. It was also useful to produce a business card or letter emblazoned with, for instance, the name of the local Maersk CEO, and ask, innocently, 'Shall I call him? Perhaps he can help?'

The other factor that determined how well or not these interactions went was my mood. If I'd just been enjoying a conversation, or had slept properly the night before, or had had a couple of wins that day, then I'd be able to take the attention in my stride. But if I was worried about how things were going with Le, or money, or I'd had a setback, then the moment a flashlight was shone in my face would be the trigger for a sulky kind of misery and resignation.

A real source of comfort was the strong feeling of community that very often emerged on the bus. You'd have sixty other people watching you sympathetically because they understood that this was the sort of thing that happened in their country. Although I would feel bad on their behalf for causing the delay, they rarely seemed bothered; they were used to it.

But, of course, they weren't frantically trying to cross a border before their visas ran out.

\* \* \*

On the morning of 28 December 2015 I woke early in Douala, Cameroon, to try to arrange my journey to Gabon. I spent the morning working through some admin, then in the afternoon visited the port, where I discovered that the next boat going to Gabon would not leave for another two or three days, perhaps longer. Instead, I made a deal with a taxi driver to collect me the next morning

The next day I got up at 4.30 a.m., skipped breakfast, and was waiting on the street from 5 a.m. He did not show up. I waited for a while, enough to give him a fair chance, then moved on to another option. A motorcycle taxi took me to a bus terminal, but all the seats had been sold. I had more luck at the next terminal I tried, where I secured a ticket on the 6 a.m. bus to Cameroon's capital, Yaoundé. We arrived four hours later. I bought another ticket, this time to the border with Gabon. We arrived at 5 p.m., an hour before immigration closed.

Flush with the success of my journey I raced into the office. Here I was told that although my visa was acceptable, I needed an invitation letter. I produced the letter. 'It's no good.' I tried to argue. But it was clear nothing I could say would move the impassive, severe man sitting behind the glass window.

That night I slept in the border town of Kyé-Ossi. I woke early, skipped breakfast again, and returned to immigration, where I was told to wait for a short while. Three and a half hours later, the chief of immigration eventually appeared. He took thirty seconds to dismiss me, having demanded a new letter of invitation. I slunk back to Kyé-Ossi.

The frustration and anger I felt was only partially offset by the kindness of an immigration officer on the Cameroonian side. Each morning, he would stamp me out of Cameroon and wish me good luck. Then I'd head into no-man's-land; whatever hope I had inside me slowly dying as the sun wound its way across the sky. Sometimes I'd manage to catch an official's attention. When I did, they'd simply ask for another document I didn't have, and I'd return to Cameroon conscious that another wasted day had gone by. Mostly, however, I would just wait. Then wait some more. There was little to break up the maddening tedium. A few of my fellow inmates in this baking hot limbo would chat to me. I spent hours playing Snake on my Nokia 1100. But a lot of the time I'd watch seething as yet another person was let in before me.

Then, on 31 December 2015, I gave up. I was in a damp, windowless concrete room whose only light came from a half-opened door. I was sitting on a hard bench, insects agitated the sticky air around my head. A few minutes earlier, I'd been told that although my letter of invitation was now perfectly fine, they had discovered a problem with my visa – I wouldn't be able to enter for two months.

Something inside me collapsed. I feared I was broken, perhaps irreparably. I had been defeated. I had given this project everything I possibly could; I had emptied myself trying to succeed, and for what? There was no point in what I was doing. Nobody cared. The number of people following me on social media was dwindling, and I had come to believe that only a tiny fraction of the people I encountered understood what I was doing. I couldn't see that the Red Cross was benefiting in any way from its association with me, and my quest to show that the world is a better place by far than most people think was floundering.

I felt completely, excruciatingly alone. There was nobody who knew my state of mind: I'd hidden my struggles from Le because I hadn't wanted to distress her. I was finding it harder and harder to explain even to myself what I was doing, or why. I could not remember the last time all of this had been enjoyable rather than a constant, attritional grind.

I hated the bargaining over prices: a relentless round of bluff and counterbluff where, as I grew more tired, less able to contemplate walking any significant distance at all, my ability to hold my nerve would often crumble and I'd pay more than I needed.

For months, I had been trying to force myself to work for twenty-four hours a day, then beating myself up because I couldn't. It was impossible to work when I was sleeping or eating or going to the bathroom. These things that my body needed had come to feel like hindrances. Obstacles that stood between me and where I needed to go.

I had largely lost any of the joy that most people find in eating. It was a question of: what does my body need for me to perform? Do I need more protein? I'd buy an egg from one of the roadside vendors who sold them sprinkled with chilli. Do I need more carbohydrates? I'd see if I could find some manioc or bread. Am I lacking vitamins? Time for an orange. Am I lacking potassium? OK, I'll pick up some bananas.

When I'd been in Europe, I'd frequently skipped eating: one way to save money is to eat two, not three, meals a day. A regular meal when I was staying in hostels was pasta boiled in stock, which I called soup. In more expensive countries I'd go to a supermarket and buy bread, cheese, cucumbers, tomatoes, and then go and sit in a park to eat them. But if I needed to reset my body – sometimes you need to eat something that you *know* – I'd get a sandwich from Subway, assuming they had branches in that country.

I don't think I saw my body as part of me any more, rather as a machine I relied on to get me visas or across borders. It was no different, in my eyes, from the trains and buses and taxis that were taking me around the continent.

This was all set against the fear that Le, who I loved more than anyone else on the planet, was slipping away from me. I wasn't even halfway through the journey, and I knew that the hardest parts of my quest – the unimaginably vast expanses of the Pacific – still lay before me. My sponsorship with Ross had collapsed and by now, for the first time in my life, I had started to suffer from those dreaded migraines. Until this point I had thought that migraines were simply severe headaches. Now I realised how wrong I had been. A friend who had been afflicted by them for longer than me once explained to me that when they strike, it can be so bad that if somebody offers you a pill that gives you a 50 per cent chance of removing the pain, and a 50 per cent chance of killing you, you'd swallow it without hesitating. They felt to me as if the two halves of my brain were pulling in different directions and my head was about to split. There was nothing I could do. Closing my eyes did nothing, nor did hiding under my bed covers. I could barely drink water without throwing up, and I had become excruciatingly sensitive to even the slightest sound. Stress was acting on my body like a vice. (The migraines would flare up once more when I was stuck in Lebanon. The attacks were so violent that I vomited from the pain. I've never had one since.)

*This is madness*, I thought, *this is madness. I have wasted two years of my life that I'll never get back. I am destroying myself on every level. Why am I doing this?*

I walked out of the immigration complex and instantly saw a taxi parked close by. This, I told myself, is going to take me to the airport. Who cares about my bag? Who cares about the project? This is as far as I go. The madness ends now.

I reckoned a bus journey to the airport would take me two days; it would surely be a matter of hours in a car. I was willing to pay the driver whatever he wanted to take me and could sort out tickets when I got there. There is a photo of me from this moment. I cannot remember whether I took it deliberately, or if it was the result of a moment of clumsiness. You can see the weariness on my face; my lips are pursed, pressed together by weeks of angst; but the most striking thing is my eyes: they are a visual manifestation of defeat.

I was escaping this mad spider's web of a place, I was going home! But as a man who had been overwhelmed. A man who had given up.

It was at precisely this moment that Abdul Karimou arrived. He was a motorcycle taxi driver who operated in the borderlands. We had struck up a basic kind of friendship while I was in the area, albeit one limited by the fact that we had no language in common that went beyond the basics of: 'Take me there' and 'How much do you want?' These were the building blocks of so many of my interactions around this time; supplemented by the dumb shows involved with showing people banknotes or pointing to stuff. It was enough to make things work, but I had this constant sense of being cut off from something important.

Africa is a talkative continent that is dense with languages. In every country, alongside French, or English, Portuguese or whatever their colonisers spoke, there is a proliferation of local languages and dialects. A single country can have hundreds.

Unfortunately, I never had the mental capacity or energy to explore them, so I had to stick to the colonial tongues. This was fine where English was spoken widely, but my French is limited and extremely functional. (And there was not a single soul for hundreds of kilometres who spoke Danish.)

I think it was a while before I realised how isolating it was to reduce almost all of my human interactions to stumbling attempts to buy food, negotiate with taxi drivers or book a room. In fact, it was only once I'd reached Nigeria – home to more than five hundred languages but where English is spoken routinely – that it hit me. Suddenly, people were making jokes and I could catch the punchline. When you can both laugh at the same thing, share a sense of humour, you know you're connecting on a deeper level. It was a relief and at the same time it was sad to be reminded about how much I was missing so much of the time.

Abdul Karimou had a way of helping me get past this. He was a life force. The kind of person who smiles with not just his mouth and his eyes, but an entire body that radiates happiness. He was short, slender and irrepressible. The police had once told him that he was forbidden from riding around without a helmet, so he'd gone out and found himself a yellow Bob the Builder-style hard hat.

He saw me sitting there, crumpled in on myself, came up to me and started talking to me in a language I did not know. He gestured to me to climb on to his bike – I am not sure why I followed him, but I think by then I had surrendered so completely that I would have agreed to anything. We then rode perhaps 50 metres down the road, certainly no more – it would have been easier to walk. Here, we stopped by a rough plastic table surrounded by a jumble of chairs where a street vendor was serving people drinks. While we waited for the tea Abdul Karimou had ordered us, I sat there feeling lower than I had ever been at any point in my life. *I've been struggling so hard. I've been through so much to get to this point. People have no idea how rough it has been for such a long time; they don't know what the journey has actually been like.*

Abdul Karimou had not stopped talking. He seemed completely unbothered by the fact that I obviously did not understand him, and had not responded in any way since he had first opened his mouth. I looked up. Words continued to stream past me, but something of his infectious joy and optimism found its way into my slumped body. We were still within sight of the immigration complex. There was the same taxi I'd seen before. Something inside me shifted. *They're not going to beat me. They're not going to decide my destiny. I will find a way. I'm tougher than this system, I'm going to prove them wrong. There is only one way: keep on keeping on. I will keep fighting until there is not a single drop of blood left in my body.*

I opened my passport. It was the last day of my Cameroonian visa; I had to leave the country by the end of the day. But there were still seven days left on the Congolese visa I'd obtained some months previously. I opened Google Maps and began to work out what I could do. Two hundred kilometres lay between me and the border with the Republic of Congo. After that, I would need to travel a thousand kilometres down through Congo and then up again to meet Gabon's southern border, which I'd crossed without trouble once before. The people in charge there seemed far more inclined to follow the actual rules.

I asked Abdul to go to Kyé-Ossi and find me a driver willing to undertake the journey. He returned shortly afterwards with a man called Said Kiyosse, who had borrowed his brother's car. We entered into a long negotiation; he came out the other side with what I was sure was the better deal, a sum that equated to twenty-five days of my budget. But I didn't care. I'd found a way through.

CHAPTER 9

# You Sleep Here Tonight

*Republic of Congo, Cameroon, Equatorial Guinea, January 2016*

It was that night that we were stopped by the three drunken soldiers. Eventually, at four in the morning, we reached the border between Cameroon and the Republic of Congo. By this point it was already light. I could just about make out the crossing. A small settlement, Mbalam, barely a village. More a huddle of houses and round huts in the middle of thick jungle. There was no fence dividing the two countries, just a square little shack beside a gate and a flagpole.

Nearby was another collection of huts in a clearing carved out of the jungle. Here, the new year's festivities were still in full flow. In the village's dusty centre, boozed-out women performed a slow, drunk dance to music that blasted out of a stack of huge speakers. Men watched from a bench inside the porch of a white wooden house, each of them clasping an enormous bottle of beer.

I knew I would have to wait a few hours for anybody to turn up, but if I was used to anything now, it was waiting. At seven, a truck filled with beer arrived at the gate. I talked to its driver, who told me that immigration wouldn't open for a little while longer. Then it was 40 kilometres to Cabosse in the Congo. This was too much for me to walk. I negotiated a price with him to carry me, and returned to my waiting. About an hour later, we heard a distinctive roar that could only belong to a powerful motorbike. The sound came closer, and closer, and then suddenly a white Suzuki 600 ridden by a man in full leathers and helmet sped into view.

I struggled for a while to process what I was looking at. Its presence made no sense. We were in a region populated almost exclusively by banged-up old Toyota Corollas and mopeds. *This* didn't fit.

The apparition took his helmet off and introduced himself as Djamila Augustin, the immigration officer. He was also happiness personified. 'OK,' he said, breezily, his face wreathed in smiles, 'let's hoist the flag.' He disappeared for a moment inside the shack and then re-emerged with the Cameroonian flag, which he ran up a nearby pole before indicating that we should salute it. It was hard to work out what he was going to do next. 'Now, before we get down to business, let's go and have breakfast.' With that he indicated that I was to hop on to the back of his motorcycle.

Once I'd climbed on, we sped off to a tiny café – little more than a wooden house with a few seats – with the truck driver following. Over eggs, tomatoes and coffee Djamila asked me where I was from: 'Denmark? Oh, I love Denmark. Hans Christian Andersen.' The room was dark, they only turned the electric lights on at night, but Djamila's presence alone made our meal feel almost like a celebration. The events of the night before receded, beginning to feel more like a horrible nightmare rather than something that had actually happened to me.

Once he was satisfied we'd all eaten our fill he took me back to the shack, where he looked at my visa. For the first time since I'd met him, he appeared to be struggling with a negative emotion. 'I don't think they will let you cross,' he said sadly.

'Why not? It's still valid.'

'No, well, yes, technically, but they will say it's expired. Look, it is a sixty-day visa and it was issued almost sixty days ago. In most countries you're supposed to start counting that sixty days from the day of entry, which makes more sense. They're supposed to do that too, but they won't. They'll say it's expired.'

'I have to try it,' I said, 'I've come this far, I can't go back.'

There was little more either of us could say. He stamped me out of Cameroon and wished me good luck. The beer truck took me through the gate and along the bumpy road that led to Congolese immigration.

Everything was a tiny bit smarter, more modern on the Congolese side. There were even fences, which were guarded by a group of soldiers, also drunk, sitting in the morning sun. Armed with my Cameroonian friend's warnings, I approached the immigration hut and tried to do all the things I knew could help my cause. I waited until I was called to enter, I took my hat off, and did not sit down. And to begin with, everything seemed to be going fine. The man in front of me was short, really short, in fact, with extremely crooked teeth. What was strange was his eyes. It was hard to say exactly what was wrong, or different. Just that there was something off, almost sinister, about them that, once detected, became impossible to ignore. And yet he was kind and polite. He was friendly as he invited me in and asked for my passport. But then, as if something had snapped inside him, his demeanour changed.

Dismissively, he threw my passport so that it thudded into my chest. 'The visa has expired. You will not be able to cross.' Instinctively I reached inside my pocket to find my Nokia so I could call the French Red Cross in Brazzaville, who I thought might be able to help. *Damn.* My hands grasped empty space in my pocket and I remembered that I'd lost it and the important sim cards strapped to it a few days ago in a taxi. I still had my smartphone, but I was reluctant to bring it out because it only contained my Danish sim card, so had no signal. I also knew that by doing so I'd instantly mark myself as somebody who had money to spare. (Yet almost everyone I encountered in Africa had a smartphone. A lot of them wanted to take a photo of my old Nokia. The joke, for them, was how ancient my phone was.)

As I was trying to process what the loss of the phone and the number stored on it meant, I was also trying to make my case, pointing out as politely as I could that my visa still had seven days left.

'You are going nowhere,' he told me, unmoved by my arguments. 'Who is immigration?' he asked, a vicious glint creeping into his eyes. The situation was deteriorating rapidly. 'Am I immigration or are you immigration?'

'No, no, of course you are immigration.'

'So I'm telling you, it has expired. You cannot cross, you cannot enter.'

'There must be something we can do. I cannot go back to Cameroon. My visa has expired. If you're not letting me into Congo, then I'm stuck here between two countries.'

'That,' he said, appearing to enjoy the sound of the words as they emerged from between his crooked teeth, 'is not my problem. Find a truck, get back to Cameroon.'

With that, he sent me out. He seemed convinced that the matter was closed. I was desperate to prove him wrong. And yet, for the moment, how exactly I was going to do this wasn't clear. Losing the sim cards meant that my smartphone was functionally useless, so I approached the dozing soldiers to see if they could help in any way. As well as quoting me an outrageous price to borrow one of their handsets, they told me that a German man, who was working on the construction of a modern border crossing nearby, might be worth speaking to. I wasn't sure how I'd contact him, so paid what they were asking and called Jérémie, a guy I knew at the French Red Cross in Congo. He asked me where I was and promised to try to speak to some of his contacts, and so I ended the call feeling cautiously optimistic.

This coincided with the reappearance of the immigration guy with crooked teeth, who was annoyed to find me still there, very obviously *not* working on getting back into Cameroon. I tried to explain what I was trying to do, but the more I spoke, the more I seemed to upset him. Just as he was approaching a crescendo of anger, he was interrupted by the arrival of a Filipino woman riding a scruffy, dented motorbike – the damaged, far less powerful cousin of the beast I'd been on earlier that morning.

Speaking in perfect English, she instantly took charge of the situation. She asked me who I was. I explained that I was Danish, and that I was stuck. 'Oh,' she said, 'my husband is German, he's working on a project nearby whose manager is Danish. They will surely be able to help out. Come,' she said, indicating I should join her on the motorbike, 'I'll take you.'

I moved towards her but found my way blocked by the immigration officer. At this, the Filipino woman launched a volley of incandescent French at him. He responded in kind, his anger mounting all the time. He was obviously not somebody who enjoyed losing face. Very quickly, they started screaming at each other, while I, increasingly bemused, looked on. Eventually the Filipino woman brought the shouting match to an end by announcing that she was going to tell her husband. 'Stay here,' she told me, 'wait until I come back.' Almost as soon as she'd arrived, she had disappeared in a cloud of dust.

The man with the crooked teeth surged up to me. 'Get out of here. Get back to Cameroon.' A new kind of urgency now accompanied his anger, as if he was worried that he was going to get into trouble if someone found me lingering around his station.

I, on the other hand, was doing everything I could to delay my departure in order to give what I hoped would be my Danish saviour enough time to come to my aid. This, in turn, made the tiny Napoleon even madder. I was beginning to worry he might actually go insane.

Eventually he screamed an order at the soldiers, who up until this point had been lazing in the sun, enjoying the spectacle. For the second time in a matter of hours I found myself confronted by men pointing guns at me. There was not the same supercharged, deranged menace as the night before – I'm not sure these guys had either the will or the energy to pull their triggers – and yet it was still unpleasant.

They prodded and pushed me towards a waiting truck and the immigration officer ordered its driver to take me back to the border. The driver made a brief, futile attempt to ask for money, then submitted. I watched the immigration officer hand my passport to the co-driver: 'Don't give it back to him until he's back in Cameroon.'

This was not good. My antagonist had me by the arm, pushing me forward; in response I tried to walk slowly. Sensing my intransigence, he grew ever more aggressive; crazier, louder, spinning out of control. Eventually they bundled me into the truck. I could only do so much. The truck had just begun to trundle off when the Filipino woman's husband zoomed up on his motorbike. I shouted across to him in German: 'I've done nothing wrong. I have my paperwork in order. I'm supposed to cross. Please help me.'

The German guy started trying to argue my case, doing his best to calm the immigration officer down, but the time when he might have been willing to listen to reason had long since passed: he was *gone.* The German pointed out how much trouble he would be in, and tried to make him see how much sway the Danish project manager had locally. No use. I watched, impotently, from the slowly moving truck. It wasn't clear what my next move should be. 'Should I try to jump off?' I shouted across to the German, who was now further and further behind us. At that moment, I remembered that the co-driver was holding my passport. I leaned across to try to snatch it, but he was a split-second faster than me, and now he was on his guard against me trying the same stunt again. There was no chance of getting it back and thus no longer any point in trying to jump out.

As we bumped along the dusty track to Cameroon, the end of the project suddenly seemed extremely close.

I was welcomed back into Cameroon by Djamila, the friendly motorbike rider from before. 'Yes,' he said, as cheerful as he had been earlier that morning, 'I told you so, but I'm sorry it didn't happen. I know that immigration officer. I also know that his sister wanted to go to Europe but was denied a visa. This was his opportunity to take a small revenge. Let's see if we can help you.'

I told him my Cameroonian visa had now expired. This was no problem, he said, and began the process of producing the paperwork I'd need to travel back to Yaoundé and get a new visa. 'OK, come and we'll get a room for you.' With that he ordered a subordinate to pick up my bag. Before I knew it, they had disappeared. For a moment I thought, *I don't know these people. I don't know where my bag is going.* But I was overwhelmed by a defeated feeling that was compounded by stress, hunger, lack of sleep and the weakness that always follows diarrhoea. On top of all this was the experience of having had guns shoved in my face twice in a matter of hours. I had yet to process this, so it sat, uncomfortable and undigested, inside me.

The women were still performing their slow dance. Drunkenness had robbed it of any of its sensuality. My friend shooed the men who had been sitting watching off the bench and encouraged me to sit.

Someone gave me a beer. I drank it, almost mechanically. I could hear somebody explaining to me that they could get me somewhere to rest my head – that this was why Cameroon was a better country than Congo. All of this took place at one remove, as if it was happening to somebody else. I was dead to the room. 'Tomorrow,' my new friend told me, 'we'll put you in a car. You can go back. You sleep here tonight.'

The room was small and dark, with no windows. There was a small candle on the concrete floor and a mosquito coil, and I could just make out a bed against the wall. I was desperate to have a shower to try to wash off the dust that caked my skin and had seemed to cling to every strand of my beard, but the last thing I remember from that day is sitting on that bed with my bag open and a clean pair of boxers in my hands.

I woke fifteen hours later, still clasping my underwear, my legs sprawling over the side of the bed: I had collapsed backwards from exhaustion. Equipped with my new paperwork, I clambered inside a bush taxi: a poorly serviced and dangerously overloaded Corolla. It was perhaps only ten years old, but it bore the signs of having been used every day in some of the most difficult terrain on the planet. The seats were worn and covered with dust, as well as a layer of grease and slime left by a decade of passengers eating meals in motion. There was little point in washing the dust off the car because everyone knew that within two minutes the same amount would have cascaded in to replace it. In an extraordinary feat of engineering, the driver had forced nine adults into the car.

Two sat on the passenger seat (quite common) and two were squeezed on to the driver's side (less common but not unknown: it meant that four legs hovered over the pedals). There were five people in the back. This was the most complex part of the puzzle. The two people situated beside the doors, as well as the person sitting right in the middle, sat as far back in their seats as they could. Then, the two other occupants sat as far forward in their seats as they were able. This just about works because, if one puts one's legs together, it is narrower at the knees than at the hips.

What's more, a couple of my fellow passengers had children on their laps, and we were also surrounded by everyone's luggage. Luckily, I avoided being crammed in like this and found myself in the front, between two other passengers. The driver blasted off, the Toyota's old engine straining to carry its hefty cargo. At some point, I realised with a vicious jolt that we would pass the checkpoint manned by the men who had threatened my life the night before. We pulled up, my anxiety mounted as they shot me another series of evil looks, and then drained away as they quickly and efficiently processed us.

Normally on a journey like this there would be conversation, with me as an object of curiosity. There would be questions. Why are you here? Where are you from? What are you doing here? Why are you not in a taxi on your own? And we would stop at every little hole along the way.

Not today. Perhaps the cumulative effect of the new year's festivities had subdued them. Everyone seemed to be affected, including inside the bush taxi, where the rest of the passengers appeared to be falling asleep around me. One after another, I watched people's heads droop, until the only two people still awake were me and the driver, a slender, cleanshaven man about the same age as me.

I tried to sleep but each time the car tumbled up and down another rut in the road, I was jolted awake. Everything was hot, anything metal was so warm that it was uncomfortable to touch.

There was no air conditioning, so we just did what almost all passengers here did: open the windows and hope for the best. My nose filled with the smell of sweat and unwashed, greasy bodies. We were all covered in dust – it clung uncomfortably to my hair and beard – and our clothes stuck to our skin with sweat.

An hour went by, then another. Journeys like these were always a reminder of the continent's almost incomprehensible scale. We were travelling at 90 kilometres an hour on a dirt road. The whole car shook as the worn tyres scrambled over stones and ruts. Wind whipped through the vehicle's open windows, entombing each of us in more dust but also offering a welcome relief from the punishing heat. On our left was thick forest, on our right a ditch with a steep cliff rising up on its far side. I looked across at the driver. His eyes were narrowing. He had obviously been up as late as all his passengers. Any loss of control would either smash us into a solid wall of trees or send us hurtling into a ravine. I began to consider the consequences of any kind of accident. We were in a part of the world where the chances of any ambulance arriving were tiny. In the unlikely event that one did come to your aid, you could not expect it to arrive in mint condition. It would be highly unlikely to carry oxygen or gloves or painkillers, and it's possible your first stop would not be a hospital but a petrol station. In fact, what with one thing or another, being picked up in an ambulance in Central Africa might well decrease your chances of survival.

A country like Denmark has all kinds of systems in place to make sure that no matter how far you fall, you'll never actually crash right to the bottom. You could see these as forming a kind of safety net. If a visitor to Denmark is attacked in the street, the police will come. If the hotel they are staying in starts burning, they will be saved by the fire brigade. The hospitals are clean, well-stocked with medicine. Whatever happens to you, you're highly likely to get back to your country in one piece.

There are some parts of the world that do not have a safety net. This does not mean that these places are relentlessly bad. It's perfectly possible that you will visit Afghanistan or Syria and have an exquisite time. You'll visit extraordinary mosques, eat delicious, unusual food, and have rewarding cultural exchanges with people you meet in the street. But when things go wrong, they go wrong all the way. If your finger gets caught in a machine, your finger is gone. Nobody is going to reattach it. You might bleed out before anybody comes to help.

Central Africa has no safety net. If there was an accident, my chances of walking away and continuing my journey were minimal. The driver began to nod. I could see his grip on the steering get looser, his shoulders start to slump. I had a vivid flash of what it would be like to veer out of control, of the carnage that would be visited on this speeding lump of metal, of my blood washing out of me into the road's orange dust. There were no seatbelts, no airbags. Any survivors would probably be maimed for life: victims of a tragedy that would probably not even merit a single line in a newspaper.

The Toyota started to edge towards the ditch. I realised that I was the only person in the car who knew what was about to happen. In a moment of pure instinct, I extended my arm across the sleeping figure on my left, grabbed the steering wheel and corrected our course.

The driver woke with a start and saw my hand on the steering wheel. Anger clouded his face, and then, as he realised what had just happened, passed almost as quickly as it had come. He remained silent, but nodded knowingly at me, as if to say: 'Let's keep this between friends.'

The rest of the passengers continued to slumber, blissfully unaware of how close they had come to disaster. The driver did not fall asleep again.

\* \* \*

The guy who eventually got me inside Equatorial Guinea was Sébastien Lescouet, a French expat working for a French company. I'd met him by pure chance on the Cameroonian side of the border crossing into Gabon. I watched him as he spoke to somebody else on the phone. There was something about this man, with his shaved head, dark glasses and a polo shirt that displayed his strong arms, that made him look like a human being capable of exerting control. I thought: *He would make a great ally. I need to see if I can get him on my side.*

I waited for him to finish his call then approached him: 'Sorry, do you speak English?'

He smiled and a cocky look spread across his face: 'Yes, *and* French and Spanish.'

But the most important thing he understood was the right attitude to take when confronted by people in authority: when they said jump, you said how high?

The people in uniform had the power and could do anything they wanted with you. That was an unarguable fact; there was no value in trying to dispute it. The sooner you got your head around it, the better. He had almost lost count of the number of times he'd been thrown into a Guinean prison cell. Sometimes this had been for ten minutes, sometimes for five hours, sometimes longer. They would rob him of his freedom, take him out of his vehicle, drive him somewhere and lock him up.

This was something I'd thought about a lot during the time I'd spent by myself on trains and buses during my journey. One subject that nagged away at me was morality. Are people inherently good? Am I a good person who sometimes missteps or am I a bad person who's doing the best I can, without much success? And after many years, I came to the conclusion that both are probably true. More than that, I thought, morality is a question of circumstances.

We may not be inherently good, but the context of our lives gives us no reason to show the darker side of our nature, so we come across as decent. In Denmark, for instance, a comparatively equal society, there aren't massive disparities in people's salaries, they have the same size television set and house, so there's a balance in society. But if you disrupted that, if you took a handful of people and entrusted them with huge power and great wealth, the chances are that unless they're buttressed by a Gandhi-like morality, those 'gifts' will deform them. They will use that power cruelly, to manipulate or punish others, or will begin to believe that they deserve this unearned money because, in some obscure way, they are better than the plebs on the street.

Of course, most people are not in that position. Most people just have their families and their jobs. What you see of them is the good, everyday side. You might then infer that people are inherently good, but if you changed their circumstances, you might see that good disappear.

Central Africa bore out the truth of this argument. Anyone in a uniform was the devil. I saw it time after time. People, like the immigration officer, who were given a small amount of power *used* it. He could use that authority and then go back home to his sister and say: 'Guess what I did today?' The same is true of the petty Napoleons insisting that I use a particular colour of ink when filling in a form.

Sébastien was unbothered by any of this. For him, it was simply another facet of life in this part of the world, like the punishing heat. You couldn't fight it, so the only thing to do was find a way of living with it. He explained that he would be going back to Gabon the following day, and from there on to Equatorial Guinea. This was perfect. It was always easier travelling with someone who spoke proper French, and two is always better than one.

It turned out that he'd been working in Equatorial Guinea for many years. He knew people in the capital, Malabo, and wouldn't be affected by the border shutdown. In the space of a few seconds everything just changed. I had three days left before my visa for Equatorial Guinea would expire. I'd spent three months trying to get that visa. Then I'd been grinding my teeth for twenty-seven days trying to *use* it. But now I had this guy. He showed up the next day in his Toyota Land Cruiser. We took a dirt road towards the border, passed through immigration and then, here I was, at last: Equatorial Guinea. The expat turned to me, his face deadly serious: 'Do you have anything in your bag you're not supposed to have? If so, then I need to know *now*.'

'No, everything's legit. Everything's fine.'

'OK. When we arrive, I do all the talking. Even if they speak directly to you. Say nothing, I will answer for you. It is essential that you remain silent.'

We pulled up to immigration and I followed his instructions. I was asked a question and remained mute, staring blankly back at my interlocutor while the Frenchman leaned behind my back and spoke.

Then he got out of the car. By this point we were surrounded by a circle of men in a mix of uniforms and civilian clothes. My new friend went up to each of them and shook their hands. I suspect each handshake concealed a gift. At a desk sat another man, operating an ancient-looking computer, beside which sat a ledger in which somebody had recorded a great deal of information incredibly tidily.

There was more conversation, then the Frenchman came over to explain. 'They cannot write your name in that book because the borders are closed, but you're good to continue.' Somebody typed into the ancient computer, then we were waved off. That was where the tarmac started. A perfect road through the jungle; smooth, with rails either side. It was like a version of Dubai in Africa. This, I told myself, is what oil money buys you.

The next two days were pleasant, if a little strange. I'd initially considered simply hiding in the jungle for twenty-four hours before hopping back over the border. Instead, I let the Frenchman take me into the heart of the new capital that the country was creating in the middle of the jungle. Everywhere around me they were building schools, retirement homes, government offices, luxury hotels, golf courses. An artificial paradise in the heart of darkness. Again, I was reminded of what oil money can buy you. Again, I thought of Dubai.

That odd sense of being lost in a half-completed dream persisted even as I made my way out of the country. I encountered the same people who had ushered me in just forty-eight hours previously, and yet this time they looked at me wonderingly. 'How did you get in?' they quizzed me, their puzzlement seeming genuine. 'The borders are closed. How could you do this?' I considered trying to argue with them; then quickly thought better of it. Still, they punched an exit stamp into my passport, which now sits there looking slightly adrift without a corresponding entry stamp.

That dreamlike dislocation fell away as soon as I mounted the small truck that took me back into Gabon, replaced by a wave of exaltation. I had returned with a livid scratch on my cheek and bite marks on my hat – the legacy of a surprise encounter with a group of chimpanzees on a golf course – but as I sat there beneath a shining sky on that truck, surrounded by its cargo of bananas and four or five other passengers, I could not help reflecting on the turn in my fortunes. Just twenty-six days before, I had fallen to the lowest moment of my life. I had been prepared to abandon the project and fly home. Now, here I was, with a body that felt as if it had been transformed into one big smile: an exhausted, tattered, utterly ecstatic symbol of happiness.

Realising this, I took another photograph of myself – a counterpart of the shot I'd captured of the bleak moment I thought my journey was over. I still have them now, a reminder that I should never give up, that no matter how bad I'm feeling *right now*, it will not last. My mood will change, the situation will improve. Things can turn around. Things will turn around.

Time changes everything. Back when I was a boy scout, we went on a trip to Norway. There was a hike one day and the leaders divided us into three groups: fast, regular and slow. We could pick which group we wanted to walk with. Obviously, I went for the fast one. But after a while I began to lag behind the others. I was too small to keep up. One of the leaders stopped me to ask if I was OK. I explained that I wasn't ill, I was just no longer capable of putting one foot in front of the other. He told me that his group would continue without me, and that the next, slower group would catch up with us soon. I was fine with that.

I sat there thinking, alone in the stunning Norwegian landscape watching the others grow small as they approached two mountain tops in the distance. It hurt that I couldn't keep up. And yet I knew that, sooner or later, I too would pass between those two mountain tops. I would recover my strength, or enough of it to do what I needed. It was just a question of time. The way you feel in any given moment does not determine what you end up doing. All I had to do was wait a bit longer. A better future was there if I was willing to hold on.

In a similar way, my time in Central Africa became like a reference point for me throughout the rest of the journey. It was the place where the *real* adventure started. I knew it would never get that hard again. Nothing would, or could, come close; though I was glad that I'd faced these challenges when, relatively speaking,

I still had youth, energy and optimism on my side. If I had survived that experience – the segment that should have lasted six weeks, but ended up taking me nine months – then there was nothing that could stop me.

## CHAPTER 10

# The Question

*Mount Kenya, Kenya, November 2016*

Here's the thing: the overwhelming, obsessive priority in my life, completing the project, was also what threatened to wreck what was perhaps the most precious thing in my life, my relationship with Le.

If I was no longer in a relationship with Le, then I'd have nothing to come home for, and so the constant pressure I felt to make progress would be removed. I could start to stay longer in each country, I could actually enjoy myself. It wouldn't matter if the journey took twenty years. But that was exactly the point: she was my reason for coming home. I did not want to give up what we had. And I could not have kept going without her.

Partly that was because of how sustaining I found the support she could give me. She had a talent for centring me, calming me on those days when my angst or worries grew out of hand. But also because I always believed that *she* would stick it out.

Le never asked me to give up or come home. She made a point that she wouldn't. Of course, that's not the same as saying that she wouldn't have preferred to have a boyfriend who lived in Denmark with her. Sometimes I've wondered what I'd have done had she given me an ultimatum: it's me or the project. Early on, our relationship wasn't developed enough, we didn't have enough history, so I would have finished the project and come home to nobody. Later, in Hong Kong, for instance, I probably would have abandoned everything and got on a plane. The question gathered more weight the further into the journey I got.

She had flown out to see me as often as she could, eight times already before I'd left Central Africa (she'd go on to make twenty-seven trips in total). I saw her in Scotland, just two weeks after I'd left home, she saved my life in Ghana, and I shouted at her in the middle of a jungle in São Tomé.

I knew how complex I had made her life. Le was going to places she had never considered travelling to. This was almost always a good thing. But the logistics involved were never easy. My erratic progress did not marry well with the demands of the world she lived in, which was organised along more predictable lines: flights that ran according to an inflexible schedule; a working life that required her to book holidays in advance.

And she was flying out to meet a man who was often preoccupied, or frustrated, or disappointed, although always *ecstatic* to see her.

I looked forward intensely to every single trip Le made. But I ended up working twice as hard when she visited, because I was still running the project, still trying to make progress, while also attempting to ensure that everything about her holiday went perfectly. I wanted her to travel home with love hearts in her eyes. My fear was always that we'd have a bad time and she'd return with a mind full of doubts, that would marinate and fester while we were 5,000 kilometres away from each other.

There were also certain places where I'd already got used to the environment's particular dangers and challenges. With Le it could sometimes be like walking around with a child; I'd constantly be on guard trying to make sure she didn't get run over or cheated or scammed. Still, wherever we were, there were things we always tried to do so that, even if it was just for a few days, we could follow the rhythms of a 'normal' relationship. We'd go for sushi, we'd play cards, we'd find a cinema and watch a film, we'd go for day trips. There were other rituals that were particular to us. In the time in-between Le's visits, I'd let my beard grow wild – grooming was one of the first things I was always willing to let go when I got busy – then, when she arrived, we'd trim it.

But none of the visits could obscure the central fact of our relationship. It was easy, too easy, for a relationship to get into a very dangerous atmosphere when there are thousands of kilometres between you. And it gets harder to fix things.

You can only do a certain amount through video calls. Video calls are so much better than text messages – you get facial reactions, you can see if the other person just had a haircut and what they're wearing – but they're so much worse than being in the same room, especially if you're speaking – as we often were – through a patchy internet connection. You need to be near somebody if you want to communicate something important. There is so much you miss if you cannot give your loved ones a hug, or wipe tears from their cheeks. I was also conscious of how much was happening in Le's life that I couldn't know. I worried sometimes that she was putting on a show for me for the thirty-minute video call, then collapsing in tears as soon as we'd hung up.

All of this becomes more acute when things are not going your way. A strong relationship can take a lot of damage before it starts to become unhealthy. But the same is true of something that feels broken. It's extremely hard to put it back together, even more so if you're on different continents.

Our relationship came damn near to breaking when I was in Cameroon. This was when I was appallingly stressed about the mess I was in with visas and borders, and she had lots to think about in her own career as a doctor. We were tired, our lives were full, and for a long time we had been in a state of disconnection, like we were trying to communicate on different frequencies.

As I went through Central Africa I knew that, in one way, the best thing I could do would be to explain all the things I was struggling with. It would help her relate to me. But I also didn't want to worry her – because she is extremely compassionate, if she knew I was unhappy, it would pain her – so I hid elements of my situation from her.

I also knew that it probably would be better if I understood what she did each day, what time she got up, who she met with, how her studies or work were going, whether her back was aching – as much as possible. And yet that would have been an overload. Did I really need to know what she had on her toast for breakfast?

The other extreme would have been for us to reduce our communication to the barest essentials, because we both had other stuff demanding our time and interest. But when you're that laconic, you end up knowing nothing about the other person. You need to keep an interest, you need to keep a connection, because it's an easy leap from there to dangerous questions like: what does it mean to say that we're a couple? Or: why am I even in this relationship?

That balance between superficial and deep is easier to maintain when you're under the same roof. All of our communication was superficial: *How are you doing? It's been a rough day. I'm going to bed. OK, goodnight.* We never asked, *Why was it a rough day? Is there anything I can do?* At times, we talked to each other as if we were clients or customers. Friendly, not close.

Eventually we decided we needed to have a call to discuss whether it was time to go our separate ways. I found a space in a nearby internet café, logged on and, as people around me chatted volubly, had one of the most significant conversations of my life. That was the closest we've ever been to breaking up. We agreed that we would think about it during the day, then speak again that evening to make the decision. I started considering what I wanted, and very quickly stopped, because the answer was overwhelmingly obvious: she is definitely the one. So I used my time to put together a list of twenty reasons why I thought we should stay together, and emailed it to her.

She replied that she was encouraged by my enthusiasm, and thought we should talk a bit more. I could tell she was trying to keep me on edge. She asked me to explain the first reason, then the second, then the third . . .

We agreed this was something we both wanted and needed; we would work harder. She would come to visit me more frequently. We would do more video calls, and would try to engage more, and learn more about what was going on in each other's lives. Things got better and better and better.

By the time I had reached South Africa, not only was my relationship in a completely different place, everything about the project had become far easier. The big change came when I crossed over from Angola – the last country in Central Africa – into Namibia in Southern Africa. It was like going from one world into an entirely new one. No more checkpoints, no more wrangles over visas. I was in a place where ambulances would actually come if you had an accident. There was a Burger King! I had to sit quietly in a chair for a few days in an attempt to process the fact that the game had changed. Everything was so different that I felt a kind of shell shock.

So perhaps this contributed to what I was planning to do next, because my mind was now liberated to think about other, happier topics. I went from Namibia to Botswana to South Africa, a beautiful country. It's often referred to as the rainbow nation, a reference to the diversity of its population. But to me the phrase is equally applicable to its geographic qualities. When I took bus journeys, I noticed that the landscape kept changing. It felt to me as if every film I'd ever seen in my life could have been filmed in South Africa.

And it was here that I decided I would ask Le to marry me. I wanted to spend my life with her; I just hoped that she felt the same way. I carried on through the soft south of Africa: Lesotho, Swaziland, Mozambique and then Zimbabwe, where Le joined me, staying by my side as I progressed into Zambia. Her visit was important for two reasons. The first was that I could see Le again. The second was that she brought with her a new hat.

The one I'd set out with had made it to 101 countries – I'd finally lost it in the DRC. In fact, the day before I lost it I'd made a cocky social media post boasting about having brought the hat across so many borders. Then the next morning it was gone, its fate one of the enduring mysteries of the whole journey.

Its loss destroyed me, it was like a pet going missing. I tried to reconstruct what might have happened. I was staying in a room in an old colonial-style compound (complete with a monkey on a leash in the courtyard) rented by a man who'd reached out to me to see if he could help. We'd been drinking that night – unusual for me – and I had a memory of going to a lake an hour or so away. I didn't have a memory of the hat coming back with us. I was so distressed that I started offering ludicrous rewards to anybody who might be able to recover it.

I paid someone to drive to the lake. No luck. I looked in all the ordinary places one might have expected to find it. Still no luck. By the end, I was opening the fridge and staring intently inside it: hope had displaced any sense of rationality or proportion.

For a while after, I looked for a new hat. Sometimes I'd wear the hats I was given by Red Cross offices; I experimented with a paper hat; and in Botswana I briefly flirted with a colonial Dr Livingstone-style number before I realised that it wasn't a look that would endear me to populations who still had living memories of European rulers.

In the end, though, my dad gave my sister the money to buy a hat similar to the one I'd lost from the same hat shop. She handed it to Le, and I wore it right through to the end of the project. It's still there in my apartment, impregnated with years of sweat and filth. I don't put it on though – that thing could start a new pandemic by itself.

From Zambia I went to Malawi, then Tanzania. Here a Norwegian couple, Helene and Eivind, who ran a beach-side guest house and had been following my journey's progress, reached out to me. They told me about a mineral called tanzanite, which was only found in Tanzania's volcanic soil and was a thousand times rarer than diamonds. Depending on how you twisted it in the light, it could be blue or violet or purple. Perfect, I thought, a special stone for a special woman. Operating under conditions of the strictest secrecy, I contacted Le's twin, Pil, to see if she could discover her sister's ring size. She delivered. I got a ring made. All I needed to do now was work out the best way to give it to her.

After Tanzania I continued my journey, first travelling to the island nations of Comoros, Madagascar, the Seychelles and Mauritius, then retracing my steps back up the continent, returning to South Africa and Tanzania among other countries, before passing through Burundi, Rwanda, Uganda, South Sudan and Uganda (again).

Eventually, I crossed into Kenya, the hundred and twenty-first country in the project, where Le was going to be joining me. As I arrived in Nairobi, a bustling, traffic-choked, sporadically clean metropolis whose population had long since outgrown the space that had been built to accommodate it, I was still turning over ideas for the proposal in my mind.

The first building block came from the local Red Cross. They were very different from a lot of their brothers and sisters in the movement, which sometimes attracted criticism: namely that they were run more like a business than a humanitarian organisation. There was some truth to this, as they were phenomenal operators and fundraisers. But this allowed them to do a great deal of good. For instance, they organised the second-largest ambulance service in the whole of Africa, which ran on a subscription basis. They'd pick you up whether you had a subscription or not, but those who did have a subscription would end up paying less. They also owned a five-star hotel called the Boma, in Nairobi, which offered locals unprecedented opportunities for vocational training – all its profits were invested back into the Red Cross.

I'd learned about the existence of the hotel the year before, in Haiti, from another Red Cross representative, Ruben Wedel. It sounded so amazing that I told Ruben then and there that I planned to stay in it. He laughed and said that I had no chance, it was too exclusive for the likes of me. A bet was born: if I managed to get a room there, he'd have to buy me a beer served in Belgium (ask a beer nerd, and they'll tell you that the Belgians make the world's best). If I failed, it'd be me buying the drinks. I don't think he believed I was serious. I guess he didn't know me that well.

My way in was a speaking engagement. I delivered a talk to seventy members of the Kenyan Red Cross, talking passionately about my plans for the project. And then, Anthony Mwangi, their head of external relations with whom I'd discussed the proposal, prompted me to talk to them about my plans for Le. It was time to swear seventy strangers to secrecy. I explained that they were in a unique position to help me achieve two ambitions. First, winning my wager with Ruben. And second, getting Le to marry me. All they needed to do was secure me a room in the Boma. It turns out that there's very little you can't accomplish when seventy Kenyan members of the Red Cross have got your back. Within a couple of days, and with the help of the hotel's general manager, Jürgen Grübel, I'd got a reservation.

That still left the question of where I would ask Le to marry me. The answer was looming above us: Mount Kenya. Ever since I'd scaled Kilimanjaro in 2007, I'd wanted to tackle this, Africa's second highest peak.

With that decided, my plan quickly took shape. We'd hike up the mountain during the night. Then, when daylight broke, I'd get down on one knee. After that, it was in the hands of the gods. I think Le had a first inkling that something was up when I collected her from the airport and brought her back to the Boma. 'How are you paying for *this*?' she asked, gesturing at our plush surroundings. When Le had come to see me before, we hadn't stayed in hostels, but nor had we ever set foot in anything on quite this level. I opted to remain as vague as possible. 'I know people,' I said offhandedly. She looked at me again, obviously not convinced.

Before Le had arrived, I'd called a few of my married friends and asked them what I should expect, and what I needed to do. Their answers were pretty consistent. They told me that I needed a ring. Well, that was covered. I had what I thought was the best ring. But that wasn't the most important thing, they said. You've got to have a great location. Again, I felt as if I had that covered. I imagined the sun shining down on us, like a kind of benediction, as we gazed happily at the panorama below. In my more expansive moments I thought perhaps some of the local wild animals might even bow, as if they were extras from *The Lion King*.

Great, they all said. Though, of course, *that's* not the most important thing either. The most important thing is the mood.

You can have the best ring, the best place, but if the mood is not there, do not ask her. This was the thing I was anxious about. You can help create the conditions for a good mood, but you can't make it happen. There are too many factors outside your control. Still, notwithstanding her suspicions about the hotel, and the fact that I was keeping my cards close to my chest – including the exact nature of what we were about to do – Le was happy to be here.

We chose not to read anything into the fact that the guide who met us in the Kenya National Park's name was called Laban Wanjohi. In Danish, Laban means crook. Laban was tall, handsome and very capable looking, which it turns out is just the sort of person you want by your side when you break the news to your girlfriend that she's about to go on a surprise three-day hike to the top of Mount Kenya.

Le's first reaction was to point out that she'd never climbed a mountain, and didn't possess any mountaineering equipment. I wasn't worried by her first objection: she was a woman who ran ultramarathons. More to the point, she *enjoyed* doing them. And I'd taken steps to deal with her other objection by arranging to have some extra gear brought for her.

'What are you waiting for?' I said.

We began our climb, making our way up through scrub dotted with succulents that appeared in almost impossible architectural configurations. We stopped occasionally to help our bodies acclimatise to the elevation, and to take simple meals of popcorn and tea, or onion and cucumber, which somehow tasted better than any onion and cucumber I'd ever tasted in my life. At some point that day, we crossed the equator. Usually on my journey this had been the occasion for extreme heat. Now, however, we were high enough that the temperature seemed to be falling with every step we took. All the time, the same jumble of thoughts swirled through my mind: *Am I really going to ask her? Is she truly the one?*

*I'm going to be away for at least three more years of risk and struggle, so is it fair to her to ask her to make this commitment? Will there be the right mood? What if she gets altitude sickness?*

We spent the first night of our expedition in a hut, before recommencing our journey at 3 a.m., which I hoped would ensure we reached the summit at sunrise. It was dark and fearsomely cold. As we climbed higher there was ice; even the flowers below our feet were frozen. Flurries of snow billowing around our heads signalled that whatever progress we made, it was unlikely we'd see the sun.

Worst of all, I was beginning to worry that I might have miscalculated in bringing Le up this mountain at this time of year. Neither of us had clothes, such as gloves, warm enough to protect us in this environment, and Le's shoes did not have sufficient grip. I don't think I had realised that this was not simply a question of endurance; if it had been, Le would have been fine. There is a skill involved in keeping one's balance on terrain like this that can only really be acquired through long practice. Laban and I had it, Le didn't. She'd have demolished either of us in a marathon, but here she was slipping and sliding over jagged rocks, occasionally clasping Laban's steadying hand to prevent her from falling.

My mind turned again to everything my friends had told me. As brave as Le was being, it was hard for anybody to argue that I had created the best mood for a proposal.

There was little I could do about that now. We carried on climbing up, ever higher, into a snowstorm. Suddenly our world was reduced to the metre or so immediately in front of us. It was difficult to say what was left or right, up or down, everything was just white. The ground was treacherous, the view was non-existent, and we shivered in our thin clothes as the wind whipped sharp cold crystals into our faces. It was a disaster. I thought: *I don't know where I'm going to kneel. I don't know if I even* can *kneel.* Almost irrelevantly it occurred to me that we were now almost 5,000 metres above Denmark.

I could just about make out Laban, who was indicating to me that we needed to get back down as soon as we could, it wasn't safe to stay here much longer. I looked about me. Nearby there was a huge rock that seemed as if it might offer some shelter. I pulled Le behind it; instantly we were no longer being buffeted by vicious gusts of wind. But there was a new danger, as I was now standing on an exposed ledge: centimetres away from a 400-metre drop. The ground beneath my feet was icy and treacherous. I knew that I had to move as slowly and carefully as my frozen, tired body would allow me.

I put my arms around her neck, looked her in the eyes and made sure she was OK. Then I congratulated her on reaching the summit of Point Lenana. We were 4,985 metres above sea level.

Slowly I lowered myself down on to one knee, fumbled beneath my borrowed poncho with red fingers that were stiff and clumsy with cold, and presented her with the ring. Even as I did so a thought slid into my mind. *What if she says no?* The idea of trekking back down Mount Kenya beside somebody who had rejected me suddenly seemed deeply unappealing.

I looked up, Le was crying. 'Yes,' she said, tears freezing on her face.

*Ah*, I thought, *this is what they mean by the mood.*

Everything changed after that. Whether it was the joy of the proposal, the achievement of having reached the peak or simply the prospect of descending, Le seemed energised in a way that was hard to explain. It was like she had the strength of ten horses. This was good, though there was nothing that could be done about her footing. She carried on slipping, so Laban walked beside her to help. I thought: *Great, just minutes after I proposed, my fiancée is already holding hands with another man.*

The descent continued. We scrabbled and slid further down, noting how much warmer we already felt. A couple of hours in, just at the moment we neared our destination, the sun broke through the clouds and the snow slowly disappeared from the sky above us. Its place was taken by a rainbow.

## CHAPTER 11

# That's Why Everyone Has a Weapon

*Valletta, Malta; Tunis, Tunisia; Zuwarah, Libya, May to June 2017*
*Syria, December 2017*

Libya had changed my life once. For years I longed to go back. I loved its culture, its history and the people who lived there. I had this grand plan that nestled inside me. I'd discovered that camels were cheap in Libya, and that you could sell them for a far higher price in Sudan. It was just a question of bringing them across the Sahara. If I could find people with the right expertise, then I knew it was possible. The excitement I felt when I contemplated the idea was sufficient to blot out the fears I had about camel spiders. But life, and world events, had got in the way of that.

Nevertheless, by the beginning of 2017 I was contemplating my return. My original plan had been to complete Africa in one go. I'd go from Sudan to Egypt and then enter Libya on its eastern border. The time I'd spent there before meant I felt I only needed to stay there for twenty-four hours, but many questions remained: where, when and how should I cross the border? Should I even be looking to cross the border? And what about the visa? An

181

invitation letter was required, and yet who in their right mind would invite me?

I met with a number of experts, including one man who had literally written the book on the area, and I even went to their embassy. The chief result of all this research was realising that while it can sometimes be frightening to know too much, it can be even more terrifying when you know pretty much nothing. The east of Libya was under the control of General Haftar, one of the warlords who had emerged from the chaos that followed the fall of Colonel Gaddafi. There was a suggestion that he was interested in courting European leaders and that therefore I would be 'untouchable' within his territory. But there was no way of assessing how much faith I could put in this idea.

The Libyan embassy in Cairo told me that if I could bring them the number from an invitation letter (not even the invitation itself) then they would issue a visa on the same day. I asked how safe it would be to travel. They paused, gave a half-smile and said: 'You should definitely enter from Tunisia!'

There was just no way of knowing what would happen once I crossed the border. Everything to the west of Egypt was an informational black hole. The only fair assumption was that, like other black holes, it would be unpredictable, unstable and dangerous. So I aborted the idea. I didn't want my journey to end with my blood spilling into the Sahara's sand.

This meant that my actual route to Libya came through Malta, which although an island in the Mediterranean, is also technically Europe, which annoyed me because now I wouldn't finish Africa in one neat loop. It was country 128, in theory a long way into the journey. And yet there was still a long way to go. I was tired, mentally and physically, and though I was able to recharge on the container ship that had brought me there, I still felt as if my batteries were depleted.

Once I'd got my bearings in Malta's capital, Valletta, I began the process of trying to find a way into Libya. One challenge was finding a boat. This proved difficult. Not many people wanted to sail to a country that looked, from the outside, as if it was collapsing. I had a moment of optimism when I made contact with a shipping company that regularly serviced this route. But this excitement was dispelled once they explained that their ship was so riddled with bullet holes from the last time they'd tried to make the journey that it was unlikely they'd be going back any time soon. The search continued.

The other challenge was getting a visa. It was acknowledged that your best chance was to approach one of the Libyan oil companies who supplemented their income – Libya's unusually thick product was still considered by connoisseurs of such things as superior to what you could find in Saudi Arabia or Venezuela – by providing a service whereby they pretended you were a businessman employed by them. They'd apply for a business visa on your behalf, they'd even provide an itinerary of meetings to make it look as if you really were travelling there for work. But, even then, it was far from sure you'd get into the country. I did everything I could, supplied every document the Libyan consulate asked for, but still somehow found I had made no progress. They never said yes, and they never said no; but each time they seemed to be trying to make things harder for me. I could not understand what they were doing, or why. What made things worse was that because this was Ramadan, a month of fasting, everything moved with aching slowness.

A brief flash of hope came when Maersk, which had no office in Malta, informed me that they did run services to Libya, which then sailed on to Tunisia, another country I needed to visit. If I could get on a ship to Misurata in Libya, then travel 73 kilometres overland to Al Khoms, I'd be able to reboard the ship, which would take me to Tunisia. I was told that the overland route appeared 'reasonably' safe. Finally, things were opening up. I just needed a visa.

I asked to meet the consul to see if explaining my situation directly to him would help. 'He's a very difficult man,' the friendly clerk behind the glass screen told me. I shrugged and said that I was willing to take that risk. He was in a meeting, so I was instructed to take a seat and wait. Two hours passed. Finally an important-looking man materialised behind the glass window and spoke with the clerk for a few minutes. Was this the consul? I looked up expectantly. The man glanced quickly at me, before resuming his conversation with the clerk. Then he disappeared. The clerk called me up to the window and said: 'He doesn't want to see you. I'm sorry.' He appeared genuinely sympathetic, but it was clear that I had reached the end of this road.

I knew that travelling to Tunisia and trying there was an option, but I held out hope I'd be able to make progress in Malta. The problem was that ferries to Tunisia only sailed once a week. Each time I missed one, I was condemning myself to another week in Malta. I thought about how I might try to influence the consul. Could I meet the ambassador?

I got a flood of new contacts. A lot of my meetings took place in nightclubs at three in the morning. As music banged at ear-splitting volume I met with diplomats and businessmen, some Maltese, some Libyan, and tried to work out how I would obtain both a visa, and find a boat that could take me across over 200 kilometres of ocean to the North African coast.

Lots of promises were made in those days. Many of them were broken. My frustration mounted, and my spirits spiralled downwards. I'd first entered Africa more than two years ago, and I had only three countries to visit before I had completed the continent.

It felt to me like no one cared. I felt alone. And suddenly that familiar feeling returned: I wondered if I was capable of carrying on.

There seemed such a vast gap between what people thought I was doing and my actual experience. I'd get comments applauding me for 'living the dream', or chiding me, telling me to 'get a real job'. They did not know, could not see, that I was working harder than I ever had in my life. My health was shattered. Most days I woke up miserable and angry. And for what? Why was I doing this?

At other times in the journey, I was able to rouse myself out of these spirals of depression and rage by myself. Here, though, what helped, what in fact made the difference, was the support given me by the couple I was staying with in Malta, Dave and Alex. They had been paragons of hospitality and kindness ever since my arrival; now they lifted me up, gave me the spark I needed to carry on.

I had to accept that Malta had been a dead end. I'd wasted time there, and almost broken myself in the process. I reluctantly boarded a ferry to Sicily, and from there travelled to Tunisia. And here, things began to move quickly. So quickly that I kicked myself for not having come sooner. I had not realised how many friends I had there: people I'd met before who lived there, or at the very least had good links to the country.

A Tunisian guy I'd dealt with in Djibouti, who'd been immensely helpful back then, did amazing things for me. He set me up in a five-star hotel and introduced me to so many people that almost overnight I felt as if I had a million Tunisian friends. I found myself invited to the party to celebrate the victory of a local football team, Club Africain, in the final of the Tunisian Cup – amidst the chaos and fun I even got to lift the trophy they'd brought back.

Most importantly, this web of contacts led me to a Libyan businessman, Adel, who among other things operated a chemical factory in his home country. I was introduced to him by another businessman, who took me to see this guy in his office. It was like being brought to pay my respects to a mafia boss. He sat, enormous, silent and brooding, at a table at the end of a long room. We made a stilted greeting – neither of us spoke the other's language – and then he and the man who had introduced us fell into a long, animated conversation in Arabic.

I could not follow the words themselves, but one thing was clear from Adel's expression: he saw absolutely no reason why he should help me get into Libya. I'd come into this meeting full of hope, now it began to drain out of me.

It was at this point that his two young children arrived. The thing about Tunisian businessmen is that they're all extremely savvy. My contact was no exception: those two kids gave him an opening. 'You see this guy?' he said, pointing at me. 'This guy is travelling to every country in the world without flying.' The atmosphere in the office changed instantly: the kids were extremely excited, they asked me for selfies and if they could follow me on Instagram. Their father watched, a quizzical expression on his face. He spoke another volley of Arabic, this time in a kind of cheerfully resigned way, as if to say: 'Well, now I *have* to help him.' It reminded me of something I'd learned over a decade before. In Libya, everyone looks like a real hard case. Their default setting is: do not mess with me. But if you smile, or help or amuse them in some way, then their face will crack into a beautiful grin. Their eyes will *glow*.

My friend relayed a peremptory set of instructions: go to the embassy and ask for Ibrahim, he will give you your visa. This caught me on the back foot. I hadn't actually applied for the visa yet. This was relayed to Adel.

'It doesn't matter. Go and speak with Ibrahim, and he will know.'

I was beginning to understand that this man enjoyed a level of power and influence that went well beyond what one might expect from an exporter of chemicals.

As I'd been ordered, I headed to the embassy, where I was confronted by a scene of complete chaos. Everywhere I looked were people with paper in their hands, waving and shouting at murderous volume. It was like witnessing the early stages of a riot. There was no order to what was happening, just the clamour of a thousand different competing needs.

I stood there at the back of this throng, trying to weigh up my options. I didn't know if it would even be possible to make my way to the front desk. How on Earth was I going to find Ibrahim? Was Ibrahim even here?

A couple of seconds passed before a voice cut through the hurricane of noise in front of me. The man behind the front desk had spotted me and called over asking me if I was Thor Pedersen. I nodded yes and, after he had beckoned me towards him, started to push my way through the pulsating sea of human bodies that lay between us.

After that, everything was easy. He told me to hand him my passport and fill out a form. Once these small formalities were complete, he stamped my visa and waved me goodbye.

This visa was infamously one of the hardest to obtain. Even under Gaddafi getting in and out of the country had come with its share of problems. Back in 2006 I spent an entire month as an effective hostage in a hotel room while the company I worked for tried to resolve a tax dispute with the government. It was a luxurious captivity that saw me wake up each morning with burger sauce on my face before heading downstairs to demolish a pile of pancakes for breakfast (I put on 10 kilos), but it was captivity nonetheless.

And yet, here I was with a visa in my hands. This was the strange thing about the journey I was on. Sometimes you could spend months hammering on a door, hoping and praying that there was even somebody on the other side. At other times that door just swung open without you needing to do a single thing.

My run of luck continued. Adel was flying to Libya for Eid, the celebration that follows the thirty days of Ramadan. Join me there, he said – his children's enthusiasm clearly had a long half-life. He told me to trust him and promised to take care of me.

The timing of the invitation was also in my favour. You'd truly have to be the most extreme of extremists to commit an atrocity during Eid – it's difficult to claim you're doing God's work if you set off a bomb during a religious festival.

Still, nobody else seemed to want me to go to Libya. The day before I left the head of the Danish diplomatic mission in Tunisia called me to ensure that I knew that the Danish government strongly advised against doing so. The International Committee of the Red Cross requested that if I insisted on travelling to Libya, I should strip away any connection I had to them: no logos, emblems, paperwork or mentions of the Red Cross at all. They told me I should avoid doing any interviews and warned me again about the risk of kidnapping.

And, at the border, almost everyone I spoke to seemed baffled about my desire to cross it. 'Why leave Tunisia for *that* madhouse? Are you not aware of the situation?'

Yes, I told them, I was aware of the situation. They shrugged their shoulders. If I wanted to kill myself that much, then I was welcome to try. On the other side of the border I was met by Radwan, a tall, slender policeman in a shirt and sunglasses who spoke a very pleasant variety of broken English. We hopped into his car and set off along the coast for Zuwarah, which was about 56 kilometres away, bumping along sandy, pot-holed roads that clearly had not been repaired in years.

I'd had a vague fantasy of making it as far as Tripoli, which was another hundred kilometres or so further away; I'd even made contact with the hotel I'd been confined to eleven years before. If I could make it, they'd let me stay for free.

This desire to travel to the capital started to dissipate once we started to pass through a series of hardcore checkpoints on the perimeter of Zuwarah. Each was manned by a number of menacing-looking troops wielding big guns; there was no way I was getting through these on my own. We'd slow down in front of yet another imposing barrier, a soldier would peer in, recognise the policeman, and wave us back on without even exchanging a word.

Zuwarah itself seemed like a sleepy fisherman's village with a good-sized port attached to it. At some point, somebody had obviously intended to make the place a little grander. At intervals one could see the hulking shells of abandoned construction projects. The seafront was a mess of huge concrete blocks that should have become hotels. Cranes had rusted, then collapsed on to the bricks.

'It was a Gaddafi project,' someone told me, flatly, without emotion, 'but he's not around any more.' He didn't seem to feel the need to elaborate.

The policeman was keen to get a selfie that we could post online. It was just as we were struggling to get a good shot in the blinding Middle Eastern sun that an expensive-looking black car pulled up near the beach we were standing on: the businessman and his two children had arrived.

I was beckoned into the car. The policeman's work was clearly over. We headed for Regdalin, an Arab town twenty minutes south of Zuwarah. All the while, Adel talked to me through his children, who spoke perfect English. Abrar, the girl, told me that she was nine, but she carried herself as if she was far older. She was not coquettish, or precocious, it was something else, far harder to define.

Adel welcomed me to Libya and asked me how long I planned to stay. With these formalities done, his expression changed a little. He seemed sad as he explained that I had to understand that Libya was now the Wild West: there were no rules; licence plates were optional, there were no speed limits.

The towns were controlled environments, that's why the entrances to them were guarded so heavily. If you were inside them, it was like being on a safe island – every settlement was a separate entity existing in relative peace. If you left them without the right protection, you were taking a terrible risk. The desert was home to fighters from the Islamic State or rebel groups – the list of malign actors was as long as it was complicated.

'That's why everyone has a weapon. They need to protect themselves. If someone tries to steal the car, I'm ready.'

'Really?' I asked, looking around the plush interior of the car.

A wry smile. 'Yes, there's a gun under your seat right now.' He reached down and brought out a 9 mm Belgian handgun, then handed it to me. I started looking at it. I had not held a firearm like this since my time in the army.

'We can go and shoot it if you want. We could fire it at a tree or a burned-out car.' The businessman watched me coolly, as his daughter translated, as if assessing me. It did not feel like an invitation, more a test of what sort of person I was. What were my values? Was I an action junkie? (Libya has a shortage of trees. Under Gaddafi, harming them in any way was considered a crime: another sign of how much the situation had changed here.)

'No,' I said, 'I'm good. That's fine. I don't need to do that.'

The moment passed and Abrar starting talking guilelessly in her bright birdlike voice about what she wanted to do when she grew up. 'Maybe a lawyer, or a doctor, or an architect, or maybe I want to be a CEO in an oil company.'

She was still talking as we approached yet another checkpoint. This one was equipped with a large machine gun, which sat there, menacing but still, like a warning. 'That gun can fire a hundred and fifty-five rounds a minute,' Abrar said, pointing at it and speaking in exactly the same tone she'd been using to discuss her plans for her future career. 'Shall I tell you about my favourite doll . . .'

I was not able to take in much of what followed, something about this irruption of abnormality into the happy flow of her conversation momentarily winded me. This was not something a girl of her age should know. I was still in this distracted state when we arrived at their home, an imposing compound with several families living in it.

The sun was setting, and we got ready for the last Iftar – the fast-breaking meal – of this year's Ramadan. The fast would be over at nightfall and Eid al-Fitr – a kind of New Year's celebration where families and friends come together to say sorry for any wrongdoings and confess their love for each other – would last the next three days. In deference to the festivities, the men had swapped their normal jeans and trainers for the more traditional djellabas – long, flowing robes that buttoned around their necks.

We lay in their courtyard for a while, eating dates, drinking tea and talking – a very Libyan way of passing time. As we did so, the children played with fidget spinners. Some of them were emblazoned with the logo of Supreme, a popular streetwear brand that had almost overnight become incredibly fashionable; suddenly wherever I went everyone was wearing Supreme caps or T-shirts or bags, which were often knockoff products. It was always things like that which reminded me that if the world wasn't small, exactly, it was incredibly well connected. Trends travelled *fast*, and penetrated deep into places you'd never expect. But what really caught my eye was one kid, a slightly chubby boy, whose fidget spinner was decorated to look like Captain America's shield. Slightly taken aback, I took a photograph. It seemed amazing to me, given Libya's complex, barbed history with the USA, that this boy should be playing – happily, unselfconsciously – with a toy decked in the Great Satan's flag.

While I was turning this over in my head, one of Adel's cousins, who spoke a little English, came up to me. 'They're fighting right now,' he said, referring to two of the factions in the country's unending civil war, 'not far away from here.' Occasionally he'd speak into his phone, then return to our exchange. 'They're shooting at each other. We can drive over there and sit on the hilltop and look at the fighting. Do you want to do that?'

Again, I felt as if I was being tested. Again, I said, 'No, there's no need for that.'

An absurd comparison popped into my head: in Iceland they often drive towards erupting volcanos with a few cold beers. And I had friends who I knew would have been desperate to take him up on his offer. They'd be taking selfies and shooting videos as people killed each other in the valley beneath them. But I did not want to become a spectator of somebody else's misery. He looked at me, his face betraying neither pleasure nor disappointment. Nevertheless, I felt as if I had said the right thing.

That night they put me up in a hotel rather than my staying in the compound. They didn't explain why. We returned to Zuwarah, which was bursting with life. The relentless heat from the Libyan sun had kept people indoors all day but now they were shopping, chatting, socialising. The roads were crammed with cars (many of which had Swiss registrations, I never found out why) and lots of boys were running about with plastic toy guns playing soldiers or a modern-day version of Cowboys and Indians.

I thought about how different this all was to my first spell in Libya. Back then we were staying in a camp in the desert, with a wall around it. Outside there were sand and snakes and scorpions, inside it was like a slice of Eden; there was grass, a swimming pool. But for the first three months of the project, I was pretty much on my own; there was nobody around me who was my age, or if they were I had little in common with them.

From five in the afternoon, the camp would be empty, with everyone retreating to their homes to watch television. To pass the time I went to a nearby village to get a glass box made up. I put some sand and rocks inside and made it a home for the scorpions I had started to collect. I was lonely and bored. and there was something dangerous but alluring about these creatures that were so utterly different to any beast that lived in Denmark. The first night that one was in my room I could not sleep for fear that it would escape.

Eventually I was joined in the camp by a group of guys closer to my age. On our days off, we'd go into the desert to explore. We'd encounter everything from Roman and Greek artefacts to leftover materiel from the Second World War; there'd be stuff that reflected centuries of Bedouin culture. And then, of course, the endless expanses of sand and blazing blue sky.

None of us were naive. We knew that Colonel Gaddafi was a hardline authoritarian. We always knew that somebody, somewhere was listening to our conversations. It might be a local informing on us after overhearing a conversation about a forbidden topic, or the clicking sound our phones made, or the way that sometimes our computer screens would go funny for a second or two. It was common knowledge that at least 10 per cent of the workforce were government spies.

However, we could wander pretty much where we wanted without fear of being murdered or kidnapped. In fact, we could enjoy freedoms unavailable to us in our own countries. Here nobody would stop me from climbing to the top of a two-thousand-year-old temple. In Denmark, that same ruin would be fenced in and ringed with cameras. In Libya, I could drive a car at 140 kilometres per hour. I'd be fined if I tried that on the streets of Copenhagen.

The collapse of order in Libya meant that I could only exist here in an inhibited fashion; there was no chance of a freewheeling expedition out into the desert; I would not have the same opportunities to meet in the same informal, unguarded circumstances. I did not wish for the return to the brutality of Gaddafi's rule – it was not my place to tell the Libyans what they did or didn't need – but I found myself hoping that this country that I loved so much would find something approaching peace sooner rather than later.

The next day I took the opportunity to explore a bit more of the town and the surrounding area. When I'd asked Adel if I was OK to walk about by myself, he assured me that I could do so safely. People knew that I was under his protection, I could go wherever I wanted and nobody would touch me. Once more, I found myself wondering exactly who, or what, he was. Was it usual for a mere businessman to wield such power?

The town seemed like a land of plenty. The supermarkets were well stocked, the fruit and vegetables being sold by a man in the street looked glossy and abundant. There was even, oddly, a shop selling expensive glassware. Occasionally I'd hear a noise, a car misfiring, somebody dropping their shopping, and whip round, convinced that the fighting had come to this peaceful town. Each time I realised, quickly, I'd made a mistake.

I carried on exploring the town's edges, walking through empty streets in which only a handful of cars lazily drove past me. I passed a new-looking football stadium and eventually managed to locate the local branch of the Red Crescent. It was closed, nobody was about. I looked around their site for a little while, took photographs and was struck once more by how normal and quiet it was.

By this point, the day had started to heat up and most of the locals had retreated inside. I had asked Adel if I would be OK to go down to the seafront, to take a look at the beach and port area. My relationship with Maersk meant that I was always keen to take a photograph of one of their containers if I could.

'Yes, no problem.'

Libya has 1,800 kilometres of perfect Mediterranean coastline; in theory it should be a paradise for tourists and hotels. However, for obvious reasons, it has never become a holiday hotspot. Even before Gaddafi's fall, when everything was reasonably calm, they never had more than three thousand or so visitors a year.

I stepped on to a beach of pure white sand. Everything around me was blue, with the brilliant cobalt of the sky giving way to the turquoise of the sea. Birds wheeled above me, their cries merging with the gentle lapping of the waves. The beauty of the moment was only spoiled by an unpleasant smell, as if something nearby was rotting. Probably seaweed, I thought to myself, and put it out of my mind.

I took a shot of the sea then moved along the beach towards the port, my eyes searching for a Maersk container. It was a long beach, so I kept walking along the fine sand. Then, as I took another step, I froze. Perhaps 50 metres away, on the periphery of my vision, I could see a black heap in the near distance. *Was that a body?* I felt my legs turn to lead. My entire body was gripped by terror. *Why is there a dead body?* My mind began to fill with the events of the last twenty-four hours. I thought of the armed guards at the checkpoints; the fighting that was taking place so close to my friend's compound. I thought of everything I'd been told about this country before I'd even set foot in it. The torture, the terrorists. I felt out of control. *I really shouldn't be in Libya. Why am I here?*

*Should I be looking at this? Will I be next?* I checked myself and took a couple of deep breaths. *That's not a dead body, it's too far away for you to be able to identify it. It's just some seaweed and plastic arranged in an odd fashion.* This calmed me down.

I carried on walking towards whatever it was that I'd seen, feeling a little more at ease with the situation, though I remained in a heightened state of alertness. I got closer and closer, then froze again. I could see a body and a head. There was no longer any doubt. This was, or had been, a human being. My mind began to race. *What is going on here? Why is there a body?* I was too afraid to come any closer to the corpse. Some strange, irrational part of my imagination elbowed its way to the front of my thoughts. *What if it gets up and becomes a zombie?* My head felt full, as if *everything* was in it, all at once. Numbly, I lifted my phone and took a picture. I didn't think too much about why I did this. For years now, I'd been taking pictures; this sight seemed significant.

Then I turned round and walked the other way. There was a second body. Like the first it was splayed, half-buried in the sand, in an unnatural position. It had been close to me all the time I had stood there while taking that photograph, but I hadn't noticed it. I could see this one in greater detail. I could tell that it was a man. An Arab. He was still in jeans, sandals and T-shirt. Just like any number of the other men I'd been speaking to since I'd come to the country. His face was contorted, with bloated skin, and his dark, salt-stiffened hair flopped on to the sand beneath him. The nails on his hands were neatly trimmed. I guess that he'd been dead for a few days.

I took another photograph and moved closer, walking around the corpse. I noticed, with an unpleasant shiver of surprise, that even after little more than a minute I was already at ease with my proximity to dead humans.

I walked further down the beach. Another body. Nothing made sense to me about what I was seeing. *Why are there dead people? Is this where they kill people? Is this where they dumped them?*

Nobody else was around. It was just me and the ocean, a sandy beach and three corpses. Close to the third body I found a tangle of clues as to their fate: life jackets, some timber and tarpaulin. These were refugees whose boat had sunk. They had drowned and their bodies had washed up on this beach.

Close by I found a fourth cadaver. Its body resembled the others: partially covered by sand, wet clothes, bloated skin, sandalled feet. But the similarity ended at the neck. Its skull was perfectly white, even more so than the sand it nestled in. Every single piece of flesh and skin and hair had gone. I thought, absurdly, of Yorick's skull in *Hamlet*.

I realised that I'd been lucky in my life. My experience of dead bodies was limited to funerals, and a single corpse in Eritrea. And none of those matched the visceral horror of what I was witnessing. I felt overwhelmed by a queasy discomfort. The idea that I might ever feel at ease again suddenly felt impossible.

I looked up again. My discomfort mounted as I spotted, 400 metres in front of me, a section of the beach populated with umbrellas and sun loungers. As I got closer, I saw locals playing happily in the sparkling water. I could hear piercing shrieks of joy from their kids.

*This is insane*, I thought, *people are lying on the sand in the shade. How can they do that with dead bodies nearby?* I turned round to check – at that distance you couldn't tell what they were. But then what about the ones who are out there swimming? What if another body floats by while they're in the water? You could be playing with your child, throwing a ball and then feel something bump gently into your back.

I carried on walking along the beach, thinking all the time about the surreal horror of everything I had just witnessed, and emerged on the other side. A man strolled past me and fixed me with a strange look that seemed to me to be suffused with shame and awkwardness. For a moment, I did not understand what was going on, then quickly things became clear.

I spotted another body. This time somebody had put a stick in the sand beside it. They obviously wanted to show somebody what was lying there. (I learned later on that the Red Crescent usually picked up these bodies, but had not done so today because they were closed for Eid.) One thing I noticed about many countries across the world is that their people are deeply proud of their country. It's a benign kind of pride, concerned mainly with showing you the best that their home has to offer. That man knew I was about to see the corpse; I think he feared that it would colour my feelings about Libya.

I realised that I had to get away from the beach. It was hard to process everything I had just seen. I found it impossible not to think about the individual tragedies and hardships that had driven these men to step on to that boat, and to wonder what each of them must have thought when it became obvious that their fragile craft was about to be torn to pieces. They must all have known that they would not escape.

But I thought too about everything I knew of Libyan culture. It would be highly offensive to my hosts if I told them about finding dead bodies on a beach. So I kept it to myself. When I got back, they asked me how my day had been. I smiled and told them, 'It's fine, everything's fine. I had a good time,' before excusing myself to go and take a rest.

We ate well that evening, then sat for a while drinking tea and talking. Adel asked me how much longer I was planning to stay in Libya. He was planning on pushing on to Tripoli to celebrate Eid and would be delighted to take me. The rule he and his family had was that you judged the safety or otherwise of any given route based on the experience of the last person who had travelled it. Someone had recently made the journey without too much trouble, so they thought it wouldn't be too dangerous.

I paused for a second to collect myself. The idea that I might want to go to Tripoli had imploded at precisely the moment I first saw that corpse. All I wanted to do now was leave. But I didn't want to give them any sign that I was being torn up inside, that all I could think about was dead bodies lying crumpled on a hot beach. As calmly as I could, I said, 'No, well, I think this is enough. I'm ready to go back tomorrow. I think it'll be good to continue with the project.'

The conversation moved on. At some point someone suggested we visit the businessman's chemical factory. So, at two in the morning we drove there. Along with another person who, for reasons I could not follow, was also being given the tour, I walked, dazed, past forklifts zooming about carrying drums filled with oil. There was a nice office that somebody had decorated with small Libyan flags. I took little else in. Occasionally I'd say something polite, or complimentary, to show gratitude and that I was interested in what they were showing me.

That night I read Karen Blixen's *Seven Gothic Tales* into the early hours. Sleep stubbornly refused to come. Every time I fell asleep my dreams would fill with terrible nightmares of dead people and contorted bodies. I'd wake sweating, my heart racing, my breath coming in jagged gasps, hoping desperately that what had just passed through my mind was only a nightmare. That I hadn't actually seen those things. That those five men hadn't actually died in the course of their desperate attempt to carve out a better life for themselves. The sporadic explosions of fireworks, set off to celebrate Eid, added to the almost hallucinogenic quality of those hours.

Morning, when it finally came, was a relief.

As soon as I was back across the border I activated my Tunisian sim card and called Le. I told her everything I had witnessed. Then I called my friends Kris and Lars and did the same. I talked and talked as if in doing so I'd be able to unburden myself. It destabilised something in me. It pushed something within me. None of us are supposed to die like that. I knew that if there had been women or children, then I would have gone straight home right then, abandoning the project. That would have broken me entirely, it would have been the final straw.

Over time, the horror faded a little as I managed to get some distance from it. But for more than a year afterwards I did not, could not, go back into the ocean.

Six months later, as I went through the countries of the Middle East, I was still thinking about this tragedy, which had unfolded just a hop and a skip from Sicily and the islands of Greece.

There is a great deal that the Danes do not understand, because they're not interested in understanding it. Our sympathy for others is incredibly parochial. I remember I was in Western Africa at around the time of the Charlie Hebdo attack in Paris. I noticed that a lot of my Facebook friends in the West had changed their profiles to include the French flag's colours. But this outrage, in which seven people were slaughtered, made little impression where I was.

Soon after, there was a ghastly attack in Nigeria by Boko Haram in which they killed upwards of two hundred people. The Facebook friends I'd made in this part of the world started to add Nigeria's white and green to their profiles, while the people I knew in the West largely ignored it.

We care about our household, our neighbours, our colleagues, but we don't have to get very far removed from those close connections before we get to the point where we don't really care whether strangers live or die. It's always horrible when a ship sinks and five hundred people die, but then we remind ourselves it was in Bangladesh, and then our mind wanders and we find ourselves asking: what's for supper?

We sympathise with what we know, and struggle to summon up the same humanity when the victims are more distant. For the Danes, if something happens in Germany, it's horrible. The Germans aren't Danish, but close enough; they live in more or less the same way as we do. But Nigerians, who knows how they live? They probably live in huts.

We forget how similar we are. People are creatures who need to sleep, they need to eat, they need to be seen. (That seems quite important. This isn't about being on stage, but about our time on this planet, our existence, being acknowledged.) They love sports, music, movies, entertainment games, internet. They do not like rain or getting stuck in traffic. Much, or all, of that would have been true for those men whose bodies washed up on a Libyan beach.

But what we also forget is how quickly we can be dislocated from the terrible things that are happening in places that are by any measure quite close to us. By the end of 2017, Syria had long been a fixture in the Danish news. We consumed horrifying stories while reassuring ourselves that all of this was happening in a strange, faraway country. But then I got to Lebanon, Syria's neighbour, and realised that this war still did not feel present. I wondered how close you needed to get to a conflict before you could feel its hot breath on your neck.

After a lot of negotiation with local contacts, I travelled across the border into Syria with a Red Cross representative. As we drove to Damascus I looked out of the truck's window. There were cultivated fields, a few stalled-looking construction projects but no signs that this was a nation in the grip of a civil war. There were no refugees, no burned-out tanks. I started to ask myself: how far *does* a bullet fly?

This almost surreal normality persisted once we'd arrived in the city, where I was going to be staying in an apartment that the Red Cross used. Here I was issued with a special cell phone, controlled by the International Committee of the Red Cross (ICRC), which would inform me every time there was an incident.

My contact explained that every so often, people on the side of the city where the fighting was fiercest liked to remind the rest of Damascus that they were still in a war, and set off rockets or mortars in their direction. The phone beeped several times a day. I was also told that the city was divided into colour-coded zones, and that for my own safety I was forbidden from visiting the most dangerous. These included the ancient quarters of Damascus that I was most interested in seeing.

I was in a five-storey building in one of the wealthier parts of the city, an area of sports cafés, people on phones, flatscreen TVs. The shops were full of fruit and vegetables, police calmly directed traffic, children in uniforms went to school. Being there reminded me of something I'd been told earlier in my journey: the rich never attack the rich. Fighter jets screeching across the sky above us were the only sign that something might be different. You knew where they were going, and what they were going to do.

The happy noise of the day faded once night had fallen. I'd go up to the top floor of my apartment block, stick my head out of the window and listen to the city. At first, all seemed perfectly quiet. But listening more carefully revealed lonely gunshots, and also, in the background, the thunder of bombs raining down on human beings no more than a few thousand metres from me; ripping homes apart, killing. I would not have to travel far to hear children screaming, or their mothers crying.

During the days I drove around Damascus in a taxi. Its owner became my guide. He told me that he worked in the bourgeois part of the city, then every night he'd return to the neighbourhood that was being bombed. There was no self-pity or drama in his voice when he spoke, just a fatalistic understanding that this was the reality of his life.

Once, he took me up to the very edge of where I was allowed to travel. We sat in a café, smoked shisha, and watched the news on a television mounted on the wall. It showed an unsparing sequence of images: buildings beyond repair, bodies being blown to pieces, ragged women sobbing. Hell on Earth. And yet it was just twenty minutes away from where I was staying.

I looked out of the window, half-expecting to see refugees screaming as they ran past, their belongings clasped by panic-stricken limbs. The street was empty.

CHAPTER 12

# *Sisu*

*Ulaanbaatar, Mongolia, November 2018*

The project had stopped being fun, or anything like it, after two years. That idea died somewhere amid my slow, swampy progress through Central Africa. I felt as if I'd reached my limit then, I was ready to go home. I had the same questions constantly swirling around my head: *Why do I need to do this? Why am I so ambitious? Why am I so stubborn? Why try to write 120 different stories about the same organisation when nobody working there seems interested?*

Generally speaking, my capacity to feel wonder or joy had diminished, and with it my enthusiasm for trying to seek out new experiences, or new sights. Why bother getting up at 6 a.m. to get on a clanking, crowded bus that takes you four hours in the wrong direction to see a waterfall? I'd seen plenty of water falling by this stage. The most positive spin on this state of mind was that I was working on the basis that it is nice to leave something undone, or unvisited, in a country, because that gives you an excuse to return.

Really, though, I was full of resentment at a journey that I was beginning to feel had trapped me. For years there had not been a single day when the thought of packing up and heading home did not enter my mind. What I was doing was not making me any happier. It certainly wasn't making me any healthier.

I did make efforts to look after myself as much as I could. I was eating food that I knew would give my body the fuel it needed to keep going. I drank vast quantities of water every day. From Africa onwards, once it had become clear that the journey was going to be a long haul, I stopped ordering sugar in my tea, and in fact avoided sugar where possible because I didn't want to risk a dental emergency. (I went to the dentist's three times while I was away: in Lebanon; Hong Kong, where I had a filling; and in Fiji, after a caramel I'd eaten had pulled out a filling – a Korean dentist fixed it.)

For the first seven years of my journey, I barely touched a drop of alcohol. I was drunk perhaps twice, at most three times. I'd never been much of a drinker, anyway, and there had been so much to do, my life was so regimented, that I tried to keep away from something that I knew would interfere with my system. (That changed in 2020, when I reached Hong Kong. I think it probably had to.)

And if circumstances and my energy levels allowed, I'd exercise. There were times when I got into push-ups, and running, as it had been since I was a teenager, was incredibly important to me. My head is a messy place. It's my stress release. Whatever my frustrations, whatever knockbacks I might have received, it would always feel better if I went out for a run. I'd leave angry, and come back feeling as if everything had been shaken into place, that I could see more clearly.

I generally kept things like grooming to a minimum, because it didn't feel like something I had the bandwidth to care about. Usually, I'd get my hair cut by cheap street barbers, who delivered mixed results. For a while I carried a trimmer around with me, but before long it broke. Because everything broke during the project, including me. Nothing is designed or built to survive a journey like that: the extremes of hot and cold; the damp that seeped into the mechanisms of anything mechanical, and the dust that clambered into every crevice of every item I had with me; the being bumped around in the holds of buses, or crushed by people walking past.

Very few people travel for more than six months at a time. It's too tiring. I'd been on the move for over five years by this point, entering a new country, on average, every twelve days. And the discipline that was needed to just keep going was brutal. It was so tempting to procrastinate, to idle, or sightsee. But I knew that if I did not get up each morning and start working, then I'd never get over the finishing line. As well as the Red Cross visit, the social media and the post I made for the Red Cross each time I reached a new country, there were all the tasks involved in getting to the next nation. Visas. Transport. Accommodation. Tangles with bureaucracy. Over and again. Over and again. Over and again. My enthusiasm for any of this had long since atrophied – sometimes it felt as if all I had left to keep me going was discipline. Everything had to be as optimised and efficient as I could make it: I couldn't afford to lose any time, at any point; I had to make my money stretch as much as I was able.

My soul was worn down and threadbare. At the same time, my senses had been so overloaded for so long that I felt like somebody being forced to eat when they're already full.

And there was little I could do to alleviate the cruel exhaustion that had seeped right into the marrow of my bones. But I knew that no matter how often the thought of giving up tempted me – if I did actually get on that plane the regret at having failed would probably consume me utterly.

So, sometimes I'd try to break through the gloomy fog that surrounded me and give myself something to look forward to. An event, or a sight, that would give me a break from the grind of trying to locate a branch of the Red Cross (who would probably be indifferent to my arrival, or might even refuse to see me), or sitting on seemingly endless bus journeys, or queuing for yet another visa. In 2014, when I got to Peru, I decided that enough was enough, that I might never come back to this part of the world again, I was going to do something for me. I took a week-long break from my schedule and hiked through the mountains all the way up to Machu Picchu.

Usually, I was able to make a fairly clear distinction between wanting and needing something. It was when that distinction became harder that I'd realise it was time to find another carrot. In the normal run of things, it was hard to make the case that I *needed* to visit Machu Picchu. It would have been difficult to argue that it was something I could not go without. But when you are running on empty, when you need something to keep you going, that line gets far fuzzier.

After leaving the Middle East I'd been through Georgia, Armenia, Azerbaijan, Iran, Afghanistan, then Central Asia, threading my way through the countries strung along the route of the Silk Road – Uzbekistan, Tajikistan, Kyrgyzstan, Kazakhstan. I was dizzied by the beauty of the madrasas in this part of the world; the sheer size of them, the way they've been decorated with beautiful blue colours and tiles. And then there was the strangeness of Turkmenistan, which is one of the most unusual countries in the world.

Turkmenistan is a Muslim country where they drink a huge amount of vodka, or arak as it is known there. You'd sit down with somebody for lunch and they'd put a bottle on the table, then throw the cap away. After a few shots I'd be lost, my day over, while they simply got back into their car and drove back to work. It's horse country too. They adore horses there, in fact, they *idolise* them. But in the marble-clad capital, Ashgabat, they also have a fetish for white. Everything there is white. This even extends to cars. It's this odd, unacknowledged, almost secret thing, but pretty much everyone drives a white car. It's as if there's a law mandating this, or some kind of financial inducement.

Then, via a detour through Russia, returning there five years after my first visit, and a four-day train ride, I arrived in Mongolia's capital Ulaanbaatar. It was November 2018, the temperatures had plunged to minus twenty (Ulaanbaatar is the only capital in the world that has an average temperature that lies below zero). Each time I breathed in it felt as if I was taking ice into my lungs; this was followed by a satisfying plume when I exhaled. But despite the cold, I was feeling hopeful and positive.

My plan was to go from Mongolia into China, before travelling on to Pakistan, which was where the carrot I felt I deserved after covering all this ground was located.

The thing I was desperate to see was the Karakoram Highway, one of the highest roads on the planet – at times it goes above 5,000 metres – and a feat of engineering so stupendous that it is often described as the Eighth Wonder of the World. I had seen photos of this highway, which begins in China then sweeps down into the Punjab, and it looked gorgeous beyond belief; vertiginous snow-capped mountains bank each side of the road.

Like so many of its neighbours, Mongolia was exhilaratingly unfamiliar. It had the same uncanny, fairytale quality that comes with travelling to places that aren't in Western Europe. The people's faces there were like stone carvings: they watched you, giving nothing away of themselves. The sounds, the smells, the buildings, the clothes, all of it is different. And yet there were odd echoes of somewhere I'd been to before. For a while, this resemblance plagued me, I couldn't put my finger on it, then one morning I had it: Greenland. There was something about the way they pronounce words, the way they look, the small population in a large country, the strong primal connection to nature, the wide-open landscape.

Ulaanbaatar is an island of modernity surrounded by the endless grass of the steppes, where men and women live in the same way as they have for centuries. In the city, though, they had swapped their horses for hybrid cars. Instead of eagles soaring overhead, the people gaze up at enormous buildings that were increasingly coming to dominate the city's skyline. It was hard not to feel conscious of the way that the past and present of this country, which is lodged between the global powerhouses of China and Russa, intermingled. It had, after all, once been the home – if that is the right word for a nomadic people – to one of the greatest empires the world has ever seen. And yet monuments to its more recent past, such as the country's national hero, Damdin Sükhbaatar, who had helped liberate it during the Russian Civil War that followed the 1917 revolutions, were more significant than any tribute to figures such as Genghis Khan. Ulaanbaatar, which means 'red hero', was named in honour of Sükhbaatar. There was also a statue of the Beatles, in which John, Paul, George and Ringo were depicted in relief against a giant red apple. I'd seen a couple of similar tributes to the band across Central Asia, and had read them as celebrations of freedom, love and peace, perhaps even rebellion. It wasn't clear how neatly this sat with the rougher, less-forgiving virtues embodied by a man like Sükhbaatar.

But, as always, there was work to be done. I knew that it wouldn't be straightforward to get my Chinese visa. For one thing, the Chinese embassy didn't open every day. And on the days it did open, they had strict limits on how many visas they were willing to issue: no more than a hundred, and only ten of those could be given to foreigners. I'd not encountered any other nation that had similar restrictions, but what could I do about it?

I was also aware that the Chinese were strict to the point of paranoia about a number of things. They had an aversion to bloggers, because they didn't want to invite anybody in who might disturb their carefully constructed narratives. Although there were cats and dogs with more followers than me, I still had a presence online; it was clear that talking too loudly, or even at all, about the project might cause complications at a time when I was trying to make things as easy for myself as I could. Which is why I also booked a room at the Hotel Hilton in Beijing, and bought a plane ticket, which I would cancel once I'd got inside the country.

But I also reassured myself that it was winter – in the summertime, overlanders on bicycles, motorcycles, vehicles or foot are said to line up the night before the embassy opens – surely they'd be a bit more easy going in the cold season? After all, as another traveller had told me, there wouldn't be anybody else there.

The following morning, I climbed out of bed early, then decanted myself on to Ulaanbaatar's frigid, dark streets. I was bleary, underslept and felt a churning, queasy sense of discontent. It was in this mood that I arrived at the embassy a few minutes before they opened, to wait in the raw cold of a Mongolian morning for a further forty minutes with a handful of other foreigners: Canadians, Australians and a couple of Indians. Just as it felt as if my toes were going to fall off, we were allowed in.

Small actions, or accidents, can have outsized and often completely unexpected consequences. They are like the small tear in your bag that slowly, steadily, and without you ever noticing it, grows and grows until finally you realise all of your possessions have fallen out.

At some point on my journey through Central Asia an official had put a barcode sticker on the inside cover of one of my two passports (in Denmark we're allowed to have two at any one time).

I didn't want it there – it didn't belong there, I always removed tags of any kind that offered information I did not need to share, and, to be honest, I felt annoyed that he'd been presumptuous enough to stick it in – so as soon as I no longer needed it, I pulled it off, which left a sticky residue. In the process of trying to separate the last page of the passport from the inside cover, I tore the page slightly. This did not feel as if it would be a problem, so I thought little of it at the time.

The first inkling that it might be a bigger issue than I'd thought came when the Russians refused to give me a visa because of the torn page. On one level, this was fine, because I could resubmit my application with my other passport. But I hadn't wanted to use the second, unripped passport because it was stamped with visas from countries like Iraq and Yemen and Sudan, the sorts of places that would alarm the Chinese.

Still, the Mongolians hadn't been at all bothered by the small tear buried deep in my passport, I'm not sure they even noticed, so I decided to use it here too. I passed it across to the woman at the counter, she flicked through it unhurriedly, her face impassive. I began to exhale, this was going to be OK. Then she stopped and looked up at me, then back at the page. Her finger was resting by the rip.

'I'm not happy about this,' she told me. 'I'll see what I can do, but it might be a problem. Also, you don't have an entry visa for Mongolia, so I can't give you a visa.'

I had learned that it generally didn't pay to reveal that you have two passports. It's the kind of thing that makes anyone working in immigration instantly suspicious, as if you're a spy, or a drug smuggler, or at the very least a person with something to hide.

But it was clear that I had little choice but to show her the unripped one. I tried to explain that this was completely normal in Denmark. 'OK,' she said, clearly unconvinced, but extending her arm to take my document. Suddenly she could see everywhere I'd been, some of the world's most troubled, dangerous areas. The sorts of places that are infested with terrorists, or criminals, or refugees; the sorts of places that ring alarm bells for anyone in a position like hers, let alone somebody working for a country as mistrustful as China.

The expression on her face had not changed, and yet it was immediately clear that I was not going to be walking away with a visa today. 'We must look into this. Come back at four o'clock.' I nodded, aware that I was helpless to do anything else. Everyone else around me was trotting off to the bank. I, however, was mired in uncertainty.

I returned that afternoon, and watched as all of the other travellers, bar one Indian man, were given their visas. 'You have two options,' the woman explained to me, now, for reasons I did not quite understand, seeming quite upset. 'We need to spend more time investigating your application. This work will take place in Beijing. We'll take your passport and send it there. It'll take a month, and we can't guarantee that we'll give you a visa. The alternative is that you withdraw your application.'

This was the worst thing she could have said. If it were just a question of a missing document I could try to provide it. If she had asked me to resubmit my application, I could start all over, no problem. What was one more form?

But a one-month delay would be fatal, because by then my Pakistani visa would have expired. I'd really struggled to get that one – in theory you're only supposed to apply when you're in your home country – I couldn't see myself being able to repeat that good fortune. I walked out into the biting cold with two passports, but no visa.

A futile investigation played out in my mind as I tried to second-guess what had torpedoed my chances. *Was it the two passports? Or the dodgy list of countries? Were they suspicious of my hotel reservation or plane tickets? Had I screwed myself in some other, completely unrelated way?* My attempt to deceive them by buying a plane ticket meant that I couldn't try to use the project as a means of persuading them to help me.

The journey through China to Pakistan was approximately 6,000 kilometres. It would have been tough, I knew, but it was straightforward and would have given me a good chance of reaching Pakistan before my visa expired in a month's time. Now it was off the table.

I began to frantically work out what other options I had. One possibility was returning north into Russia and from there back to Kazakhstan, where I could get a boat across the Caspian Sea to Iran, and go from there to Pakistan. But it was a completely unfamiliar route; I had no idea when the ferry would leave, or if it was even functioning at all. And with winter setting in, many of the roads in Central Asia were already closed by snow. There was little chance of them opening again until spring. There was too much uncertainty in this route. Reluctantly, I discarded the idea.

My only choice was returning to Russia. If I travelled east, I would be able to get to Japan, which I'd be able to use as a springboard to much of the Far East. I could tick those countries off then return later to Pakistan. But this would be a fundamental alteration of a plan that I was already five years into, plus I couldn't be confident that I'd be able to get another visa for Pakistan.

As I stood in the street outside the embassy, locals huddled into thick winter jackets passing me, I suddenly felt consumed by rage. I'd been dreaming about the Karakoram Highway for months, and now there was no way I was going to see it. I'd been denied a visa to China. Whatever choice I ended up making would force me to retrace my steps, or take an enormous diversion, which would involve wasting money and time that I just didn't have.

I could feel hot prickles of anger all over my skin. My mind began to spiral out of control. Suddenly, I was angry at everything and everyone. I was angry at Mongolia and its frigid, bizarre unreality, I was angry at China and every single person who staffed its immigration authorities, I was angry at the existence of an engineering phenomenon that I would never get to see, and I was angry at everyone who had got the chance to see it. Most of all, I was angry at myself and the stupid journey I had set out on five years before. And nagging at me was the thought that always emerged at my lowest moments: *You could just go to the airport.* I imagined reclining in a comfortable seat on the plane and for a brief second my fury abated, before returning stronger than before. It felt to me as if my world was falling apart.

The *illusion* of control is very important to me. I need to at least feel as if there are options and routes I can take. That's why I always try to have contingency plans stored away so I can stay in command even when life throws a curveball. I'll know how to get out of that aeroplane, or into that building. If I can't go through something I'll have plans for how to go under, over or around it. But it always kills me when a plan falls apart or things don't go my way. The transition to the backup is more painful than it should be.

On my way back to my hostel I spotted a mother holding her young daughter's hand while crossing the road. The little girl turned her head and saw me. Her face cracked into a smile and she started to wave frantically. Again, my mood changed. I smiled and waved back. She briefly acknowledged my reply, then turned her head away and disappeared across the road with her mother. I raised my hand to my eye and felt tears brimming.

When the anger returned it drove me to walk in circles in my hostel, my feet slamming bitterly into the ground with every step. One thing that often helps me calm down is drinking water, so I took deep gulps from my bottle. Eventually, my mind cleared enough to allow me to return to the problem before me. I knew that if I let this rage continue unchecked, it would destroy me. I had to find a way of channelling it into something I could use.

I told myself that the actions you take in the face of situations like these are what define you in life. Who ever achieved anything by giving up and not trying harder? Not Ibn Battuta, not Marco Polo, not Vasco da Gama, not Roald Amundsen, not Edmund Hillary, not Tensing Norgay, not Ernest Shackleton.

In Finland, where my mother comes from, they have a word, *sisu*. Loosely translated into English, *sisu* means stoic determination, grit, bravery, resilience and hardiness. It's the mindset that allows individuals to face up to adversity and reach beyond their present limitations. There were times in my past when I believed I had embodied those qualities.

In Eritrea, I ran a desert marathon that I hadn't trained for. The sun lacerated my skin, I had to drag myself across a plateau 2,300 metres above sea level, and halfway through I was smashed into a ditch by a truck's wing mirror. The truck drove off, while I was left to regain consciousness in a ditch filled with the skeletons of what I hoped were cows. I climbed out, picked up my blue UN cap, and, sometimes walking, sometimes running, I hauled my body to the finish line. It took me five hours fifteen minutes.

The next marathon I did was in Berlin. I'd been carrying a knee injury, so hadn't prepared for this one either, I just turned up. This was a time when I was short of cash, so I was wearing trainers that I'd glued together after they'd split in two. Very soon, I was in excruciating pain as a result of my quick fix. Not longer after, my knee blew up. I completed that run too, determined to beat the time I'd set in Eritrea.

Now, I was facing another situation where it would have been easier to give up than carry on. If I could draw on whatever reserves of *sisu* I'd inherited from my Finnish ancestors, then I thought that I might have a chance of making it through. It was time to get to work.

My first port of call was the Russian embassy. Next, I would get new travel insurance for Russia (the only other country in the world who also demanded this was Gabon) and make a new visa application. A new plan was forming in my mind. That's the thing about anger, it can smash your thinking into pieces, or give it a cool, hard-edged clarity. I could leap from Russia to Georgia, then into Armenia, Iran and finally Pakistan. I'd been to all these countries already, I knew them, the buses, the trains, the distances, the borders. There were people I knew along the route who could help me. It was a way of wresting back some control. The detour was plan C; I'd need to cover 10,000 kilometres, cross several time zones and secure several visas before the month was out. The prospect of it gave me a kind of vertigo, and yet amidst the rage that still coursed through my body I could also feel a little pulse of defiance. *This could work.*

This spark was kindled further by the person I spoke to at the Russian embassy, who was surprisingly friendly and helpful. A 'special military operation' in the region close to the border of Russia with Georgia would mean a ten-day delay in approving my visa. But, she told me, if I could find another route, they could give me a visa the same day. Her helpfulness persisted when she discovered I had no access to the internet. She passed her phone to me beneath the glass screen and shared her wi-fi. I opened Google Maps and stared at it for a couple of moments before a new possibility emerged. I could take a train from Moscow to Odessa in Ukraine, then travel from there, adding another 2,000 kilometres. And yet here too geopolitics threatened to sabotage my personal plans. Russia had snatched the Crimean Peninsula only a few years before, and they were now sponsoring an insurgency in

Ukraine's east; would they give me a visa to travel through to Ukraine?

The answer, to my great surprise, was yes. I had to rush back to my hostel to fill in a new application then print it out, before sprinting to the embassy. They were as good as their word. In just three hours I'd acquired a visa. When you only have three weeks to travel 12,000 kilometres, every minute counts.

I worked late that night. I'd met up with a Danish student I'd encountered before on my travels – in Lebanon – who had also washed up here. We went to a Korean restaurant, ate spicy beef soup, then stepped back out into the city's icy streets. I was still seized by anger, and also stressed by all the tasks I had left to complete.

The next morning, I stepped on to a train to Russia. I'd breakfasted at my hostel with two young German travellers who had just checked in. As we talked over tea, bread and jam, I was reminded of a saying: you should be careful not to open your mind too much, as it might fall out. We ranged over conspiracy theories, religion, existence, the future and a lot of other lofty subjects. Then we headed out to hear the monks chant at the Gandan Tegchinlen Monastery, which is the centre of Mongolian Buddhist worship.

After that, I hurried to catch my train. Once the elation of making my connection had subsided, the anger returned. The rage filled me as I took my seat, and stayed there as I went to bed. I woke up angry and the anger clung on throughout that day and the days that followed.

For five days I travelled on an almost empty train through endless tracts of blank, snowbound steppe. Winter had covered any sign of life, rendering the world outside as lonely as the train I was travelling on. I woke each morning to darkness. When I had the energy, I read a book about a Danish expedition that took place between 1761 and 1767. Five scientists left Copenhagen to explore

'Arabia Felix', the 'Happy Arabia', which is today known as Yemen, a journey over land and sea paid for by the Danish king. They saw great wonders, but were struck down by malaria. Only one man returned alive. I tried not to take this as a sign.

Otherwise I took pictures, stared out of the window or just slept. Three times a day I'd shuffle unsteadily through nine equally uninhabited carriages to the dining carriage, where I ate alone, staff hovering pointlessly over somebody who was at times their only customer. The food was good here, though expensive and in such small portions I'd always leave unsatisfied; I found myself thinking about the hot pots I'd enjoyed in Mongolia, as well as grilled horse, the first time I'd tried it, which was served simply and deliciously with cabbage. Afterwards, I'd make the 300-metre return journey. This was my only exercise.

Each time you moved from one wagon to the next, you'd press a button, wait for the door to open, then step outside into a micro-Narnia. The temperatures had already fallen to minus 22 degrees; everything was frozen. Each time, this felt like an act of faith: there was always the fear that you would press the door that led to the next wagon, and it would not open. A handful of times there was a heartstopping delay, long enough to make me think: is *this* how it's going to end? Then, after what seemed like minutes, but can only have been seconds, the door opened and you could escape into the enveloping warmth of the train's interior.

Even days into the journey, every thought that passed through my mind was negative. My pulse raced, I ground my teeth so hard I was surprised that I did not wear them into dust, and my fists were permanently clenched. There was no moment I felt at ease, the idea of relaxation felt like a distant dream. The anger was so consuming that it spread to the world around me. I'd stare, glaring at the carriage: *Stupid table, stupid seat, stupid window.*

It consumed me, but it also kept me going. It pushed me on, it agitated and shamed me in ways that I probably needed more than I realised. And it had still not abated by the time I reached Moscow.

I was in the Russian capital for long enough to run to the Danish embassy and apply for two new passports, which would be sent ahead to Delhi for me to collect; the list of conflict zones in my old passports had, I'd decided, caused me enough trouble already. After this, there was another train journey, another day's travel – by this time the act of staring out of the window at the winter landscape had come to resemble staring into a fireplace. I was no longer really seeing anything. It had all become a perpetual landscape speeding past me. But I noticed that my rage seemed to dwindle with each extra kilometre I covered and every administrative hurdle I leaped over.

At 3 a.m. in a little port, Burlacha Balka, some 18 kilometres from Odessa, I caught the ferry to Georgia. An Uber driver, steering what seemed like the world's smallest Skoda, drove painfully slowly along empty roads. He threw me out 500 metres short of our destination because there were so many cargo trucks ahead of us. I stepped into the road and strode in the half-light between ranks of vehicles towards the customs house. Petrol fumes and dust filled my nostrils. I shivered a little and adjusted the bags on my back. This was now an extremely familiar experience; I'd crossed so many borders in so many countries in precisely these circumstances.

A tired woman checked my passport and waved me into a dark dusty room where three other passengers were also waiting. I was ten minutes late for the ferry but it could not have mattered less. A series of sleepy people in uniforms guided us to a series of different rooms. We waited, had our documents stamped, then waited some more. Finally, we were ushered on to a cold bus that brought us to the ferry. A young guy guided us on board towards the passenger entrance. In a rapid flurry of gestures, he demonstrated that the only way to actually get there was to crawl under a truck. An old lady stared at him in disbelief then, realising she had no option, squeezed her ancient frame into the only space that would allow her to get on to the boat.

I was sharing cabin 8110 with four other passengers. The first to arrive was a young Georgian, who desperately needed a shower. The stench of stale sweat was almost overwhelming. He spoke no English but was friendly enough. I took the lower bunk.

The ferry steadily filled up. A little later, at 8 a.m., the speakers crackled into life to announce that breakfast was ready. We were still moored, with little sign that we were about to move. Lunch, at 1.30 p.m., came and went and we had still not left. It was only at 6 p.m. that with a great groaning of engines we set off into the Black Sea. The wi-fi stopped working. I felt a brief stab of annoyance, then realised that I didn't care. We were on our way.

What I did care about was my Georgian roommate. He behaved like a teenager alone in his bedroom, appearing to be completely unburdened by the fear that anything he did might annoy or inconvenience his fellow passengers. He would frequently embark on long, loud telephone conversations, usually at precisely the moment I was trying to sleep. When he wasn't talking he was playing music. On those occasions when I did manage to drift off, I'd be woken by light streaming in from curtains he'd opened without checking to see if anybody else wanted him to. It was a huge boat, he could have gone anywhere on it, at any time, and yet he seemed to have chosen to stay within our cramped cabin and persecute me.

I found myself torn between the impulse to stay polite and a growing desire to tell him what I thought. In the end, I opted to keep my grievances to myself, partly, though not entirely, because the language barrier meant I wasn't confident of being able to express my rage at him adequately.

The boat continued its trundle across the Black Sea, the throb of its engines resonating in its every corner. I lay in my bed fuming at the Georgian cacophony above me and wondering anxiously if I would arrive in time to catch my train to Tbilisi.

The train had long since departed by the time we docked. As I clambered down the ferry's gangway I decided to dig into the anger that had driven me on so effectively a few days ago. What followed was not easy. I spoke no Georgian, few people spoke English. With no direct route available my only alternative was to compose a jumbled hodgepodge of a journey assembled from a number of disparate bus routes. Each leg was exhausting, involving long waits, tense moments in which I worried that a late-running service might never actually arrive. I travelled through mountain landscapes, snow-capped mountains, desert, forest, rivers, I made my way through Georgia and Armenia and eventually, at 2.30 a.m. on 11 December 2018, arrived at the Iranian border. An Armenian passenger approached me to ask where I was from. He spoke a variety of English so broken as to be almost unintelligible. On learning that I was Danish he launched into a long, meandering speech, from which I picked up the following: Copenhagen, Legoland, something about his child winning a competition, that he imported rocks from Iran, that business was good, that he preferred his cottage in the forest with the rabbits (here he paused for long enough to phone – and no doubt wake – a friend to ask him how to say 'rabbits' in English), and that he loved Denmark.

There was no customs check and the immigration officer stamped me out of Armenia almost immediately. I made the same journey across no-man's-land as I had two months earlier. Idly I tried to count the number of countries I had been to this year, then gave up; my brain was too tired to produce the neat list I was looking for. The first passport control in Iran glanced at my papers, smiled and said: 'Welcome to Iran.' By 3 a.m. I was in the waiting area hoping that a bus would come soon that would take me into the country's interior. The Armenian man from before approached me again: 'Brin Gamleth . . . Brin Gamleth. Schaggspar?' After a while I got it: Prince Hamlet. Shakespeare. Elsinore, the castle where the story takes place, is in Denmark and there is a famous line from the play which goes: 'Something is rotten in the state of Denmark'. At 3.47 a.m. I was in the bus.

One way of describing Iran is as a repressive theocratic state that's also home to millions of incredibly nice people. I'm not sure there's any nation where there's such a disconnect between government and its population. The garbage that comes out of the mouths of its leaders bears little relation to the feelings of the people in the street. I remember once walking past a building covered in an enormous mural of an American flag in which the stars had been replaced by bombs. The friend I was with shuddered as we looked at it. 'We didn't put that up, the government did, but who's going to touch it?'

Every time I went there, I seemed to make new friends. This visit was no different. A guy I encountered set me up with a contact near the border with Pakistan who was used to briefing people who were travelling overland into Pakistan. Balochistan, the province that we'd be entering – the historical region actually sprawls across Iran and Afghanistan too – has a reputation as Pakistan's Wild West because of the level of conflict between the authorities and separatist insurgents. Its own government provides visitors with an escort of armed guards.

My contact, Ahmed, a dentist, lived in Zahedan, a small Iranian town not far from the crossing into Pakistan. The train arrived early in the morning, then I took a taxi to the place where we'd agreed to meet. I texted him and he came down on the street to greet me, then took me up a flight of stairs to his apartment. He was friendly but there was something a little glazed about his expression; he did not seem entirely present. He opened the door to a room full of dentistry equipment like chairs and drills, all of it covered in a thick layer of dust. It was as if I had stepped into an abandoned museum. This wasn't his clinic, he said. That was elsewhere. This property was just used for storage. Well, not *just* storage. The next room was, in the most literal sense, an opium den. He went to a table and picked up a pipe and an enormous chunk, almost a rock, of opium.

'Make yourself at home,' he said, then sat down on the floor and lit his pipe. He inhaled deeply, then offered it to me.

'No, I better not.'

'OK,' he said, shrugging to show that he was not troubled whether I did or didn't. Then, with the air of a man sinking into a relaxing bath he explained that opium's chief benefit was allowing you to focus on one task in great detail. Our conversation continued. He told me about two French travellers he'd hosted a while back who had started smoking opium with him. They had stayed for a whole fourteen days, leaving only when their visas expired.

I started taking pictures of my extraordinary surroundings. I picked up the lump of opium, smelled it. Everything about this place felt decadent and strange; it was hard to know what sort of story it belonged in. I fired a series of questions at my host. He was like an encyclopaedia, seeming to know everything about the drug, which he said had been smoked by kings for centuries. Speaking in a floaty, almost distracted voice, he discussed the long-term effects of opium, how it is harvested, and gave me detailed instructions on how to prepare the pipe and smoke it.

'This town,' he said, 'is three things. It's money, weapons and drugs. That's what it is.' Its location at a point where three countries – Iran, Afghanistan and Pakistan – met, and the fact that the antipathy between their respective governments meant that there was little to no cooperation ensured that it was essentially a free-for-all for criminals. There was nobody there with the will, or the means, to fight them.

I listened to him, knowing that he was trying to warn me about the many risks of the country I was proposing to travel to. I was grateful for his concern, woozy as he was. And I knew that I would at times be in danger. But as he talked, my mind was not on terrorists, or drug smugglers, or corrupt policemen; I was thinking about what I'd achieved over the last fortnight. I'd crossed over 11,919 kilometres of land and sea. In order to do that, I'd taken four trains, a ferry, two minibuses, a bus, five taxis and three metros. I'd passed through six countries – Mongolia, Russia, Ukraine, Georgia, Armenia, Iran – and secured two visas. I'd spent just two nights in a regular bed, the other twelve I slept while I moved. And now, I was here, just a few metres from Pakistan, with three days to spare before my visa expired.

I had come up with an extravagant plan and I'd pulled it off. And though I realised that I would not be seeing the Karakoram Highway, as I hadn't entered from China, I had proved something to myself: maybe I, just like my Finnish ancestors, had my own measure of *sisu*.

## CHAPTER 13

# Paradise, Loser

*Singapore, the Solomon Islands, the Marshall Islands,*
*June 2019 to December 2020*

R ight through every moment of the journey so far I'd been conscious that the time would come when I had to tackle the Pacific. I'd always thought this would be the biggest monster to slay. A good friend of mine, Gunnar Garfors, who has been to every country in the world twice, said that going to each country in the Pacific is a phenomenal task even if you're flying. He looked at me almost in wonder. 'I can't even begin to understand how you're going to pull it off.'

The distances involved were almost unconscionable. Fiji to Kiribati, for instance, was over two thousand kilometres. I knew that there were few, if any, ferry services. Those that still operated rarely ran according to schedule. There was the possibility of finding a sailboat but the chances were that somebody willing to take you as a passenger wouldn't actually be going where you wanted to go.

This left three other sorts of seafarers regularly tracing a path in this part of the world. There were military vessels, which were a non-starter, cruise ships, which were always a headache because generally they'd sold their tickets long before (I'd occasionally offer myself as entertainment – giving talks in exchange for a ride – nobody ever seemed interested), and also commercial cargo operations. The problem was that the island nations of the Pacific were not business behemoths, there was little to no industry, they exported minimal amounts of goods, so very few people actually needed or wanted to travel to them.

But, there were routes. If you could persuade the operators to take you, then you had a chance. Otherwise, you were out of luck. It didn't necessarily get easier when you reached the islands. The governments were famously inefficient and corrupt. You could not be sure that they would let you in. You could not even be confident that immigration would return your calls or emails. These were places where time was sticky; they were rundown, littered with rusting vehicles and abandoned structures. They were not places where you could get stuff done. The beauty of the islands, the culture and the kindness of their people: all of these would prove remarkable. But none of this helped me.

And, of course, there was the Pacific itself. A wilful ocean that had the capacity to change, almost in an instant, from placid sparkling calm to tempestuous walls of crashing water and howling wind. Later, I would ask a captain when it was typhoon season. He laughed, 'It's always typhoon season.' It was the Pacific, more than any other element, that could knock my journey off the rails. A storm at the wrong time could effectively shut off some of the more distant countries in the area. I was in the ocean's hands.

However, by the time I got to Singapore I was feeling fairly sanguine. I had this thought that Maersk would be able to help me in the Pacific. We'd had a really good relationship through the whole project; they'd been kind to me, I'd been kind to them. The problem was that their ships very rarely sailed to the tiny island nations I needed to get to. What they could do, however, was introduce me to some of the other companies they collaborated with.

They set up meetings for me with Pacific International Line and Swire Shipping, telling me that, between them, these two operators reached just about every part of the Pacific. Before I sat down with them, I made a list of the countries I still had to travel to (twenty). Then I made another one featuring just the nations I was confident I could get to (four). An uneasy feeling crept up my spine. On the one hand I was, numerically speaking, extremely close to the end. On the other, I thought that given the scale of the task before me I might as well have included the moon.

Luckily, there was Paramesh. He was one of the Swire employees I was put in touch with. My modus operandi up to this point had been to avoid looking too far ahead, to take each challenge one at a time. Paramesh was different. He went online and looked at all the shipping schedules, both for Swire and their supposed rivals Pacific International Line, and created an Excel spreadsheet in which he mapped out every country I still needed to travel to, and how I could get to them. He included everything: the different ships, their names, when they'd be sailing, what ports they'd be stopping at, how long they'd be in transit for. It was incredible. He explained the things that could cause delays, from typhoons to cranes malfunctioning, but it was Paramesh who gave me the hope that I could be home within ten months.

Suddenly there was a path back to Denmark. I could see the journey unfolding before me. I'd go from Singapore to Indonesia – I knew there were lots of ferries here, which is probably just as well, it's an archipelago of over 17,000 islands – then on to Borneo, Malaysia, Brunei, Malaysia again, Indonesia once more, East Timor, Papua New Guinea, then on and on . . . I thought: *The project is going to be a success.* I just had to hold on for a year, maybe not even that long. I allowed myself to hope I might be home in ten months.

It started off well. Le met me in East Timor. Afterwards, I was dazzled by Papua New Guinea. If there are any dinosaurs on the planet, we'll find them there. It's so mountainous and the forest is unfathomably deep. There are definitely people living there who have never had any kind of contact with the outside world.

And God, I fell hard for the Solomon Islands. Just being there felt like an adventure. Part of that was the myths that swirled around the place. There are rumours of cannibals. And it was here that John F. Kennedy made his reputation as a young lieutenant with an astonishing piece of heroism after the torpedo boat he commanded had been rammed by a Japanese destroyer. His boat exploded following the collision and JFK personally rescued three members of his crew, swimming for hours at a time in an attempt to find help, before shepherding his men to safety several days later. But part of it is that it might genuinely be one of the most beautiful places on the planet: where else can you sit on a porch by the ocean, eating a papaya as more than two hundred dolphins jump through the water before you?

I had ten days to explore because the ship that was supposed to take me onwards had been caught up behind a typhoon. *Fine*, I said to myself, *I really want to get home, but there are worse places to be.* I took one of the ferries that travelled from one island to the next because I wanted to go to the western Solomon Islands – my host in Papua New Guinea, Craig, a commercial manager from Maersk, had told me they were unmissable.

This was not a mode of transport designed to get passengers quickly from one place to another. The idea was to make a leisurely progress, stopping frequently. It was the kind of environment designed for meeting people. You got on a boat, you chatted, you learned, you laughed. And all the time you're surrounded by a version of paradise. A lot of the islands have neither roads nor cars. The water is an iridescent blue, the trees are an ambush of every conceivable shade of green, and there is an astonishing profusion of flowers that burn with an intensity of colour I had never thought possible.

Each time the boat stopped there would be a chance to buy fruit and vegetables from a stall set up beneath a roof of palm leaves. You'd buy your mangoes, bananas, breadfruit, watermelon, papaya or pineapple, then take them back to the boat. Nothing ever seemed to be a problem. Everyone was helpful, everyone was smiling and funny and kind. Very often they'd be chewing betel nut, which has a mild narcotic effect, something akin to tobacco or caffeine. It stains mouths and lips a deep red; and all across the country you'd see evidence of people having spat it out – on the streets, in the soil, even on bushes. Once it had been a ceremonial activity reserved for special occasions, now it was part of everyday life.

Halfway through the journey, as I sprawled happily eating fruit on a tractor wheel on the boat's top deck, I was joined by an elderly fellow, who introduced himself as Pastor Frazer. 'It's not in our culture to eat alone,' he said, 'come and sit with me.'

We shared our purchases, eating greedily, and letting the juices run down our chins. We talked for a while and he began to take a close interest in where I was going next. I told him I'd booked a guest house that looked beautiful. It had a hammock where I planned to rest up and gather energy ahead of taking on the next challenge.

He revealed that he was a village elder and invited me to come to visit his home once I'd finished putting my feet up. He gave me his phone number and I took a photograph of his ID card so that I had his details. We travelled together for another day or so, then went our separate ways.

The thing about paradises is that they only stay paradisiacal as long as human beings keep their distance. The second our feet step on to their bleached white sands, everything changes. JFK was here in 1943 as a young lieutenant in the US Navy because the islands were the backdrop for the Allies' struggles against the Japanese during the Second World War.

While I was staying at the guest house, I met a man who had assembled a museum of trinkets from the war. He'd begun when he was a kid, now his huge garage was full of helmets, guns, grenades, dog tags, cutlery, buttons, buckets, cups, plates, jars, syringes, pocket knives, coins, spectacles, safety pins and bullets.

Elsewhere there was a beautifully tended American military cemetery. And history is not done with the Solomon Islands. The country itself is engaged in a high-wire act, playing Australia and China off against each other, and trying to extract as much as it can from both in the process. Papua New Guinea is doing something similar.

Occasionally an enormous Chinese battleship would slide past our boat. Officially they are listed as research vessels. Or we'd see Australian tactical helicopters flying above, or Australian troops in the streets. It is not a war, not even close to it, but bigger, more advanced nations have decided that these islands fall within their sphere of influence, and they're willing to, at the very least, show force to protect their power.

These are huge swathes of water. If you control them, you can fish in them, which means you can feed your population. For China, a nation of 1.4 billion people, this is clearly a pressing issue. What is more, all of these island nations are represented at the United Nations, and as such each has a vote. So there is a clear advantage to be had for any larger nation that is able to persuade, or pressure, these smaller entities into voting on their side when controversial issues come up in the assembly.

Nobody cares about the land itself, or the people who live there.

\* \* \*

A few days later I took the several boats I needed to reach Pastor Frazer. Over the phone we had agreed we'd meet in Gizo on Ghizo Island. The first thing he said to me was: 'What does someone like you eat?'

He took me to a market, then we hopped into his tiny motorboat, and we puttered on until we pulled up on another pristine beach. It was filled with naked children playing happily in water that held and reflected the glittering light from the bright sun above us. Further out there were little ridges of coral around which tiny blue, red and yellow fish flitted. The children seemed completely, perfectly at ease in the ocean, jumping, diving, catching crabs. They were like little dolphins. When they saw me, they crowded round, bubbling with questions and curiosity.

A flat path, lined by vast thick trees that offered shade, led inland. We followed it for a while, until we reached three gravestones. Pastor Frazer pointed, matter-of-factly. 'My father, mother and brother. The village, Vori Vori, used to be here, then in 2004 the tsunami came and took everything. These gravestones were the only things that survived.' Then he pointed towards the top of the hill before us. 'Now the village is there.'

We walked up past palm trees, a man carrying firewood, and butterflies that flitted brightly among the lush vegetation that surrounded us. No matter how steep the climb, Pastor Frazer, who must have been well into his seventies, never seemed to falter. I began to wonder whether I, too, should eat fish and fresh fruit every day.

The village, home to two hundred people, was a collection of wooden huts on stilts which centred round a beautifully tended green lawn. Its tallest building was the church, which also stood on stilts. It did not have a bell, but a large gas canister and metal rod performed the same function. This was a surprisingly common, and effective, substitute.

There was no running water here, nor mains electricity. The population caught whatever fish they needed each day, which they supplemented with coconuts, fruit and roots from the forest. They collected rainwater, or drew it from a nearby creek where they also bathed. Power was supplied by a generator and a few solar panels.

A hut had been set aside for me to stay in. Almost sheepishly, I delved into my rucksack and brought out some cans containing liver pâté that Le had brought out from Denmark. I wanted to give the pastor something that felt particular to my home country. Pastor Frazer received them very gratefully, then surprised me by immediately opening one of the cans and emptying it over his rice. I had never seen anybody do that before, but it felt rude to point out that we usually consumed it on rye bread. Also, as I watched him tucking into it with obvious pleasure I realised: why *should* he eat it like I did back in Copenhagen?

Afterwards, he carried on showing me round, introducing me to some of his neighbours. Then he turned to me, a serious look on his face. 'Do you travel with a laptop?' he asked.

'Yes,' I said, unsure where this was leading.

'Do you have any movies that the children might enjoy? Maybe something with a snake?'

I thought for a moment, 'How about *The Jungle Book*?'

He had not seen it before, but once I had explained a little about the plot and characters, he agreed it sounded suitable. Within minutes I had set the laptop up inside a flimsy wooden structure that was almost completely open on every side. A gaggle of nine kids sat on the floor, staring enchanted at the screen. Occasionally I'd glance around me. The butterflies, vegetation and trees we saw in the movie felt like a mirror of everything that surrounded us.

When the film came to an end, the elder approached me once more. 'Is there any power left in your laptop?' I nodded. 'Do you have anything suitable for adults?'

I nodded again.

'Perhaps something with war?' he asked, looking hopeful.

This was how, once darkness had fallen, we ended up watching *The Thin Red Line*. I had remembered that it was both set in the Solomon Islands and filmed there. Eighty villagers crowded round my computer, which somebody had managed to connect to speakers powered by a generator.

Halfway through the film I stepped back a little bit to take in the scene. I leaned against the low fence that ran round the perimeter of the hut. It was raining gently. If I concentrated, I could hear the gentle patter of raindrops and the chatter of the insects. Above us stars shone brilliantly; there was just enough light that it was possible to make out the silhouettes of the trees around us.

And there in the middle was the flickering screen showing the carnage that played out in this country just seventy years before. The islanders engaged with the film in ways I had not anticipated. Moments of frightening violence were greeted with hoots of laughter and encouragement. When an American drove a bayonet through his enemy's face there was merriment, and one man shouted: 'That Japanese guy really got it good.'

My journey through the Pacific continued: Kiribati and the third smallest nation in the world, Nauru, which is hard to get to even if you're flying, because it's one of the most closed-off countries in the world. That ended up being relatively straightforward, unlike the Marshall Islands, which was supposed to be one of the easier ones for me to tick off my list. The ship that took me there was due to set anchor for thirty hours while it conducted various cargo operations.

Then, after we'd landed, they got new orders. I wasn't going to get the twenty-four hours I needed, because they were going to leave after just eleven.

The captain summoned me into his presence and asked me what I wanted to do. I paused, trying to process the choice before me. If I stayed with this ship, I'd be breaking my own rules. But if I disembarked, I'd be effectively marooning myself for another fortnight, perhaps more. I was following a strict schedule, having been pre-approved to join ships later in my journey. Staying here meant I would miss them and I'd have to go through the tortuous process of making new arrangements; it wasn't just a question of buying a new ferry ticket. I thought for a couple of seconds. And yet there was, of course, only one answer. 'I have to go, I'll stay on the island.'

Just as I was about to walk back down the gangway to the country's main urban area, Majuro, one of the crew handed me a box of instant noodles. 'We don't know what kind of food they have here.' Then, registering the surprise on my face: 'Don't worry, we know you'll be fine.'

I stood for a moment to watch the ship plunge back into the ocean. Then turned away, aware that by staring at it like that I was only torturing myself. There was no guarantee that I'd be able to get on the next ship. They might not be willing to let me on. Or they might have checked every box they needed before being stalled by some event, like a typhoon, completely outside their control. I knew enough by this stage to understand that nothing, ever, was a guarantee.

One idea that kept recurring to me was of the project as a very long tunnel of countries that I needed to get through. There was no sign of the light at its end, I just had to believe it was there if I managed to get far enough through. Some days I *knew* I'd find my way to that light. Others, I merely hoped.

The thing about the Marshall Islands is that life there is so strange and full of unexpected events that a man can turn up to rent a shabby room in the back of a shabby bar (the Flame Tree) with a box of instant noodles and nobody bats an eyelid. For them, whatever happens, happens. I was sleeping in what was theoretically a dormitory. There were eight rooms, but they were all empty, except for the mosquitoes that flew menacingly in circles above my bed. I quickly invested in some mosquito coils and aimed a fan towards where I'd be sleeping.

The Marshall Islands' population remained fundamentally indifferent to my existence for almost the whole time I was there. People throughout the world had been kind to me. Here, it was as if I barely existed. They might acknowledge that I was present, they might even look at me, but they would never smile or wave or interact in any other way. It felt to me as if they were keeping their distance, as if there was an invisible barrier between me and everyone who lived here. The loneliness I'd felt for the best part of a decade intensified.

The vagaries of travel in the Pacific meant that I had not seen Le for months. Almost every location I was likely to be in needed at least two and a half days of flight time to reach. It wasn't worth her committing to this if neither she nor I had any way of being confident where I was likely to be from one day to the next.

And it was not a pleasant place to be staying. I'd arrived in typhoon season. The rain, wind and grey skies seemed to match Majuro's concrete sprawl. It did not feel like a tropical paradise. The noise from the Flame Tree bar stopped me from sleeping until late every night. The island was covered in rubbish: the streets were littered with abandoned, rusting cars and refrigerators; garbage also spilled on to its white beaches and azure water. Its cinema was closed, so was its only sports centre. The Marshall Islands had once had a purpose. Their remoteness, which for centuries had been the thing that protected its population, became the thing that condemned it.

The Marshall Islands were chosen by the American government as the site where they could test new atomic weapons – on Bikini Atoll. In doing so, they forced various sections of the population to move to areas where they had no historical affinity. In a stroke, they had ripped up its social fabric. So many bombs were dropped that even now there are astonishing levels of radioactivity. This was not merely an unfortunate side-effect of their work, it was part of the design because they also wanted to assess the impact of radiation on human beings.

The Marshall Islands have a spectacular history of seamanship and navigating. The people who lived there used to be the masters of the Pacific Ocean. They had an intimate, almost symbiotic relationship with the water that surrounded them on all sides. They would set sail into the gigantic, seemingly endless expanse and navigate it effortlessly, travelling as easily between islands as we might between cities. Instead of GPS they were able to read the ocean: by looking at the swell, at the current and colour of the water, or by putting their hands into it and testing its temperature, they were able to locate tiny outcrops of land – which sometimes jutted only 1 or 2 metres above the surface. It was here that I was first introduced to star maps. Sticks and seashells would be tied together in a mesh-like configuration that resembled a spider web. The older sailors would use this to teach youngsters about the different constellations in the sky, who would then memorise what they had learned so that they would be able to sail by night.

This culture was all but destroyed by the atomic testing. The Americans knew what damage they had caused. In a fit of guilt, they showered the islands with intermittent bursts of investment. That's why its streets are littered with expensive goods.

The Americans' other big gesture – their way of saying 'I'm sorry we destroyed your country' – was to offer citizenship to any islander who came to live and work in the US. This means, in practice, that anyone who's bright or ambitious or wants something else from life leaves.

They are a tiny nation surrounded by other tiny nations. The only country in this part of the Pacific of any real size is Fiji, which has a population of nearly a million. It's big enough to support proper universities and companies and industry. But all the other island nations have far smaller populations, rarely more than a hundred thousand. Your options are limited: the young, the ambitious, they don't see their futures at home, but abroad, in Australia, New Zealand, Hawaii, maybe Fiji.

This, combined with their isolation, results in a kind of hopelessness.

It is impossible to be a modern state and an island paradise. You can either be the sort of place where people wear Levi's and have iPhones and go to universities, or you can live off the land. You can't have both. This is also true of somewhere like Greenland. They don't want to go back to seal hunting and living in basic ways. But the only way they can achieve any kind of modernity is to rely on the support of other nations. Greenland gets bags of money from Denmark. That's the reality. And they don't like it. It's the tragedy of living between these two worlds.

I felt that tragedy too, for the first couple of days I was in Majuro. It was impossible not to. Then New Year's Eve came along. That was the night when I fell in love with the Marshall Islands: I'll defend that place till the day I die.

There was an almost magical transformation, both of the people and the place itself. There's a single road that runs through Majuro. The local authorities closed off a couple of kilometres to make space for a party, putting a stage at each end and stringing bright lights across it. On one stage was Rosie Delmah, a big-name artist from the Solomon Islands who'd been imported from her home in Australia for the occasion. The majority of the crowd was here, hundreds of people in brightly patterned Bula shirts milling about, eating and drinking, enjoying the firework display. I ate raw salmon with salad and rice I'd picked up from a little stand, and drank coconut water. There was an openness about the people that had been absent before. They were all smiling and nodding to each other, greeting friends and strangers alike with warmth. I had spent days feeling like I had been shunned, now I was included in the festivities. It was as if they had all needed the best part of a week to warm up to this strange foreigner who had appeared in their midst.

All of a sudden, I was reminded of the small Danish community I had grown up in. A place where everybody knows everyone else, and nothing ever happens without the whole population knowing it. People know the best and worst of their neighbours and live together in a sense of unity in spite of it. Maybe because of it?

I spent the evening talking happily with some of the people I'd encountered since I'd arrived. The African missionary whose school I had spoken at (he danced beautifully, I . . . did my best), the friendly American ambassador; several members of the local Red Cross.

On the other stage was a local band of teenage boys. They were playing their hearts out, their enthusiasm more than making up for limited technique. I wandered over to watch them towards the end of the night. There were at most forty others in the crowd. The band played on, a clanging, whirling, crashing ball of energy, until, abruptly, they halted in a squeal of feedback and clattering drums. It seemed they had exhausted their repertoire. They were done for the night.

Except that some of the audience had other ideas. A couple of voices started calling for Radiohead's 'Creep'; soon they were joined by everyone around them, a chorus all shouting, 'Play "Creep"! Play "Creep"!'

The boys looked at each other wonderingly. They had forgotten they knew this one. Guitars and drumsticks were picked up again and they launched into the song. As the chorus started, we all joined in, singing up into the warm, star-scattered Pacific sky, 'I'm a creep, I'm a weirdo. What the hell am I doing here? I don't belong here.' You could see the band pick up on the surge of energy from the gaggle of figures beneath them; their playing became more intense and in turn this energy surged back into the crowd.

The force of those lyrics hit me hard. They somehow expressed both the alienation I'd felt over the last week and the unifying, bonding experience of the last hours. I shouldn't even have been here; I had been cold-shouldered, made to feel as if I did not belong, and yet I had spent the evening feeling embraced, supported by people who probably felt that they also were not supposed to be stranded on this island nation in the middle of a gigantic ocean.

Three days later, I sailed away in high spirits. I was making progress. The Pacific was tough but so far it had thrown up nothing I couldn't handle. I thought: *This is good, I'll be home soon.*

CHAPTER 14

# The Ice Floe

*Hong Kong, January 2020 to November 2020*

When I was a kid, I loved reading about the race to reach
the South Pole. I was enthralled by the accounts of how the
Norwegian explorer Roald Amundsen had trained in Greenland
with a dog sled and seal skin and technology that was already
obsolete. And yet, because of his skill with maps, his clever
distribution of essential stores, and his luck with the weather, he
was able to pull off almost the perfect expedition. I loved his
bravado too. When he reached the South Pole, a month ahead of
his British rival Robert Scott, who had been struggling along with
his superior modern machinery, he erected a tent in which he left
some extra boots, some supplies of food and a sign saying:

*Dear Captain Scott,*
*As you are probably the first to reach this area after us, I will ask you*
*kindly to forward this letter to King Haakon VII.*

*If you can use any of the articles left in the tent please do not hesitate to do so.*

*With kind regards*

*Wish you a safe return.*

*Yours Truly*

*Roald Amundsen*

I found the tragedy of Scott's failed journey just as compelling. The harrowing thought of their desperate attempt to make their way back. They were assailed by frostbite and gangrene, exhausted, unable to find their depots. Each night they would shiver in tents that were almost being ripped to shreds by the howling wind, effectively waiting to die. The image that stayed with me most was of the ailing Lawrence 'Titus' Oates, who knew he was sicker than any of his comrades, and decided to sacrifice himself rather than consume any more of their dwindling stock of rations. He walked out of the tent into a blizzard he knew would kill him, saying to his comrades: 'I am just going outside and may be some time.' It was, as Scott wrote at the time, 'the act of a brave man and an English gentleman'.

I never wanted that tragic end for myself. I always wanted to be Amundsen. The successful one, the one who knows what he's doing, where everything goes according to plan. I wanted to be the kind of explorer where, even if the first plan faltered, I'd have a backup.

Then I ran into a global pandemic and realised that I was faced by a different kind of story, one that did not rely on my ability to plan or think on my feet. The situation I had found myself in was closer to the experiences of Ernest Shackleton and the crew of the *Endurance*. After their ship was trapped, then crushed by pack ice, in the winter of 1915, they were forced to drift helplessly on ice floes, waiting for a gap to open up that would allow them to escape.

They survived not because they were clever, or brave, or resourceful, though they were all of those things. It was because they *held on*. That would become my challenge.

I had stepped on to the *Kota Hening*, the ship that would take me to Hong Kong from the Marshall Islands, via a stop in Micronesia, just as the news was full of stories about how the world was about to change, perhaps for ever. Tensions between Iran and America after the US assassination of Qasem Soleimani, the leader of the Iranian Republican Guard, on 3 January 2020 were ramping up quickly. I remember feeling worried. It seemed as if there was a real chance that things could escalate. Were we on the cusp of a new conflict? Was it going to be another Iraq? Newspapers and television programmes were warning of the possibility of World War Three.

The ship had no wi-fi for the crew, so for the next eleven days I heard nothing more about what was going on. In the absence of any solid information, my mind filled with increasingly lurid fears. I was thinking: *I wonder if we'll get to Hong Kong and find smoke rising from bombed-out buildings?*

Perhaps that is why I was so puzzled when, as we approached Hong Kong, I went up on the bridge and saw that the captain was wearing a face mask. He handed me one and said, 'You better wear this,' before telling me that there had been a virus outbreak in Wuhan. I was so ignorant at this point that my first question was, essentially, 'What is a Wuhan?'

He carried on, explaining that although the government had assured the population that everything was under control, it was best to be cautious: 'In China, we do not trust the government when it tells us there is nothing to worry about.'

As soon I was in the port complex I logged on to the free wi-fi and looked at Google Maps to see where Wuhan was in relation to Hong Kong. It was a thousand kilometres away. I started laughing.

I thought I knew something about how distances in countries worked. If you were in Egypt and riots broke out in Cairo, everyone you knew would be concerned for you even if you were 600 kilometres away. When I was in Kinshasa, the capital of Congo, volcanoes erupted in a place called Goma and I had loads of messages asking if I was OK. And of course, I was, I was 2,000 kilometres from where the lava was flowing – Germany and Portugal are closer to each other.

I thought: *Are you kidding me? Like, OK, I'll put the mask on, but this is never going to have anything to do with me.* All of this felt like the same media hysteria that just a few days earlier had been whipped up about a war between Iran and the USA.

Earlier in the project I'd passed through Guinea, Sierra Leone and Liberia during the Ebola epidemic – this was a disease that at one time had a 40–70 per cent mortality rate. I'd also travelled through Angola in the midst of the 2016 yellow fever outbreak. And that had a fatality rate of 8.7 per cent. I'd escaped unscathed then, and saw no reason why it would be any different now. To be honest, I was more struck by how cold Hong Kong felt compared to the tropical nations I'd spent the last months in.

Anyway, I was only going to be here for four days; and then I'd be on my way to Palau, the next country I had to visit. I thought about the sharp but short-lived panics about SARS and swine flu. Surely this would be the same.

A couple called James and Cassie Savagar, who both worked at Maersk, along with their two boys, Edward and Harry, had offered to be my hosts while I was in Hong Kong. I was going to speak at the Danish Seamen's Church and at the Maersk office there (in return they were going to give me a Lego Maersk container ship, something I'd always coveted). And I needed to buy a new iPhone to replace the one I had busted in the Solomon

Islands when I had walked into a waterfall – I figured I was in the perfect place.

The agent who'd been appointed by the shipping company came to get me: I noticed that he was wearing a mask. But after I had said farewell to the ship and we were safely in his car, he took the mask off. I looked at him and asked, 'So, no mask?'

'No, there's no virus in Hong Kong. Hong Kong's fine.' He was behaving as I thought he should. As we pulled up to immigration he pointed at my face, 'Put on the mask for the authorities.' We passed through and he offered to drop me off. I handed him the address I'd been given. 'Oh yeah,' he said, with an air of confidence, 'I know it.'

I was about to be surprised again by Hong Kong. We drove for twenty minutes, leaving the skyscrapers and gleaming office buildings behind and weaving our way through forest, mountains and villages. This was not what I had expected. 'Are we still in Hong Kong?' He smiled, and nodded. Twenty minutes later, my anxiety mounting, I asked again, 'Are we still in Hong Kong? We're not going to China, are we?'

Me, the great world traveller, had not realised that three-quarters of Hong Kong is countryside. I had thought it was just a city. For the next two years, the territory's countryside, which until just now I had not known existed, would be my salvation. I would soon fall in love with the lush, green, almost primeval ferns that were home to every sort of animal, from monkeys and snakes to wild boar and the cows that had been set free by farmers who no longer wanted to tend them, allowed to roam and graze unhindered. You'd see them wandering into the small mainland villages or obliviously blocking roads. Hong Kong has mountains that tower four times above Denmark's highest geographical point, and beaches that equal the most paradisiacal of Thailand or Malaysia. Even seven years into the project, I still had so much to learn; there was still so much about the world that could shock and surprise.

I arrived at the home that this family, who had never met me, had generously allowed me to use while they were in Dalian, where Cassie was from, to celebrate Chinese New Year. They had left a maid, Arlene, to look after me (though before long she left to see her husband in Macau), a long letter from James welcoming me and telling me how to get my bearings, and a charming note from the children, explaining how to use the TV control.

Over the next day or so, I began to be aware that something was shifting. First, Maersk closed their offices and sent all their staff home. My speaking gig was cancelled. Even now, my main concern was losing out on the Lego swag. The event at the seamen's church went ahead, but there were gaps in the audience; clearly people were worried about the virus. The organisers gave me some Danish sweets. *Great*, I thought, *I don't have a sweet tooth but I can give them to the crew on board my next ship.* As far as I knew, it was still leaving in forty-eight hours' time, with me on it.

The drip, drip of new, unsettling information continued. James and Cassie wrote to say that they were still in China and were uncertain about when, or even if, they would be able to make it back. Travel restrictions had been imposed; suddenly just catching a flight had become a complicated business.

Life went on, and they returned. When I got a message telling me that due to Chinese New Year, the port only had half its usual numbers of staff, and so my departure would be delayed by seven days, the Savagars let me stay longer without blinking. Eleven days in Hong Kong? No problem.

Days five, six and seven came and went. The reporting on the virus changed. It began to feel as if, actually, there was something different about this one. All at once, it was the only thing any of us could talk about. Then Palau closed its border to greater China (China, Hong Kong and Macau). I still had my berth on the container ship, and it was still slated to travel to Palau, but there was no point in me walking up its gangway because I wouldn't be allowed to walk down it again when it docked. Reluctantly, I told Pacific International Line that I would stay in Hong Kong.

This was not good news, and yet nor did it feel fatal. I'd lost count of how many ships, trains, buses that I was supposed to be catching had been cancelled over the last few years. No part of me was thinking: *I need to get out, because unless I get out now, I'm not going to get out at all.*

Still, things were crazy in Wuhan. We watched the robots in the street telling people to go back inside and the body bags piling high in corridors of funeral parlours. We knew that they were building walls around certain apartment blocks and were welding doors shut. However, there hadn't been a single case recorded in Hong Kong, or Beijing, or Shanghai. We felt safe, protected from what was going on a thousand kilometres away.

And life continued, after a fashion. Cassie and James were working from home, and their kids' school was shut, so we, along with Arlene, were all in their home. This wasn't a problem; they were still gracious and friendly and kind, and their house was big. I started talking about different options for the journey to Palau. And yet each time I came up with a new plan, it was quickly rendered obsolete by a pandemic that was moving at a bewildering pace. I thought about going via Seoul, an idea that was doomed as soon as a religious sect who had made a trip to China returned to South Korea, bringing the virus with them.

More plans formed – going via Taiwan, or Singapore – then dissolved as soon as they made contact with the new reality. One repeated suggestion was that I should buy a boat and simply sail it myself. This foundered on several points: the sheer scale of the

Pacific, as well as the likelihood of being caught in a typhoon; the fact that I had no experience of sailing such craft; and the fact that I'd never be allowed to cross Chinese territorial waters. I'd also heard about another man who had set out on a sailboat adventure just before the pandemic and was waved away every time he approached a port. He was stranded on his own boat, becoming perhaps the most isolated man on the planet. I was not ready for that.

The virus was speeding from nation to nation, and suddenly it was in Europe. People in Italy were dying and singing from balconies. That's when I *really* started talking. Trying to follow up every contact, every friend of a friend, every possible avenue. Trying to build up a network, because I realised that there was no way I was going to solve this on my own. The game became: how many human beings can I meet? I'd post on social media, then follow through on every hint or tip I got. Word about me spread quickly. I became a curiosity. People would invite me to dinner parties. I'd talk and drink wine with fresh faces. Each time I'd make more contacts. Someone else who might, potentially, be useful. My cause was helped by a wave of media interest prompted by a CNN piece on me, followed by a feature by the vlogger Nas Daily. Having felt ignored for years, I was suddenly fielding hundreds of requests for interviews and podcast appearances.

If you looked at my phone today, you'd probably find the contact details of half the Hong Kong population there. My days went by in a blur of activity, until finally, in March 2020, one, then another senior shipping executive told me that there was no way I'd be joining a ship for the next four months, at least. (One kept my hopes up for a while longer by telling me that their ships were operating according to schedule – their crews would have to rotate on and off, so in theory there was scope for taking a passenger on. Nothing came of it.)

This didn't hit me as hard as you might think. I once read that time is not something that passes. It's something that comes. I like that. I like the idea that you have this infinite amount of time that's just washing over you. I thought of this, or at least tried to, whenever I was frustrated by delays. I'd tell myself that now I had this time that I could use for something else.

I felt sure that everything would go back to normal soon, or that people would work out systems to get people back on ships. It seemed inconceivable that the world was going to close. There was nothing I could do. I had been emptied by my experiences of the last few years. This was my opportunity to build myself up, ready for the big push through the last nine countries. I'd eat well, sleep well, exercise, read a bit, clear my mind, become a little bit more human.

Hong Kong had already been changed by its brush with SARS in 2003. Its population had been terrified by this mysterious virus that spread in ways nobody could understand, and that seemed to resist any attempts to defeat it. Summer was what killed it, not vaccines or public health measures.

Its legacy was a new kind of carefulness. When you take an elevator in Hong Kong you'll notice that the buttons are covered in a plastic sheet, which makes them easier to wipe down. When they set the table in a restaurant, you are given two pairs of chopsticks, one white and one green. One is for transferring the food to your plate, the other is for putting the food into your mouth. And everybody wore masks; there was no need for a government mandate.

In 2020, there was a belief, or perhaps it was more of a hope, that once temperatures rose, this new illness – by now it had been named and categorised as a pandemic; we were beginning to acquire new vocabularies, to understand what words like comorbidity meant – would fade away, just as it had seventeen years before. Then COVID-19 spread into some of the hottest places on

251

the planet, and that hope died. Hopeful talk of a vaccine coming soon had been succeeded by warnings that the testing process for these sorts of drugs usually took ten years. And yet that was also in some ways a relief. Everybody was affected. Everyone was in the same boat. It was no longer a problem for just me. This distinction really helped.

At the same time, I was also distressed by the lack of control I had over my own life. Even in my journey's bleakest moments I had been able to convince myself that I'd find the right door eventually, and I always had. Now, a global pandemic had snatched that possibility away. Robbed of my main reason for being here, I tried to set myself other challenges. Stuff that was neither too easy nor too hard. I found the name of Hong Kong's highest mountain, Tai Mo Shan, and tried to see if I could make it to the top and back in the same day. This was actually pretty simple – if I'd known Hong Kong better this wouldn't have been a surprise – still, the experience left me feeling good. If only for a few hours, my fate was back in my hands.

Then I found out about the MacLehose Trail, which runs across the entire 100-kilometre extent of Hong Kong, with 5,000 metres of upwards elevation, which is more than half the height of Mount Everest. I decided I'd complete it in three days, setting off with just my hammock, my mosquito net, my hat and a water purification kit. I began working my way through a book of hikes James had, as well as tackling Hong Kong's other three ultra-distance trails. Every time I went out, I was challenging myself to do the route harder and faster, pushing myself as much as I could.

Sometimes, this had unexpected results. One late afternoon I was on my way back to Cassie and James's home from Hong Kong city centre, where I'd spent the day. I had an evening meeting I needed to get to, so pressed on in the gathering dark, anxious to make sure I wouldn't be late. I remember climbing up a concrete staircase, music playing on my headphones, my eyes focused on each step ahead of me, sweat beginning to pool in the small of my back, when suddenly I saw a movement from the step above. Then there was elegant uncoiling; a long, black body darted sharply up, then flared its unmistakable hood and hissed. There, right before me, lit from above by the streetlamps that lined the path, was a cobra. I'd seen many snakes in Hong Kong, and hadn't been too bothered by them. This was something else.

I leaped up, hoisted skywards by adrenaline crashing through my body, and the cobra flowed swiftly beneath me, down the steps where I had just come from. For a wild few moments, I followed the snake, filming it on my phone; it was slowing down now and I wanted evidence of the cobra I had jumped over. I thought again, wondering whether it was worth the risk. Luckily, good sense prevailed.

As the world grew sicker and sicker, I became stronger and fitter than I had been in decades. But, more important than that, I was making new friends.

Until Hong Kong, my friendships had always been quite atomised. I'd never really had a clique or a gang of comrades, and had always felt the lack of it. As if something was missing from my life. I was never into team sports, so I didn't have people from that. And although I had served in the military, there was no group of us that met up to drink and reminisce about old times. This was exacerbated by all the time I had spent abroad.

I fell in with a group of five Danish businessmen who were also stuck in Hong Kong.

We started hiking, meeting each Thursday at 6 p.m. At the beginning, we might grab a beer or a sandwich afterwards, later we started going back to somebody's home for food and red wine.

We'd take it in turns to organise the whole thing. Eventually, the drinking and the talking became far more important to us than the relatively gentle exercise that preceded it. We started calling ourselves the 'The Dictatorship' because we all had to show up each Thursday, no excuses.

At a time when I didn't know when I was going to see Le again, the support and comradeship these men provided made an incalculable difference to me.

My living arrangements had changed too. After five months staying with Cassie and James, I'd moved to an apartment in Wong Chuk Yeung village for a month. The place was organised by two of my new friends from the hiking group.

There was a group of expats from Denmark, which among others included everyone from 'The Dictatorship', that I came to call the Danish Mafia, because they seemed to be involved in everything. You'd find the same people in the Danish Chamber of Commerce as you did on the Danish Church's council. And it was this last connection that saved me when I came to look for somewhere new to stay. There were two apartments attached to the church, but no minister or assistant to stay in them. Which is where I came in. To begin with I stayed in the reverend's flat, which was so absurdly large that I had to shut sections of it off, but for the first time in seven years, I had somewhere that felt like a home.

CHAPTER 15

# A Prison of My Own Making

*Hong Kong, November 2020 to January 2022*

The shadow that hung over me was my residency. I'd been given the right to stay for three months when I first arrived. This felt laughable at the time because I was only going to be there for four days. Then, to begin with it was easy to keep extending my paperwork with Hong Kong immigration. I'd just show up, fill out the form, pay the money, and my extension would come as a matter of course. Everybody understood that we were in a nightmarish situation.

Time passed, however, and their attitude changed. Immigration became more reluctant to let me stay for longer. They began suggesting that I look into flights home. I talked about my big, beautiful project, but this left them unmoved. Two-month extensions gave way to one-month extensions. Then just a fortnight. I could see where this was going. Suddenly, it seemed terrifyingly possible that unless I could find a solution, I'd be deported. I was thinking: *I'm nine countries from finishing this, and it's going to end with a deportation during a pandemic. This is insane.* It felt to me as if I had spent seven years carefully, painstakingly constructing a house of cards, a process that had almost emptied me. To begin with, the stakes were fairly low, my hands were steady. If it collapsed after a year, then what, really, would I have lost? Now, though, the edifice had grown higher and higher, become more intricate and also more unstable. I was haunted by the idea of it collapsing because of events that were completely out of my control. Seven years of my life would be wasted utterly, unrecoverably. As I added each new card to the pile, I could feel myself holding my breath.

At least three boats that I travelled on have since sunk to the bottom of the ocean. My malaria might have left me in a coma. Either case could have seen me evacuated by air, or dead. If I'd not grabbed the wheel of that car in Cameroon I might have woken, limbs mangled, in a local hospital, knowing that whether I liked it or not, I was going to be put on a plane home. There could have been an emergency in Denmark that demanded my urgent return. This knowledge of how thin and tenuous was the line between success and failure ate away at me at all times, creating a level of stress that I found almost insupportable.

Immigration told me I had three options: I could marry some-one local, start studying or get a job. I called the Danish Mafia and once more they came to my aid. I was appointed junior assistant to the Danish Seamen's Church. In one fell swoop I had a reason to stay and a small salary.

My formal responsibilities were minimal. I could have got away with doing a few hours here and there, but that felt like an empty way of filling my time. I helped arrange imports of the sorts of Danish food – sweets and rye flour, pickled herring, pork liver pâté – that weren't otherwise available in Hong Kong. We started selling it through the church. I also began to email Danish ships who docked in Hong Kong, asking them if there was anything they might want me to bring them. My first couple of emails were ignored, and yet over time their enthusiasm mounted and Hong Kong gained a reputation as a good port to stop in during a pandemic. We could get stuff done.

On the surface, my life was going almost as well as it could, all things considering. I loved Hong Kong, even as I realised that I was enjoying an artificial version of it, where there were no tourists, most of the locals were keeping their distance and the friends I'd made weren't able to fly off. It was like a brilliant playground. In many ways I cannot imagine a better place to have weathered a pandemic.

I would sometimes look back on the time I was delayed in the Solomon and Marshall Islands with gratitude. Without that, I would have come to Hong Kong a month earlier, and probably left it before pandemic restrictions were enforced. I might have been trapped on a tiny island, or at sea – on a boat with spiralling suicide rates, where dead bodies had to be kept in the ship's freezers, because there wasn't a single port that would have taken COVID-ridden corpses.

Some of my attraction to Hong Kong – somewhere I came to know more intimately than any other place I have lived, even Copenhagen – was obvious. The food is cheap, and excellent; I loved the dumplings, the beef noodle soups with their deep, fragrant broths. And I have never been anywhere more efficient. It's a region of over seven and a half million residents who have made a system that functions. You might approach a bus queue that seems endless, so much so that you convince yourself you'll never get the bus you want. Then within minutes ten buses will have arrived, whisking away everyone who had got there before you.

Other elements are odder, more difficult to explain. The waft of incense when you enter its temples; its colour-coded taxis (they would be red, blue, or green, which would indicate where they were permitted to drive); the washing hung up to dry between buildings protected by little figurines, and the bonfires that were lit and the food left out for restless ancestors during the Hungry Ghost festival – marks of superstitions that have not yet been eradicated by the twin forces of modernity and the Chinese Communist Party. And there was a mountain there called Ma On Shan, or Horse Saddle Mountain. There are other peaks nearby, some of them taller. They, like Ma On Shan, are covered in lush green vegetation. But in ways that I cannot articulate, even to myself, I feel a deep connection to it. It's the most beautiful mountain I've ever seen. More beautiful than any other I encountered while I was on my journey, or at any other time in my life. Whenever I was near it, I felt I had more energy.

I needed that energy, because even as I was enjoying what had been some of the best times of my life, I was being ripped up inside.

I had been away from Denmark for seven years. Just a few weeks before, I'd been told that I might be home within ten months. And yet I was stranded, with no idea when my situation would change, or any means of effecting that change myself.

The hardest thing about Hong Kong was the fear that there might be no end to the waiting. Nobody knew whether I'd be leaving the following day, or the following decade. There's a reason why on railway platforms they tell you when the next train is due: it's easier to hold on if you know how long you need to be patient for.

It's why the brotherhood I found with the guys in 'The Dictatorship' mattered more and more to me.

Towards the end of November 2020 the connections I was forging provided a chink of light. Over the course of a few beers, a Danish security guard told me about a colleague of his, a British guy called Max, who was able to bring his girlfriend and two daughters over by getting married online through an agency in Utah called WebWed.

This sounded insane. But I missed Le painfully; we had not seen each other for a year and three months – the longest we had been apart since I'd left in 2013. I spoke to Max, who gave me a rundown of all the documents I would need, which made it sound a hell of a lot easier than it would prove to be, largely because the people he was working for held a certain amount of sway in Hong Kong.

Still, on 19 December 2020 HKT (Hong Kong Time), my birthday (Le suggested this to ensure I would always remember it), I got married to Le for the first time. Although technically, because of the time difference and WebWed only having a limited number of slots, we ended up being married on different days: it was 10 p.m. on 19 December for Le and 4 a.m. on 20 December for me.

There were also a number of glitches in the app, which meant that none of our witnesses were able to log on. None of that could take away from the most important point: we were married! Then we both logged off, dressed in our finery, but each alone in our own apartments. The next morning, a group of my Hong Kong friends turned up with champagne. This, too, was lovely, and yet it didn't bring the moment I would see Le again any closer.

To do that I needed to assemble a mountain of paperwork. The Hong Kong ID (supplied once I had a job) and the marriage certificate (sent from Utah and somehow resembling something Christopher Columbus might have produced) were just the beginning. I would eventually cover an entire dining table with stacks of documents, including, but not limited to: our marriage certificate, our birth certificates and pension plans, my newly acquired ID card, my employment contract, printouts from my bank account; eighteen months' worth of WhatsApps sent between Le and me (this ran to 472 pages when printed out), to prove that this wasn't a sham marriage; photos from the wedding and photos from *after* the wedding, which were difficult to provide for very obvious reasons.

In a strange echo of my time in Central Africa, I found myself buzzing from office to office getting stamps and signatures. But, eventually, I got the visa I needed, sent it by courier to Denmark, and hoped that soon I would be able to see my wife. She would be coming for three months (if there was any silver lining to the pandemic it was that it meant her employers – by this point she was employed by a company conducting medical research – were happy for her to work from 'home', which meant for the first time since I'd left, we were able to spend extended periods of time in each other's company). There was another delay after she landed in February 2021: three weeks of hotel quarantine. But at least we were back in the same time zone, within 20 kilometres of each other. Her window looked on to an internal courtyard, so I couldn't wave to her, but I could step into *her* building.

Mostly, though, I waited, and worried. It is one thing to be apart for three or four months, or five or even six months. We had not seen each other for a year and a half. This was a little bit scary, especially in a long-distance relationship. You start to ask: how much have we drifted from each other in that time? Are we still OK? Are we still us?

At other times during the journey when Le and I met up, having been apart, we fell back into familiar ways of being immediately. We'd kiss and start talking and holding hands. This felt a little more cold. We did kiss each other, but it seemed as if we were trying to force something. It was just weird.

By this stage I had moved to the assistant's apartment – Maersk were paying for the rental of both units, and it felt unfair to keep somewhere that was barely being used. This meant that our married life began, not in the lush surrounds of the reverend's apartment, which had been flanked by a large green mountain, as well as offering a view of the water and urban islands, but part of the concrete jungle that surrounded the noise and dust of the port. I'd cleared a room that she could use as her office, and then started to show her the place that had become my home, introducing her to my friends and to Hong Kong as a whole, doing the MacLehose Trail together (she nailed it in under twenty-seven hours; it was rough for her, but that was when she became 'ultra wifey').

On the one hand, we had a spectacular time; on the other, I realised that it was unfair on Le. We were living in my world. They were my friends, culture – I never stopped feeling conscious of that imbalance.

The worst thing, though, was that it couldn't last. After three months she had to return to Copenhagen. I dropped her off at the airport, before returning to my car and sitting there for a while, tears pouring down my cheek. Even now, when I think about that moment, and all the many others like it, I am hit by a wave of sadness. (Six months later, Le, who now had her own Hong Kong ID card, was able to come again; this time her quarantine only lasted two weeks.)

It was these sorts of experiences that made me appreciate even more deeply the camaraderie I had with my hiking friends. I realised that I had come to Hong Kong with almost nothing and built myself a life. I wasn't just perching in that apartment while someone else was on holiday, or travelling for work; this place where I was cooking pasta and rice was *mine*.

My frustration continued as the pandemic dragged on. The powerlessness I felt metastasised and began to erode my confidence more generally. I feared that even if I did get out of Hong Kong, I might then discover that one of the final nine countries wouldn't give me a visa. Or that the only ship that sailed there would refuse to take me. I had nightmarish visions of being deported from one of the Pacific Island nations. Nobody waits around for a ship in those circumstances; you're gone on the next available flight.

About a year after I had first been marooned in Hong Kong, one of my closest friends called me to say that it was time to return. 'You've been away for too long. You're missing out on too much. You haven't been here for my son's last eight birthdays. You haven't been here for . . .' and he listed all the births and deaths and marriages I'd been absent for.

His advice was that I should decide now how much more time I was willing to give. Three months? Six months? Once chosen, I should regard that as my cut-off – the time when I bought an aeroplane ticket home. My state of fevered not-knowing was, to him, ludicrous.

I knew he was not alone in thinking this. And I respected him and his judgement. He was only being honest with me. I also knew that in many ways he was entirely, painfully correct. I was missing out on so much. The lives of people I loved and cared about in Denmark were carrying on without me. Babies were becoming children. My parents were in their seventies. I had to ask: what is of higher value to me, fulfilling the promise of the project, which I don't even know if I believe in any more, or going home and spending time with my mother and father before it is too late? I found that many days I woke up with no real answer to the question: why don't you go home?

There was one other thing that tortured me. I have always wanted children. I had fallen deeply in love with Le and knew that I wanted to start a family with her. And yet I knew that the longer I stayed away, the less likely this would be. We were both getting older.

We began to try in Hong Kong when she was staying with me. It felt important to go for it, even if it meant that in two or three years I'd be returning to a child who barely knew me. We had no luck, and I feared that I had already overstepped an invisible line, which meant that the moment that I would become a father was no longer possible. I tortured myself wondering when this might have been. Years, months, weeks, days ago? Had the project cost me the chance to have a child with the woman I loved?

And yet I could not give up.

There were several things that allowed me to cling on during this period, like a mountaineer digging his nails into a crumbling ledge. One was that I'd already invested so much time and effort in this project. A huge chunk of the best years of my life. All the pain, all the money, all the things I'd already achieved. I didn't want those to go to waste.

And there was the public element of what I had set out to do: I was living in a mental prison, which I had created.

Years ago, long before I ever considered making a wild journey around the world, I set out on a kayak journey around the third largest island of Denmark, telling everyone I knew what I was planning to do. I thought it would be amazing. And the first day was. Birds swirled above me in the sky; the sun shone; and it was exhilarating to see my own country from such a different perspective. On the second day I woke up in pain, with hands covered in blisters. I still thought I was doing something special, but I hurt. By the third day, I resented the task I had set myself. I was uncomfortable and lonely. I no longer considered myself lucky to be on such an adventure. Instead, I asked myself why I had ever left home at all, regretted that I'd done no training for a 300-kilometre journey, and thought about how much more enjoyable it would be if I was out there with someone else.

And yet I had told so many people I was going to paddle around this island. I didn't want to come back and tell them I couldn't do it because the sea was rough or I wasn't into it. I felt as if I *had* to do it, even though I knew that probably nobody would think the less of me. They might laugh at me for a second and then moments later we'd be talking of something else. What stopped me from giving up was all in my head; it was something particular to me, buried deep inside me. I could feel that something similar was true now. There were all these people cheering me on who I didn't want to let down. I knew that if I quit, they would keep their jobs, their families wouldn't fall apart, but I didn't want to disappoint them.

The difference was that, back then, all that had been at stake was my pride. Now, with the project, I had the chance to achieve something truly important. I was also conscious that the project was at least partly driven by ego. I had a chance at making world history, and I wanted to make sure that it was me that completed the task first; I couldn't bear the thought that somebody else might beat or better me.

Equally, I'd been supported by a number of different companies and brands. I hated the idea that their generosity would have been for nothing. More than that, though, as the project had gone on, I'd found myself receiving more and more heartfelt, moving messages from people telling me how my journey had inspired them. Some of them poured their hearts out, told me harrowing things about their personal circumstances. What I was doing had given them the strength to keep going. There were people who had been considering suicide before they had contacted me.

My attitude was: no matter what wall I bang my head against, I will find a way through it, or around it: I would find a solution. Every time someone told me no, I would thank them and then try something else. There is always a door. I would still achieve my goal, whatever that demanded of me. I wanted to show people that you can achieve things in life if you work hard enough for them, and so I could not be the one who quit.

Buried even deeper than that was something else: I wanted to make my father proud. Or, rather, I wanted to prove something to him.

On the day that I graduated – one of the rare occasions when he and my mother were in the same room – he had told me that the reason that he was so proud and happy was that he didn't think that I'd finish my course. He thought I'd quit. I realised that he thought I wasn't the sort of strong character who was capable of completing what they'd set out to do.

It was one of those moments when everything else falls away. The only thing you can focus on is this handful of words that is now buzzing around your head like angry hornets. I knew that it was possible, overwhelmingly likely in fact, that he had not thought about that comment a single time since. But over the years that followed, it continued to nag at me. I also remembered his initial scepticism about the project. This was the thing I had told the world I was going to finish, and I wanted to prove this version of my father, who had cut me so deeply, wrong.

Alongside this was something more existential. The whole journey became a question about what sort of person I was. Was I the sort of person who follows through when I say I'm going to do something? Or am I someone who quits when things get tough?

I have an arrogant belief that I'm better than other people, that I'm more stubborn than other people, that I'm able to hold out when other people will quit and go. To be able to sustain that belief, I need to prove it. And that means when I do want to quit, I have to hold on.

It's a form of competitiveness that is wired deep into me. So deep that I very often find myself in competition with a lot of people who do not know that they're in a contest.

Part of the training to be a part of the Red Cross involved taking an online workshop. It was a big thing that took many hours to complete. If you passed, you'd be awarded either bronze, silver or gold, depending on how many answers you'd got right. I wanted gold. When I didn't get gold the first time, I took the test repeatedly until I managed it. I had no idea if it made any difference to the examiners, but it was *essential* to me. I wanted to be top of the class.

I'm not a monomaniac. I know that there are some situations in life when it's the right thing to give up or change course. Perhaps you're on the wrong track, in a job that's going nowhere, a relationship that's unsalvageable. In those cases, the earlier you leave the better – far wiser to use that time and energy doing something valuable, that you care about.

I suspect nobody will ever be able to count how many copies of barely touched 'Teach Yourself French' books sit on bookshelves, or how many unplayed guitars lie sadly in basements. We pick these things up with good intentions, then after a few weeks we start to think that the new grammatical constructions we're learning are too hard, or that the guitar strings really hurt our fingers. So we give up.

That has been me too many times to count. I have the French book. I have the guitar. Even if some part of me still believes I'll pick them up again, I probably never will. But the project was different.

I knew that I could relieve the hellish mental situation I was in by going home. And I could find ten bulletproof reasons that would justify me quitting. When I got home everyone would applaud me for getting further than anyone ever had before. Everything would be wonderful for a while. I'd congratulate myself on having made the correction decision.

Then, maybe six months down the line, I'd see that three of those reasons were not as bulletproof as I'd thought. I would forget how hard things had been, I'd begin to find it harder to relate to the person who had been torn up by frustration and pain waiting for the world to open up or a solution to present itself. This is why we eternally repeat doing stupid stuff. Because we forget. Because we can no longer relate to the people we once were, or the circumstances we found ourselves in.

I would start to ask myself: why couldn't you tough it out? There would be a steady, grinding process of attrition. Seven reasons would become five reasons, then three reasons. Then the moment would come when I realised that I could not forgive myself for quitting. It would destroy my relationship with Le. I would be consumed by bitterness. I'd become the sort of person who could not stop talking about how close I had come, like somebody who cannot stop themselves from plunging their fingers into a wound.

I would no longer be able to explain to myself, or anybody else, why I had quit. And I would be eaten up by this, and by the fear that someone else would do what I couldn't, and that I'd read about it and think: *That could have been me.*

Time continued to pass. The overbearing heat and humidity of summer in Hong Kong – enough to turn walls in the countryside green – gave way once more to the chill that descends in the winter. I thought more and more about Shackleton and his men, and the ways in which their position – stranded on ice floes, desperately hoping for an opening – mirrored mine. Just like me, they had set out on an adventure that had turned into a nightmare, their ambitions crushed by forces outside their control.

There were, of course, key differences. They were trapped far from any signs of civilisation in an unimaginably desolate location, the white Mars-like landscape of Antarctica. They had to contend with frostbite, blizzards, a shortage of food and the very real threat that the ice floe they were standing on would disappear from beneath them.

I was in the comfort of Hong Kong, one of the safest places on Earth. If I abandoned the project, if I gave up, it wouldn't mean death, just taking a plane to Denmark. My struggle was not one of lack of comfort, hunger or overhanging danger. The struggle I faced was entirely in my mind.

It never stopped torturing me. In fact, the pain and frustration I felt only grew as time went on. Unable to make any progress I buried myself in activity. This gave me the feeling of motion: if I couldn't secure the one thing I desperately wanted, I could at least prove to myself that I was still capable of achieving *something*. As well as the constant, hopeless attempts to find a way out of Hong Kong there was everything I was doing for the Danish Seamen's Church, a collaboration with the Hong Kong Tourist Board, all the administration involved with arranged visits from Le. I signed up for ever more extreme physical challenges: completing the 100 kilometres of the MacLehose Trail in less than twenty hours, or the 48 kilometres of the Hong Kong Trail in less than six. In the course of one of these challenges I racked up 500,000 steps in one week; pushing myself so hard that I lost several toenails and thought I might lose a toe.

These things could divert me, sometimes for hours, even days, at time. But they could not change the central, incontrovertible fact of my existence: I was still drifting on my own ice floe. I was helpless, and it was killing me.

Hong Kong was one of the first places that got the vaccine. You had a choice of brand, it was free and, like everything there, enormously efficient.

Because I'd signed up for it so promptly, I was one of the first people to be able to take it, on 17 March 2021. I'd been told that if I wanted to have any chance of escaping, then it was essential to be vaccinated. This was the first plate I could feel shifting. What I also thought would act in my favour was the fact that the shipping industry as a whole had to work out a way of rotating seafarers on and off ships – because they couldn't stay on them for ever, they needed to be relieved when their contracts ended. This was, after all, an industry that the entire world depends on: 80 or 90 per cent of anything that's sold on this planet goes through these ships. I thought: *If they can bring seafarers on and off, then how far a stretch is it to bring a passenger?*

Quite a big stretch, it turned out. As far as they were concerned, anyone coming on to a ship increased the risk of the virus spreading on board, so they had no incentive to increase that risk by taking on a passenger who has no reason to be there. So my waiting continued. I got my second and third doses of the vaccine and carried on working at the Seamen's Church.

Occasionally, there would be a glimmer of hope. A month after I'd had Pfizer BioNTech's vaccine injected into me, I spoke to Roel, a Dutch guy who'd got stuck in Palau while on a business trip there. He told me that he knew ministers there, had become good friends with the president's advisor – 'I think I can make it happen for you before Palau opens officially.' Seized by enthusiasm, I started talking to Pacific International Lines.

My pitch was essentially: you can quarantine me for the entire trip, but if I can get inside Palau will you take me?

They responded with a million excuses, so I did the only thing I could: I spent the next six months trying to knock each one of those excuses down. I negotiated with the Palau Health Ministry, the authorities in Hong Kong, and anybody else whose support I needed. But every time I felt as if I was getting somewhere, there was a new variant of the virus and these intricate plans were blown apart.

Then, finally, on 5 January 2022, after 708 days of endless waiting, I stepped on to a ship bound for Palau. After so many months when I had waited without knowing when, or if, my torment would end, it felt to me as if I were dreaming. I managed the sixteen-day journey safely, only to arrive in Palau just after their first significant COVID outbreak. The net result of six months of work was spending a fortnight in isolation on board a ship, before arriving in Palau, where I was told that I'd have to spend the entirety of my stay there quarantining in my hotel room and generally being treated as if I had an especially lethal strain of Ebola. I read books, watched films, surfed the internet and discovered how hard it is to do 10,000 steps a day if you're confined to a single room. My Dutch contact assured me that this was a mistake and that I'd be out imminently. While he continued to assure me that I'd be escaping soon, I remained locked in that room. Eventually, eight days in, I was freed.

I then had another two weeks at sea, plus a week at anchor, before I walked back down the gangway to return to Hong Kong. Here, men wearing what looked like space suits came for me, put me inside something that resembled bubble wrap and drove me to a hotel where I quarantined for two weeks.

A month later, I joined a ship bound for Australia. It was hard to process how I felt. I was ecstatic to be able to continue the project after two years of agonising stasis. And yet I was also assailed by a sense of loss, almost of grief, about everything I was leaving behind me.

CHAPTER 16

# Timeless Tuvalu

*New Zealand, Tuvalu, June 2022 to February 2023*

One of the problems about Tuvalu is that it's so unbelievably hard to get to without flying that by the time you arrive, you already resent it.

Australia had been a gas. They just seemed to love me there; they got what I was trying to do, everyone seemed really interested in the project. I found myself on several talk shows. I began to be convinced that, finally, I was on easy street. I felt as if after years of waiting and frustration I could see the finish line. I remember thinking: *Why isn't every country like this?*

I was also able to carry on drawing on the well of contacts I'd built up in Hong Kong. My friend Poul, one of the Danish hikers, put me in touch with a company called Gold Star, who for convoluted geopolitical reasons were connected to ZIM, an outfit I already had a relationship with. They had a ship that would be able to take me to New Zealand. Incredible!

That euphoria lasted pretty much up to the moment I reached out to New Zealand's immigration authorities to find out how they felt about a passenger arriving on a container ship. Not good, it turned out.

I threw everything I had at the Kiwis – I said how close I was to completing this amazing project, I talked about the historical significance – but they batted it right back. As far as they were concerned, we were still in the middle of a pandemic and I was a risk they didn't want to take. Although of course, I was welcome to fly . . .

Luckily for me, in the gap between me first contacting the New Zealand authorities and them replying, somebody else from within their customs department alerted me to a little-known loophole, which stipulated that a passenger arriving on a container ship *can* enter New Zealand, and that customs in New Zealand would be fine with this.

I sent a (slightly) smug email to immigration pointing out the relevant paragraphs, and they agreed that, yes, I could come in after all. I was set! Except, *obviously*, something else had to go wrong because sometimes the world doesn't want to make things easy for you. The shipping company had re-evaluated their position: I was no longer welcome on their boat. This meant yet another call back to friends in Hong Kong, who in turn called their friends at the shipping company who in turn re-re-evaluated their position and decided that actually they didn't mind me travelling with them.

By this point I was suffering from a kind of administrative whiplash, but, with a last-minute negative PCR test under my belt (one in a sequence of negative tests, somehow I went through the pandemic without ever catching COVID-19), I was able to join the ship in Melbourne.

It was not a happy ship. The captain and most of the crew were from Ukraine. They'd come on board before Russia invaded the country in February 2022, and so the news of the attack was broken to them while they were at sea, almost as far away from their friends and family as they could possibly be. Worse still, there was barely any internet, so their ability to either find out what was going on or contact their loved ones was severely curtailed.

You could see instantly the toll this had taken on them, how distressed they all were. Although at least they had each other for solidarity. You could not say the same of the solitary Russian sailor on board. He was nobody's idea of a Russian nationalist; he just had the wrong passport. But he spent pretty much the entire journey on his own.

It wasn't until after we'd set off that the captain told me that New Zealand had a biosecurity rule that stipulated that the ship's hull had to be cleaned once every 365 days. Without that, we'd not be allowed to even approach the country.

This shouldn't have been a problem, as our route was supposed to take us from Melbourne to Sydney, then across the Tasman Sea to Auckland. The Tasman Sea has a reputation for being really rough, but in theory we'd be able to have the hull cleaned in Sydney. Except that the orders to do this never came, and so we left Sydney and headed into the Tasman Sea. Things got a bit rowdy, as expected, but nothing I hadn't experienced by this stage. Our best hope now, I gathered, was to get special dispensation from the New Zealand authorities. They did not give it, so instead we set to drift 22 kilometres from the shore, as close as we were allowed to come. The Kiwis sent out divers in boats to come to clean the hull. But they couldn't do the job because there was a 1-metre swell, which was apparently too high. And that, for a while, was that.

We spent weeks drifting in the Bay of Plenty. Each night the Ukrainians would get together, someone would bring a guitar, and they would scream their national songs. I was left to my own devices; the Ukrainians, who had a lot on their minds, barely engaged with the strange passenger in their midst and although the captain could sometimes seem OK, he could also be a real hard ass. This wouldn't have been a problem in a modern ship equipped with a gym, high-speed internet and all the other sorts of things we can do in the twenty-first century to keep ourselves occupied. But our ship was a tatty relic of a different time.

I was left to stare at the ocean and go slowly but decisively bonkers. I tormented myself by cursing the fact that I hadn't just hitched a lift with the divers. A glimmer of hope came when a local radio host caught hold of my story and asked if any of her listeners had a boat they could use to collect me. And one man did. What he *didn't* have was a permit that allowed him to sail 22 kilometres offshore.

The situation began to look bleaker when the captain informed me that our supplies of food and water were running low – we'd have to return to Australia soon if nothing changed. Things got bleaker still when we got caught up in the aftermath of a typhoon on the other side of the island, which meant any attempt to bring the divers back had to be postponed.

Then, finally, the weather cleared and the divers returned to clean the hull. I'd begun to accept that we might have to turn back to Melbourne; instead, I put my jacket on and got ready to land in cold, wet and yet somehow clammy New Zealand.

I liked New Zealand, an exceptionally beautiful country, especially because Denmark's honorary consul-general there, Inger Mortensen, is a wonderful human being.

The problem was, there seemed to be no way to get to Fiji, which I needed to do if I was to take advantage of the help that Swire Shipping had offered me. (It was unfortunate that they couldn't get me to Fiji themselves.) I could feel depression begin to mount. *Why does it have to be so hard? Why are there so few solutions?* Conversations with shipping companies went nowhere, either because they couldn't help me or because they simply refused to engage. COVID continued to cast its long shadow. The terrible thought that had stalked me ever since I had left Denmark nearly nine years ago reared its head again: *What if I can't make it? What if there's no way through? How long am I willing to give this?*

Aware that my finances were beginning to dwindle, I rented a camper van for a fortnight, paying upfront. It would be cheaper than staying in a hostel or hotel and I thought I'd be able to see a little bit of the North Island while I was networking and waiting for messages and calling people and replying to emails.

At some point during my first night in my new home, I received a message on social media suggesting I should contact a group of Christian missionaries who were planning to sail a hospital ship to Fiji, where they would fix people's teeth (most of them were dentists) while also trying to save their souls. They'd been waiting to set sail ever since the pandemic had started, and now they were ready to go.

I spent the next twenty-four hours in a blur of activity: driving two and a half hours from Waiuku to Tauranga, where the missionaries were based, to see if they'd be willing to take me (they would); driving two hours forty-five minutes back to the rental company in Auckland to return the camper van (they refused to refund any of the money I'd given them); then using public transport to make the journey back to Tauranga.

This should have been a positive experience. I'd found a route to the next country, and the way they were helping me was an embodiment of so many of the things I wanted the journey to show.

And yet, as I climbed to the front of the ship to take a selfie that I could post online to let the world know what I was doing and to show how grateful I was for the missionaries' aid, I did not feel happy, or calm, or relieved; I felt distressed. I composed my face into a mask that I thought resembled good cheer and pressed the button on my phone. No good. I tried again. I looked at the photo and realised: no one's going to buy that. My mouth was drawn up into a rictus grin, but the message my eyes were sending didn't match. I tried one more attempt, then another. Eventually I dragged something out of myself and produced something that did the job I needed it to.

It was moments like this that made me wonder whether I was now so locked into my ambition that my sanity was beginning to fray. I don't know how mad I actually went, but I do know this: the project damaged me, and I cannot be sure if I'll ever be right in my head again.

The missionaries were beautiful people. It was wonderful spending time with them as we slalomed along the coast, watching movies and stopping at different ports and sites of historical interest along the way. But neither their religious zeal nor their kindness could disguise the generally low level of seamanship aboard. One thing I'd noticed from having spent so much time at sea over the past years is that if your captain and chief engineer are competent and experienced, you can get away with a lot. Pretty much anybody else on board can be an idiot, but if they've got good people in those two key positions, and they're willing to listen to them and – this is crucial – resist the temptation to press any buttons, things will probably run OK.

The missionaries hadn't been taught to secure things properly, which led to several instances of stuff, including a flatscreen TV, sliding across tables. That was something they had to learn quick.

When they turned the heating on it proved too much for the electrical system. The engine cut out and panic spread quickly, until the chief engineer stepped in. We had another bout of anxiety one night when the engine cut out as we were passing through a fairly rowdy patch of ocean. There was a real hullabaloo as they tried to work out what had happened. It wasn't until the following morning that they discovered the culprit: a small can of oil from the engine room that flew off its shelf as the ship pitched. In a freakish turn of events, it had hit the engine's key and switched it off.

Then, as we approached the equator, we found ourselves dead in the water for a third time. With the weather heating up they switched the air conditioning on, which was, again, a challenge too far for the electrical system.

They'd rehearsed their drills and had all the right signs up in all the right places, so I was never particularly worried we'd go down – this was no soul seller. Nonetheless, I was relieved when we arrived in Fiji. The missionaries' reputation for good works preceded them, and they were greeted with a royal welcome. The Police Marching Band bashed out tunes before the British high commissioner delivered a speech. The missionaries tried to get some of the waiting press to take an interest in my story too. This was typical of their open-hearted generosity. A couple of journalists asked half-hearted questions, more out of politeness than anything else, and then their interest subsided, and I slunk off alone to continue my journey.

I made a lot of progress over the next few months. I hopped from Fiji to Samoa, to American Samoa, then to Tonga, New Caledonia, Vanuatu (where Le joined me, and we got married a second time), and then back to Fiji where I celebrated the new year.

And it was here that I secured my passage to Tuvalu. Tuvalu, the world's smallest nation by population, and probably the least visited country in the world, was the third to last place I needed to visit. It was also, for a long time, completely closed to visitors because of the pandemic. But for months I'd been hearing rumours that they were about to open up.

I waited anxiously, frustration gnawing at me as I drew on every contact I had in a futile attempt to persuade the Tuvaluan government to approve my arrival before they opened their borders. My desire to go was not enough to shift the dial, the decision was out of my hands. Finally, the day came. The High Commission of Tuvalu announced that they would start selling tickets for the ferry that took passengers from Fiji to Tuvalu – this service only ran on special occasions, and in this instance it was to help Tuvaluans who could not afford the airfare to return home for Christmas and New Year.

I was there the first morning the tickets were available. I'd arrived early in the morning, before the staff had had a chance to even drink a cup of coffee or turn their computers on. There was no way I wasn't going to be on that boat.

Inevitably we were delayed for twenty days by engine trouble and the need to load the ship with all the goods that couldn't be flown to Tuvalu. The journey itself was supposed to last four days. Another engine breakdown extended that to five but on 9 January we reached the island, where I encountered another surprise.

I'd assumed that because of all the delays the ferry would stop for a matter of days then turn around and return to Fiji. As far as I was concerned, it had no reason to stay any longer. Of course, I was wrong. The plan was to stay for a month because the boat needed a spare part. I swallowed my frustration, knowing there was almost nothing I could do. I'd explore the islands, I told myself, I'll fall in love with the island way of life. This is not what happened.

Once I'd found a guest house to stay in, I started to roam across the archipelago. As always, I wanted to be able to understand my surroundings as quickly as possible so I could write a fair assessment on my blog. I also needed something to occupy my mind to prevent the frustration that came with waiting impotently from eating me up. As a way of rescuing anyone who had been trapped by the stricken ferry, the government had offered to buy flight tickets back to Fiji. I was left stranded, so I tried to regain some measure of power over my destiny by setting myself the challenge of exploring each of Tuvalu's nine islands, an achievement so rare that very few of its residents had ever managed it. I learned a lot about the country as I did this, not all of it good.

The problem with Tuvalu is that it doesn't really deserve to exist: it's a failed state. There is no reason for it to survive. If it was swallowed up by the Pacific – and climate change means that this will happen sooner or later – few would miss it.

Tuvalu is not a place that has been abandoned. I have no idea how much money has been ploughed into it over the last decades. They've had support from the governments of New Zealand and Australia and China and Denmark, and almost nothing to show for it.

Every single good intention founders on the islanders' almost complete unwillingness to look after anything they are given. It's a harsh environment, because they're small islands surrounded by a mighty ocean. There's salt in the air, everything corrodes, engines break down far more quickly than pretty much anywhere else on Earth. But maintenance is not a word in the locals' vocabulary.

This means that the islands are littered with the rusting remnants of a thousand well-intentioned projects. I saw fields of solar panels that have collapsed in on themselves. There was a huge area where, five years previously, palm trees had been cleared to make space for the construction of a port. Not a single thing had been done since. Everywhere there were cars that had simply been abandoned to the elements.

And yet none of this dims the enthusiasm of keen foreign engineers and government officials, or the islanders' willingness to receive their largesse. The ship I had sailed there on was not particularly old. It just *looked* it because so little care had been taken over it. While I was there, I saw a delegation from Japan, who had supplied the first ship, and were there to see if the Tuvaluans wanted another.

Few people there work. Once, they had a reputation for producing really good seafarers. The Tuvalu Maritime Training Institute used to have hundreds of students, now there are only ten. And it is difficult to blame them. Nobody wants the extra cost of picking up seafarers from Tuvalu then getting them to Fiji, where a commercial ship might actually call. They're not sought for any more. And there's no industry, and little meaningful commerce. What are you going to do with 11,000 people? You're not going to open a Nike outlet. It is an insane place. You'd be lucky to pitch a tent.

As a result, the population rely on a trust fund set up for them and administered by Australia and New Zealand, and remittances sent back from those family members that made it to New Zealand and who, living there, forget about all the hardships and squalor and instead remember it as a paradise. This is supplemented by passive income that has essentially fallen into their laps. Their internet suffix is .tv. This means that streaming companies are keen to pay Tuvalu for the right to use it. They also sell fishing rights to the Chinese and make extra income by insisting that every Chinese ship has a Tuvaluan on board responsible for measuring the catch and certifying its quality.

The Tuvaluans know that climate change presents an existential risk to their nation. The land they live on is already being washed away from beneath their feet: on one of the islands, the smallest that was inhabited, I saw how erosion had felled palm trees. They lay flat, their roots still, just, attached to the soil; their crowns with the leaves attached washing sadly in the ocean. The storms that crash into the island are intensifying. One day, on the main island, I witnessed what was known as the king tide. The waters came up terrifyingly high, flooding inland houses and gardens. There was no wind to speak of then, it was unpleasant to contemplate what a huge wave might do to those tiny atolls. However, rather than fight it, they seem to be doing everything in their grasp to accelerate the process that will end with their homes being washed away by the rising oceans.

It's a flat country, so flat that its highest point (apart from a particularly mountainous rubbish tip) is only 4 metres above sea level; and it's a small country. Both these things should have made it perfect for cycling, a cheap, environmentally sound method of transport. But the inhabitants want to ride motorcycles and four-wheel drives instead. They don't care about the stinking fumes belching up into the atmosphere. All this stuff they consume, then dump, has to be brought to the islands on huge container ships, which increases their astronomical carbon footprint still further.

Their appetite for imported goods, matched with their disdain for almost all forms of physical exercise, meant that obesity was rampant. One night while I was on the island I got talking with a surgeon working there. We walked down the runway, which had been built by the Americans in the Second World War and was now the central feature of the main island. It was where the islanders came to play a ball game called Te ano, or other sports like volleyball or football. Some Tuvaluans would sleep there, because the open space was cooler than a closed room. At other times, it was like a social venue, for people to sit and chat or play music: the Tuvaluans know how to enjoy each other's company. And after dark, it was where young couples went for privacy, because there were no landing lights.

It's the only landing strip I've ever been to that I felt had a personality; perhaps it's no coincidence that its identifying code is FUN.

That evening the surgeon complained about how tired he was. 'I don't know how many more days I can keep this up.' I asked him what it was he did. He explained he was a surgeon who specialised in diabetes. Initially, this confused me. I hadn't realised that it was something that ever needed surgical intervention. We were in the glowing half-light coming from a party behind us, where the music was playing so deafeningly that we had to move further into the darkness to continue the conversation. Tuvalu was an incredibly quiet island most of the time. The only real exceptions were the Tuvaluans' motorbikes, their parties and the awe-inspiring tri-weekly arrival of a plane from Fiji.

The aeroplane's approach is announced by a motorbike ridden by two men. One steers and the other has a handful of rocks that he tosses at dogs to get them to vacate the runway. Then there's the piercing screech of an air horn. That's the first warning. A minute or two later it goes again, and then it sounds a third time as the plane descends.

It comes within seconds, making an unspeakable noise, its wind buffeting everyone nearby, blowing left and right. It touches down on the tarmac, spins around, then comes to the terminal. People walk out of the aeroplane and the crew switch off the engines while cargo is offloaded and new passengers climb up. Forty-five minutes later it takes off, there's another incredible roar, and then silence falls upon the island once more. The first time I witnessed this I was awestruck, almost shaken. It is like watching a visit from aliens. (They are currently building landing strips on three or four of the other islands. A pilot and an aeroplane have been donated. All of this is insane.)

'No,' said the surgeon, in a voice I imagined he reserved for his slowest students, in response to my query about operating on diabetes. 'I spend my days cutting off limbs. Arms, legs, hands, fingers, I do all of this so that they can go back to cram more disgusting food and fizzy drinks down their necks.' They used to exist on a diet similar to the one I'd enjoyed on the Solomon Islands. That had been replaced by imported rice, processed meat and Coca-Cola, and the Tuvaluans had grown fat and sick.

As well as an airstrip, Tuvalu also has a prison. My landlady, a kind, very savvy woman called Penny, had told me about it. 'Who does it hold?' I asked her. She told me three murderers. I got my map out and decided to walk there, wending my way past brightly painted concrete houses fringed by unkempt gardens filled with old washing machines or disintegrating cars that would never be driven again. When I got to the location I thought it should have been in, I stopped, baffled by the absence of any building that even remotely resembled penal architecture.

I tried again the next day and, having lowered my expectations as to what a prison should look like, had more success. But, again, I was baffled. The compound's gates were open. I approached the cheerful-looking man in island clothes – baggy shorts that reached below the knees and a sleeveless T-shirt – who was sprawled on a plastic chair nearby. Earlier on that day I'd seen him walking near the edge of the runway, bending down slowly to look for a piece of grass to clean his ear out.

*He's a guard*, I thought. We shook hands and talked. Eventually I realised how wrong I had been: he was an inmate. The prisoners were allowed out as far as the tarmac during the day. Instantly, the conversation became even more interesting. He told me that he'd got into a fight that had spiralled out of control and had accidentally killed the other guy.

I left him, feeling sympathetic. These tragic mistakes happened, I told myself, it's a shame that somebody has to pay such a price.

Penny disabused me of all of this as soon as I got back to the guest house. In truth, my new friend had lured his victim to a remote corner of the island, then killed him with the weapon he had brought for that purpose.

Still, I thought, where else can you walk up and shake hands with an incarcerated murderer? He could have run away any time he wanted, but where was he going to go? He was trapped. And so, I realised, was I.

The tourist board's slogan for the country is 'Timeless Tuvalu', which has an ironic tang for me: time means nothing to the people there, but that's not something to be celebrated. Tuvalu is a place where it is hard not to reach for the bluntest absolutes. There's no progress. Nothing ever gets done. Everything there is getting worse every day. It has elements of its own unique culture, but there are a hundred unique cultures across Fiji. There are probably thousands of unique cultures in South America. What would we be saving if Tuvalu disappeared under water? How much would we be losing? Its tragedy isn't the threat of climate change, it's the fact that this place, which should be a paradise, which would have been a paradise two hundred years ago, does not know how to exist in 2024. If it had been a company, it would have long since been forced into bankruptcy.

What redeems the country, even as it makes its plight more frustrating, is that the people of Tuvalu are, almost without exception, delightful. Collectively they have a very big heart. Very often I'd be walking down the street and I'd hear a shout. When I looked round, I'd see a woman in a beautiful dress covered in a bright print of palm leaves or flowers, a flower tucked charmingly behind one ear, leaning out of her window frame to invite me to come to sit down and have lunch with the family. I lost count of the invitations I received to eat, or dance, or listen to music with the locals. This made my time there more bearable: every time the sight of waste or inefficiency threatened to send me into a spiral of rage, an act of kindness or generosity would bring me back from the edge.

And one other thing that was in my favour was my return ticket. Its presence seemed to make the authorities there feel responsible for me.

The Tuvaluan government owned four boats. They were all, true to form, absolutely infested by insects of every kind. Their filth and disrepair had made a paradise for cockroaches, who had responded to their environment by breeding promiscuously.

And, also true to form, three of the vessels had broken down. Only one was still fit to operate. Its main job was connecting the nine islands to each other and also the outside world. If somebody needed to be evacuated, it would be on that boat. This meant it couldn't be spared for a trip to Fiji. At least until it was discovered, a few weeks after I'd arrived in Tuvalu, that it desperately needed to go to the shipyard in Fiji.

The men at Tuvalu's marine office told me that it had a hole in its bottom, which had been temporarily plugged the year before, and was taking on water through its drive shaft, but if I was willing to take a risk, I could hitch a ride. A few hours later, I found myself on board an American-built vessel from the mid-sixties called the *Tala Moana*, which means 'Story of the Sea'. I had been on the island for so long by now, and spent so much time hanging around the port in an attempt to escape, that I already knew most of the crew, who began laughing at me almost as soon as I'd climbed down the gangway.

'You're sharing a cabin with Makolo, he's the loudest snorer in the South Pacific.'

I looked down at the dirty floor beneath my feet. Some of the timber was splintering and a cockroach scuttled over my shoe. Snoring seemed like the least of my problems.

Anyway, we were leaving that afternoon, and what was more important than that? Immigration and customs came and, rather than leaving again, decided to join the party, sitting with the others on deck around a large table, eating and gossiping and playing music. The party spirit that animated the little landing strip had been brought aboard by these cheerful people who were all either related or knew each other from church – almost everyone was a devout Christian – or school or a sports club.

I smiled and sang with them, before remembering that I needed to take a seasickness pill; this was a small boat and I sometimes struggled with being on board them.

I popped a tablet in my mouth. An hour or so later, as the party continued around me unabated, I began to feel drowsy. Suddenly nothing about the ship felt quite real. Blearily I started to think. Immigration had my passport, but then it was usual to surrender your documents to the captains, so I decided it was of no great importance to me. I'd go to bed. Maybe the engine's rumbling would wake me when the ship sailed off. Or perhaps it would be when we started rolling as we headed out to sea? A happy image of being woken by the sun as we sailed through the Pacific flashed through my mind. Not long after, my hands feebly trying to brush insects off my torso, I fell asleep.

The next morning, I woke to find myself, and the *Tala Moana*, still very much in Tuvalu. The same was true of the next morning, and the morning after that. More time passed. Before long, I realised I'd now spent two months in a place I'd hoped to escape within days. Occasionally our vessel would make a trip to the other islands in the archipelago. Most of the time, though, we simply wallowed in the same spot we had started in.

Nobody explained to me what was happening, or seemed at all bothered that we had not left yet and showed no signs of leaving soon. This was what everybody means when they talk about island time: everything gets delayed, everything unfurls at a super-slow pace, and no one cares. They treat these events as if they don't matter. Their attitude is: just roll with it. Don't look for an explanation or an answer. I, by contrast, had a berth on a Swire ship that would take me from Fiji to Singapore. The thought of missing it made me sick.

But I was part of the ship now. And I had a routine. On each of the twenty-seven mornings I spent aboard I'd get my breakfast of instant noodles and a cup of tea (I could take these for free, which was important because there are no credit cards on Tuvalu and no ATMs, so unless you can arrange a money transfer you have to make the cash you bring with you go a long way), then go up to the *Tala Moana*'s tiny bridge, which had just one chair for the captain, as well as space for all the buttons and displays. I'd look out of the window across the vessel's bow, at the bay and the lagoon beyond it, all the time drinking my tea and thinking: *This project's never going to end. This is insane. This is the third last country. I have no idea how I'm going to get away from Tuvalu.*

During the day I'd try to follow up on the scraps of information I'd managed to glean from anyone I thought might potentially know something useful: the marine office, seafarers, government officials, nonprofits, shipping agents. Usually they'd go nowhere. I expected this. I think I'd absorbed some of the fatalistic island spirit. When it came to other meals, I ate what people offered me. Since everyone on board was a fisherman, and the people here loved rice, I could usually guess what the main components would be. Sometimes the fish would be raw, mixed with coconut oil and spices. Sometimes it would be fried. But there was an astonishing variety of fish, including the sandfish, a local delicacy. Its abrasive skin made me feel as if I had a mouthful of sand each time I tried eating it, and it was so oily that I once vomited after eating too much of it. Generally, though, I looked forward to my meals. They were moments of pleasure and sociability in an otherwise fairly bleak schedule.

Then, one day, as I sat there in the captain's chair, his radio crackled into life. I overheard a brief conversation between the captain of a tugboat called *Katea* and *Katea*'s agent. I'd learned enough while on the island, and on the journey more generally, to avoid the trap of getting too excited. The story of the last nine years was in many ways a tale of my hopes rising then crashing in pieces back down to the floor.

But this was interesting.

I already knew that *Katea* was going back to Fiji; however, I had been under the impression that this was likely to happen in two weeks' time. I'd been trying to get in touch with the agent to see if they could help me get on board, without much luck. Largely, I discovered, because the actual agent was someone else. (This was the danger of the classic lead which begins, 'I think my cousin can help . . .' They almost always couldn't.)

All that was forgotten now, because I'd heard the *Katea*'s captain say: 'It's Saturday, we need to clear customs today because we're sailing tomorrow and tomorrow's Sunday.'

That made sense. Nothing happens on Sundays in devout Tuvalu; you're not even allowed to go for a run.

The agent replied: 'I'm working on it. Everything will be done today. No worries, you can leave tomorrow.'

And this was when I began to get really excited. I *knew* that agent. He was Mr Apisai, the agent of the only container ship that called at Tuvalu which, he had told me, was definitely *not* taking a passenger. His office, where presumably he was speaking from right now, was just a few hundred metres from where the *Tala Moana* was moored.

I leaped up, threw my tea away and sprinted to his office, bursting through the door and almost screaming, 'Remember me? Can you talk to *Katea*? Can you ask if I can get on board?'

He did, and they could. There was an extra bunk bed. I had a way out of Tuvalu. As I started to process what this meant for the project, I also tried to work out how unbelievably lucky I'd been. Coincidence piled upon coincidence.

What were the chances of me sitting there near that radio at precisely the moment the captain and agent had that very brief conversation?

But fate had taken an even bigger hand. Ships' radios are always set to channel 16; this is as true for a cruise ship as it is for a container ship or a fishing boat. Channel 16 is the open channel. Anybody can contact you, and you can contact anybody. It's the channel that you use to call agents, or issue an SOS. Once you've made contact, you might then go to channel 12 so you can speak at length without disturbing anyone. After the conversation is over, you go back to 16.

But for some reason, presumably because somebody had forgotten to switch the dial back, the *Tala Moana*'s radio was not set to channel 16, as it should have been, but channel 14, where the private conversation between *Katea*'s captain and the agent was unfolding.

You'd win the lottery fifteen times before something like that should happen. It was the kind of thing that reinforced my belief that anything that can happen will happen. Sometimes you're just in the position to experience it.

## CHAPTER 17

# Return to the Lake

It was a battle right to the end. In each of the last three countries there were obstacles. None of them were particularly significant, they were niggles really, but I had been away from home for almost ten years and my appetite for solving problems had long since shrunk to almost nothing.

Having finally escaped Tuvalu, I sailed to Fiji (my fourth visit there), where I joined another ship, which took me to Singapore. Here there was a wrangle about my visa, which was annoying but quickly fixed, and I sailed to Sri Lanka, where I arrived on 11 May 2023, having used the ship's eccentric internet connection to resolve another visa issue.

The authorities here were surly and suspicious. They were not interested or excited by my project or the fact that they were the penultimate nation on my list, they just wanted to know why I had come to their country on a container ship. I didn't make sense to them.

None of this was new, but what was new was the emotion I felt once I had finally cleared immigration, or, rather, what I *didn't* feel.

Every time I had crossed a border before, it had been joyful, because I knew that it represented both an achievement and an opportunity. Now, I felt nothing beyond a flat, grey numbness.

This troubled me immediately; I could not understand it. I still do not. My fear is that this moment was a kind of watershed. Before then, I had felt plenty of joy, even amidst the hardest moments. From that moment on, though, I would still experience the same frustration and anger when I had setbacks, when I had a win, when things went my way, I would only be conscious of an absence. And that remains true now.

This was exacerbated by a sadness that had begun to recur as I approached the end of the journey. I was still capable of smiling, laughing and getting distracted, but when I had nothing to occupy my thoughts, it would seep in. I'd feel sad when I woke up, sad when I went to sleep, and never knew why. I was aware that I'd been through a lot, and yet it had the same, inexplicable quality of my entry to Sri Lanka. Why should I be sad now with a beautiful wife who loves me, caring parents that are in good health and many friends? I was less burned-out by work, I was approaching the moment when I'd see the light at the end of the long tunnel of countries.

I was hesitant about calling it depression, I did not want to minimise the suffering experienced by those who have been diagnosed with it. And yet I had this sense, which had descended at various times during the project, that I was sinking slowly below the surface of a dark bottomless lake. Even though I could still see the outline of the sun, even though I was not lost, it frightened me.

A film I'd seen recently, about loss and depression in the ski world, made me wonder whether I was experiencing a cousin of what afflicts some professionals when they step away from the sport. For good or for ill, the project had administered various, often quite violent, rushes of adrenaline. Now they were fading, I wasn't getting them any more. I was having to face up to the idea that I was about to lose my identity as the guy who has been trying to navigate a journey through every country without flying and into the role of the man who has done it. And that begged the terrible question: what is next?

For now, though, I tried to push these thoughts aside and focus on taking the photo I would post to announce my arrival. I tried twenty times until I managed an expression that looked like a plausible impression of a happy person.

I was joined in Sri Lanka by Mike Douglas, a filmmaker who was making a documentary about me. We'd quickly formed a bond in the time we'd already spent together; it was a relief to connect with somebody who, almost instantly, seemed to understand everything I had gone through since I'd first left home. It was like having a friend. We were bonded by the same cultural language, but more than that, Mike's *full* interest was devoted to me; which had an almost narcotic impact on someone as lonely as I was.

He'd originally been commissioned by Salomon, the company that made my shoes, to film a short that could be used to help promote their products. Very quickly his ambitions and enthusiasm grew, and he told me that he wanted to make a full documentary about my journey. He had joined me for stretches in the Marshall Islands and Fiji, following me around with his camera, which instantly changed the nature of what I was trying to do. It is useless to pretend that you are assimilating into a local culture when every step you take is being filmed.

But his presence, and the sense of validation his interest in my story had given me, helped smooth over the disquiet I had felt on entering Sri Lanka, and it was exciting to have him by my side, filming, as we made the short, one-night hop to the last country on my journey: the Maldives.

Here, again, there was a bit of administrative grit that threatened to frustrate the operation of my travelling machine. I was told that because of an obscure piece of local regulation about container ships I wouldn't be able to disembark. It was maddening, because we were so close. I knew that if I simply leaped overboard I'd be able to swim ashore without any difficulty. The angry part of my mind was screaming inside me: *Where's the red carpet? Where's the celebration? Where's the welcome? Where's the well done?* But I knew it would not help to let any of this spill out. There was more wrangling, I pleaded my case, we argued some more, then it happened; they set me free.

A single small speedboat, little more than a dinghy, came to meet me. I got in, we blasted off to the shore, and I stepped on to the soil of the last country I needed to visit to complete the project. Suddenly, frustration and stasis gave way to almost frantic movement, which left me no space to think about what I was feeling, or even to savour a moment I had thought about endlessly for almost a decade.

I was hurried through a little port, and then emerged to the sight of a cluster of friends and family, who had been waiting, sweatily, in the heat for me to arrive. Le, my friend Lars, CEO of Ross Energy, and his wife, representatives from Maldives State Shipping, Gunnar Garfors, the Norwegian who's been to every country twice. Above them Danish flags flapped sluggishly. Cameras snapped, I posed for photos, shook clammy hands, embraced those I was closest to.

Still, I felt no major wave of happiness.

The pressure and the activity continued, even as I sank, or tried to, into the luxury of a resort stay that had been organised for me by a friend, Jessi, who I'd first met in Oman. There were interviews with press from across the world, I did my best to do my experience justice in a series of social media posts, I completed all of the work I had always done when I arrived in a new country, and I was whisked from one place to another, from lunch to dinner, without ever really having ten minutes to myself to try to compose my thoughts and process what had happened, and was happening still.

After five days, Mike and Le left. I travelled around a bit more, visiting Malé, the nation's capital, an extraordinary forest of skyscrapers that looked like an attempt to transpose New York to a tropical island. I walked around wondering at the fact that so much concrete had not caused this low patch of land to sink into the sea.

But mostly I was waiting for the boat that would take me home. I had made the decision before I'd arrived in the Maldives that I would not fly back to Denmark. I would close the circle. I didn't want to leave space for somebody else to surpass what I had achieved; it felt right, more true to the spirit of the project. It would have been insane to return home on a flight and be welcomed at the airport.

More importantly, I needed a long, slow journey home to give me time and space to acclimatise myself to the thought of going back to Denmark. I hadn't really speculated to myself what sort of place I would find, or what sort of shape my existence might take when I got there, and I did not know exactly how I would react to it all, but it was hard to believe I wouldn't be affected profoundly. I was worried about the shock of return. After all, I was so hard-wired now to a particular way of life. What would it be like to live in the same place, day after day? See the same people, day after day? Share a home with Le?

That this gentle re-entry was possible had been confirmed in an email from Maersk, sent while I was sailing to Singapore, which informed me they had secured berths for me on all the remaining ships I needed to complete the project, as well as take me home.

That was the moment, really, when the saga became a success. All I had to do was avoid death or serious injury. Looking back, I wonder if this knowledge explains the flatness I experienced when I reached Sri Lanka and the Maldives.

The journey home was languorous and pleasant. There was something deeply satisfying about passing a country and knowing that I had been there. Even when I couldn't actually see land, I followed our progress on the chart that was up on the ship's bridge. Everything runs like clockwork on Maersk ships, so I did not have to fear the delays and complications that had plagued me for the last nine years.

The only time I felt uncomfortable was when we entered the Mediterranean, the sea in which the unfortunate refugees whose bodies I encountered on a Libyan beach had died. Suddenly I found that I couldn't look at the water.

It was around this time that I first noticed the climate we were travelling through had changed. The air temperature fell, it became less humid. As we rounded Portugal and started heading up France's western coast, the smells drifting across to our ship became steadily more familiar. Something about the colours in the sky was different now, even the winds felt more caressing, as if they were welcoming me home.

My happiness increased as each day passed. I remember being on board while we stopped in Rotterdam to offload some cargo. I was looking, almost in disbelief, at cows grazing in a field nearby, and thinking: *This looks just like Denmark.*

Before we reached Gothenburg, Sweden, our last stop ahead of Aarhus, we left the English Channel and entered the North Sea. I went to the side of the ship and stared at the water below. *That's Danish water*, I thought. *Above us is a Danish sky. The birds soaring in it are Danish birds. The clouds floating in it are Danish clouds.*

Then, on 26 July 2023, 3,576 days and over 380,000 kilometres after I had first left Denmark, the *Milan Maersk* arrived in Aarhus.

I should remember more of my homecoming, but I don't. I cannot really tell you what my immediate response to stepping back on to home soil was, beyond a vague fuzzy happiness at having closed the circle. As with the Maldives, the energy and noise and activity that surrounded my arrival gave me little chance to metabolise what I was experiencing.

My friend Søren had done a phenomenal job of organising my welcome. While waiting for the moment I could officially disembark, I stood there at the top of the enormously long gangway – the *Milan Maersk* is one of the world's largest container ships – gazing down at the country I had not seen for nearly ten years. Beside me was the ship's captain, who had tears in his eyes.

Finally, it was time. I strode down, closer and closer. The faces of the people waiting for me gradually came into focus. There was Le, my father, and my sisters. *No more travelling*, I thought. *No more stress over visas, or pandemics, or checkpoints, or missed connections, or boats breaking down, or typhoons. No more nothing.* I stopped at the last step and lifted my foot up, letting it hover above the ground for a few seconds. Then I jumped into Denmark.

It was amazing to give Le, my father and sisters a hug. Rain started to pour from the skies as we walked from the gangway to an open shipping container with space for twenty-five VIPs and a jazz band playing 'When the Saints Go Marching In'. From here we moved to a workshop, which held fifty people, then the port office's auditorium, where Søren had gathered a hundred and fifty well-wishers, the maximum we were allowed.

Some were family and friends, others were people I'd never met before, who had just started following the project online. There was the secretary general of the Danish Red Cross, people from the Danish Travellers' Club and Tupperware boxes full of traditional Danish food. I delivered a tired, emotional speech, and I found my hands full of gifts, including Danish milk. I lost count of the number of photographs that were taken.

All of it was fabulous, like bathing in warm sunshine, and all of it now feels like a blur. Too much was happening too quickly, my senses were being overpowered by a million different sensations.

Eventually, people began to drift away. Le and I escaped to a restaurant in a small marina nearby. Finally, it was just the two of us. As we ate, we checked in on each other and, still dressed in my uniform, I tried to explain how surreal I was finding the return. Everything, even the pickled herrings and rye bread on our plates, had the hallucinogenic quality of an intense dream.

After that, we drove to Bryrup, my father's home, the village in which I'd grown up. At some point that day, Le and I decided to go for a run around the lake that had been so important to me as a boy, the first time I had done this for over ten years. We started on the more built-up north shore then jogged clockwise – as I always had when I was younger. Gradually, houses and shops gave way to open heathland, then forest.

Once you are on the south side of the lake, you find yourself far closer to the water; we were almost running beside the shore. And it was then that the smell of that lake hit me, like a memory suddenly resurfacing from a hidden corner of my mind. It was a scent completely unlike anything I had encountered anywhere else in the entire world.

Here I was then, home.

It took a while for the media interest to die down. A lot of people wanted interviews. It was odd, but not unwelcome, to swap hostels and hammocks for plush TV green rooms.

A month after I returned to Denmark, I started getting ill. I suffered a sequence of different ailments, each of which seemed to come and go after a handful of days. Parts of me would swell up, or I'd get an eye infection, or suddenly be afflicted by diarrhoea. For four weeks, it felt to me as if my body was reacting. I remember reading once how many parts of an astronaut's physique are affected after they return from space. Perhaps I was experiencing a version of this.

Three months in, something strange happened. A voice appeared in my head. I knew three things: it was in English, not Danish; it was very clear; and it wasn't my voice. Other than that, it was a complete mystery. It would come when I was engaged in routine things like brushing my teeth, or tying my shoelaces, saying: *Don't give up. Don't give up. Don't give up.* The voice would stay for a while, before disappearing, then returning a few weeks later.

It still comes, even now, though it happens less. I don't really mind it; more than anything, it leaves me curious. Is it some kind of aftershock from my attempts to hold on during the most stressful moments of the project? Or is it referring to something else entirely? I don't know, I probably never will.

I'm trying to work out other puzzles, too, like what it really means to be home, or what home even means.

Time and space allow you to see and hear aspects that aren't possible when you live alongside something every day. It was only after I went for three years without seeing my mother that I realised that she had a Finnish accent. Being away from Denmark has changed my relationship with the country. Some of this is to do with seeing it differently. On my return to Copenhagen, somewhere I'd always thought was a definitively Western European city, I was struck by how much it resembled Eastern Europe: there was its .

small metro with the yellow poles, and many of its buildings might have been found in Warsaw or Bucharest.

I think, too, that the project has accelerated something that has always sat inside me.

I have spent so much of my life trying to be more Danish, and I'm still working hard at it now. Since my return, I've been to a ton of museums in an attempt to understand my own country. I have this thought that if I know where I come from, then it will be easier for me to find my way back home. Because although Denmark is, technically, my home, it is not somewhere that I feel at home.

I know everything about the country. We all have the same IKEA glasses, the same size flatscreen TV and car; there aren't many Lamborghinis. Our walls are decorated with reproductions of Monet's *Water Lilies* and that famous photo of American construction workers having their lunch on a beam perched perilously above New York City. We go skiing in the Alps, sunbathing in the Canary Islands.

I know the language better than any other language. I instinctively know where to look for milk in a supermarket. If I see a spider crawling across the table, I know it cannot harm me – which is not something I'd be able to say with any confidence in any other country around the world. I can tell you obscure details about our electoral system, and what the etiquette around waiting for buses is. I know what village life in Denmark is like. I know what city life is like. In all these ways, it is definitely home, and yet I still feel misplaced.

I don't care about a lot of the Danish things. I'm not into football, I'm not into handball, I'm not into a bunch of stuff that everyone else here loves. I think I probably want different things to most of the people I live alongside.

There is a famous novel here – Aksel Sandemose's *A Fugitive Crosses His Tracks*, written in the thirties – about a fictional town called Jante that came up with its own rules for how its residents should behave. There are ten of them, but they can be best summed up collectively as: *You are not to think you're anyone special, or that you're better than us.* Although all of it is made up, the rules sum up a form of disapproval that's still widespread. We call it Jante Law.

You could be the greatest athlete of all time, but you cannot say: 'Look at what I did. Look how fantastic I am.' Instead, you praise your teammates, or smile and say that you just got lucky.

My project does not sit well with Jante Law. Instead of staying at home with a job and a family, I was dedicating the best part of my life to a crazy whim. It's the act of a show-off. I got messages from Danes saying things like, 'Why did you even do it? You should have been at home playing your role in society, paying taxes.'

It's not just that I didn't become the most famous person in the world, I have received barely any recognition in my own small country. Take, for example, the Danish Red Cross's website: there's no mention that I have done what I've done, even though I've been to more Red Cross offices than any person in history, raised huge sums for them and promoted the movement across the world. And, more broadly, I've found it hard to communicate my experiences to people because they seem unable to relate to them. This is something, I've learned, called exulansis. I feel like somebody trapped on the wrong side of a glass wall. Everyone should be able to see and hear me calling for help, but they carry on as if I don't exist.

I've really struggled with all that. If it wasn't for Le, I probably would have moved to a different country already. She is my anchor, the thing that roots me to Denmark. If she ever wants to go somewhere else, I will follow her. It is hard to see what else is keeping me in Denmark.

One thing that I had to come to terms with after my return was the idea of being forty-five, living in a time when I can reasonably expect to last until I am a hundred years old, and knowing that with over half my existence still to come, the greatest thing I will ever do is behind me.

The sadness, or depression, I felt towards the latter stages of the project returns occasionally. There are days when I fear that I am not really sure who I am, what it is that I'm actually *for* now. Am I a hasbeen? Someone who once did something?

And yet I know that it is possible to turn this around, to say that I'm one of the people on this planet that can look at my life and say, I actually accomplished something. That I do not need to top what I did. I know the value of what I've achieved, and this is not diminished, for me at least, by the knowledge that we no longer live in a world that cherishes, or is excited by, adventurers. In 1928 another Dane, Palle Huld, a teenager at the time, won a competition in honour of Jules Verne that gave him the opportunity to circumnavigate the globe unaccompanied. He did this in forty-four days, and was welcomed back to Copenhagen by a crowd of twenty thousand. The book he published about his experiences was translated into eleven different languages; he reportedly inspired Tintin. I was greeted by a hundred and fifty (I loved that they came, and am so grateful that they did). Nobody cares what adventurers do or say now.

This does not mean that I want to stop. I already have a plan to travel to Antarctica. I would love to go to the South and North Poles. I'd like to climb the seven highest mountains on the seven continents. I'm not even close to done, because I still want to stuff myself with as much experience as I possibly can.

This is another subject that has preoccupied me. What is life experience? Where does it come from? Do we all absorb it at the same rate?

The simple answer is that it comes simply from existing, from breathing and working and being around other human beings. What I have started to believe is that it is possible to accelerate that process. If you are doing the same thing every day, going to the same supermarket, seeing the same friends at the football club, eating the same potatoes and gravy, you're unlikely to evolve quickly. That rapid evolution only comes when you're constantly challenged, when you are constantly going to places where life and the way it is arranged do not make sense and you have to *think*. I was challenged relentlessly for the better part of a decade, which makes me wonder how old, in terms of life experience, I really am. Even now I feel heavier, as if I'm dragging around with me an enormous burden of accumulated sensory and emotional debris. Flashes of these challenges emerge at random times, suddenly transporting me back to something I haven't thought about for many years.

I am still trying to work out how the project has changed me. Even if I think I will never truly understand the ways in which it has reordered my mind and body, some of it is straightforward.

I look at the world map in a completely different way from most people, because with any country you could point at, there's a story. There are memories. To say that I've been to every country in the world is also to say I've tasted something in every country, I've heard something in every country, I've seen something in every country, I've felt something in every country, I've learned something.

My ability to empathise has expanded. A disaster in Myanmar, or Hungary, or Sudan, feels more immediate to me because these are countries where I know people, where other human beings have allowed me to sleep under their roof, have something of themselves.

Because of this, of all the experiences that my body has absorbed, there are things that I would do today that, a decade ago, wouldn't have crossed my mind. My sense of the importance of extending the same generous, open-handed hospitality that I benefited from in so many countries has been super-charged. Sometimes I feel as if I've accrued a biological debt that I need to repay.

The process of constantly having to improvise and solve problems that minutes before I hadn't even conceived could exist means that I'm far more open to trying new tasks or challenges than I was before. I know I can't do everything, I'm very aware I don't know everything, and yet there's nothing now that I won't give a go. I'm less worried about stuff not working out.

Because, ultimately, this feat of endurance was also an education. My confidence grew. I learned a lot about geopolitics, I learned a lot about history, I learned a lot about culture. The uncomfortable paradox is that I'm happy about being the person I am today because of the knowledge I possess and what I can do with that knowledge. I wouldn't want to give that up, but I wouldn't want to put myself through what I had to do to get it.

My problem has always been that I need to achieve stuff to feel more assured, less self-conscious. (There are people who are calm and at ease with who they are. They do not care what they look like or what they smell like. They are not affected by what other people think about them, and will go their own way in life. I envy those people.) Once I have achieved something, I feel confident within that area. Then I feel safe. My life changed dramatically after working in Libya because I came back home having proved to myself what I was capable of. I built on that, by running marathons, or pushing myself to get promotions or pay rises. More money, more status, strengthened my sense of what I was worth.

But the moment always comes when I realise that this is all worthless. In Hong Kong, this hit me hard. I realised that I was doing all these, on the face of it, incredible things. Climbing mountains faster than anyone I knew, walking further. They would make me feel great for a week, but the pleasure that follows achievement is short-lived. It fades away so quickly. I really don't care about having completed a marathon in Berlin fifteen years ago. It's no more than a throwaway line now, it means nothing really.

By contrast, the human experiences that I have had seem to live on for ever; there's no expiry date on the connections that I have made with others: what started out as a countries project became a people project. When I look back at Hong Kong, the memories that glow to me are of the people that I drank red wine with or met and walked in the streets with or hiked together with. It's always people. Quite soon in the project, I found that I was tired of meeting with the Red Cross, I was tired of applying for visas, I was tired of sitting on buses and trains. All of it. I just wanted out. But the one thing I never tired of was meeting other human beings. My journey would not have been possible without the hundreds of people who gave me a place to stay, who translated for me, who fed me or put me in touch with someone they knew could help, or simply smiled at me when I needed it most.

The value of reaching every country in the world in an unbroken journey without flying has a half-life that diminishes with each month that passes. What doesn't shrink, what will never shrink, are the memories of the conversations I've had, and the human connections I have made.

And soon I will be able to form another human connection, with the daughter that Le is carrying inside her as I write these words.

# Acknowledgements

Most of the pictures on my social media, or from when I did interviews, show me smiling. This was partly, though by no means entirely, a strategy: I had partners, people I needed help and support from, and if I'd been too critical there are certain ships, perhaps even certain countries, I wouldn't have been able to get onto/into. But it does show a rather one-sided view of the project.

I do not have space here to thank everybody that deserves it. Thousands of people helped me at various stages of the journey. Whether this was just a kind word when I needed it, or moving mountains to get me a visa, I always appreciated it. What I achieved would never have been possible without the kindness and generosity I received from human beings in every corner of the planet. They gave me the strength to pull through. I always looked forward to the welcome I received from everyone I met in the offices of the Red Cross and Red Crescent around the world. Likewise, I'm extremely grateful to all those who followed me on social media.

However, I must mention the members of the project group, Ann-Christina, Søren and Parth, without whom the impossible journey would not have been possible. And there was also the generous support from my father, Torben. Mike Douglas devoted immense amounts of time and care to making a documentary film about the project that does everything I could wish it to. Thank you, too, to all my friends and family for being so patient with me over the course of the nine years, nine months and sixteen days I was away.

The team at Ross Energy stood behind me, providing much of the financial support that underpinned the project's success. Many others also made valuable financial contributions – I will always be grateful to them. This book was written in close collaboration with Josh Ireland; I'm so pleased we got to work together. Thank you also to everybody at Little, Brown, particularly Emma Smith and Tamsin English.

Most of all, there is my wife, Le. I do not have words to express how much she means to me; I am so glad that a project that might have pulled us apart ended up bringing us closer together.